D1429562

POLICE SYSTEMS
IN THE UNITED STATES

OTHER BOOKS BY BRUCE SMITH
AND STUDIES CONDUCTED UNDER HIS DIRECTION

———

THE STATE POLICE; ORGANIZATION AND ADMINISTRATION

RURAL CRIME CONTROL

UNIFORM CRIME REPORTING; A MANUAL FOR POLICE

CHICAGO POLICE PROBLEMS

SPECIAL STUDIES OF POLICE ADMINISTRATION IN THE FEDERAL GOVERN-
MENT; IN CONNECTICUT, ILLINOIS, MAINE, MASSACHUSETTS, MISSOURI,
NEW HAMPSHIRE, NEW YORK, RHODE ISLAND AND VIRGINIA, AND IN
BELGIUM, CANADA, FRANCE, GERMANY, AND GREAT BRITAIN

REPORTS ON POLICE SURVEYS IN BALTIMORE, BOSTON, CHICAGO, CIN-
CINNATI, KANSAS CITY, NEWARK, NEW ORLEANS, PITTSBURGH, SAN
FRANCISCO, ST. LOUIS AND OTHER CITIES

POLICE SYSTEMS
IN THE
UNITED STATES

SECOND REVISED EDITION

by

BRUCE SMITH

Revised by Bruce Smith, Jr.

HARPER & BROTHERS, PUBLISHERS

NEW YORK

POLICE SYSTEMS IN THE UNITED STATES
SECOND REVISED EDITION

CONTENTS

v

LISTS OF CHARTS AND GRAPHS

LIST OF TABLES

PREFACE TO REVISED EDITION

The first edition of this book appeared in 1940. Several reprintings have since been made, at which times a few minor textual changes were introduced. But a more general revision seems now to be in order.

In approaching the task I have tried to keep in mind the occasional suggestions of friends and critics for improving the presentation and treatment. The text also has been extensively revised and brought up to date at many points and an additional chapter, dealing with police aspects of the traffic problem, has been added.

No one can complete such a review of recent police developments without being impressed by the steady advance of police standards. In parts of the United States this constant striving toward better service is so widespread that the strictures appearing in this book will appear to some to be unjustly applied. I have carefully weighed what seem to me to be the relevant facts and have decided to let the broad judgments stand. If present rates of progress are sustained, however, the passing of another decade may witness such major changes in police standards that a reappraisal of police effectiveness, and one couched in more moderate terms, will be in order.

—BRUCE SMITH

Institute of Public Administration
684 Park Avenue
New York 21, New York
June 15, 1949

Bruce Smith, Sr., foresaw clearly the advances which the police in the United States were soon to achieve, as his preface to the first revision witnesses. He passed away September 18, 1955, too soon to see many of the improvements in the police profession to which he devoted the full energies of a life's work.

This second revision is prepared in a spirit of respect for the book's author, yet is revised in many respects to reflect the changes of the past decade in police administration and performance.

—Bruce Smith, Jr.

Consultant

June 15, 1959

CHAPTER 1

THE POLICE PROBLEM

The police problem in America is as old as our system of local government. Springing from the creation of the first police establishments on these shores, it has continued to grow in complexity with the passing years. It is still a prominent feature of the American scene largely because of errors of long standing in the organization and management of police and in the methods employed to assure popular control.

Our police problem also is due in part to inactivity and neglect. The early settlers in America were too busy subduing a continent to give much thought to the nice distinctions upon which successful police administration often hinges, and probably did not even become aware of the existence of a police problem of major proportions until the growth of great cities was well under way. By that time it was already too late to rescue police from the control of the partisan political machines which have since exploited them so thoroughly, and with such devastating effect. Nor was it then feasible to create new organic relationships among police units which had been produced in such bewildering variety that they defied orderly classification.

So it has come about that our police systems have "grown up with the country." Since that growth was one of extraordinary rapidity, police service in the United States has never really enjoyed an opportunity for orderly and consistent development. From the earliest days of modern police forces, and down through the six score years that have followed, police have been the object of attack by press and pulpit, bench and bar, civic and commercial associations, labor leaders, professional politicians, ambitious office

1

seekers, reformers, and criminals. With so many social elements joining in the attack, the charges have naturally ranged between some rather wide extremes. Police have been denounced as relentless man hunters, as oppressors of the weak and helpless, and as the tools of sinister influences and interests. They have also been described as largely ineffective agencies which fail to realize their objectives and in any case cost too much.

Obviously, not all these charges could be fairly directed at any one police force, but at various times and places each has been convincingly proved; hence the widely held belief that even the unproved charges rest upon secure foundations of fact and that our entire police organism is rotten from top to bottom, and from periphery to core.

The situation thus presented in the United States is not altogether unique. It has arisen in all parts of the world, and under all types of governments. No police force, regardless of its form, qualities, or accomplishments, is ever quite free of the taint of corruption; none succeeds in wholly repressing or preventing criminal acts, or in effecting arrests and convictions in any large proportion of the total offenses reported; many are deeply involved in political manipulations of various kinds. Rarely does a major piece of police work receive the accolade of general approval. It may even be doubted whether any single instance of police action has ever been wholly satisfactory to all concerned, since an otherwise perfect example of police work is likely to be viewed with something less than enthusiasm by the thwarted or apprehended offender, and to inflict hardships upon his innocent dependents. The environment in which police must do their work is therefore certain to be unfavorable. Good immediate results are difficult to secure and may bring new and unexpected factors into operation. The chain of circumstances thus forged proves a burden to even the best police organizations.

While police forces everywhere suffer from such handicaps, those of the United States seem to have been particularly affected. Few have escaped the direct influence of political patronage, all live within its shadow, and some are tarred from head to heels with political corruption and criminal participation. From such as these, the observer turns away in disgust, and very likely with the conviction that no police system can even remotely approach its objectives.

There is as yet no conclusive evidence that this gloomy view is unfounded. In any event, most Europeans and perhaps a majority of Americans share the belief that American police systems are beyond all hope of reconstruction, and that in the future, as in the past, they will merit little of public esteem. These paint a dark picture. There are, however, certain features which upon closer examination offer more than a little hope.

For one thing, the lessons of history lean to the favorable side. Police service has come a long way from the days of the "thief-takers" who were themselves convicted felons and were employed as such. The counterparts of Jonathan Wild and Vidocq have long since disappeared in England and in France, although political police with their *agents provocateurs* still operate in parts of Europe. The paid informer, or "stool pigeon," continues as an active though unacknowledged police aide, and even in England and in certain of our own federal and local police units is compensated either directly or indirectly from public funds. But the day of flagrant police corruption in England is definitely past, and with it has gone that open public hostility to all police arms which persisted there until well into the nineteenth century. British police now generally enjoy not only a considerable degree of public confidence but also something akin to real popularity, despite occasional outbursts of angry criticism. On the Continent, likewise, and in many other parts of the civilized world, police perform the necessary tasks of law enforcement under conditions generally favorable to them and their work. Such advances are significant. They indicate that even though there is no royal road to police perfection, the way to improvement is not barred by hopeless obstacles that are inherent in the police function.

What of police in the United States? Is the judgment of almost all foreign observers, as well as that of the majority of Americans, correct? Are American police in a position of hopeless inferiority, with little prospect of improvement? Such questions invite an offhand answer, but one not contributing to a solution of the problems that arise on every hand. Still a few generalizations may be made, which should at least serve to give greater clarity and precision to the questions themselves.

Politics and Police

Political manipulation and law enforcement seem always to have been closely associated in the United States. Even during the larger stages of the colonial period, when our democratic patterns were just beginning to take form, there were traces of this alliance. Colonial sheriffs exercised a large political influence, their powers in the conduct of elections were frequently abused for partisan advantage, and the collection of taxes, often entrusted to them by law, was sometimes employed for political as well as personal ends. With the appearance of cities and great metropolitan areas the effect of such influences was magnified.

There can be no doubt that the greatest handicap of modern police administration is derived from partisan politics. Its pressure is applied under all systems and always affects management. No system is entirely free from it. In most countries it is exercised chiefly by the ruling class, and thereby becomes completely identified with police administration. The result may be an efficient though irresponsible police machine.

Here in the United States there is no such well-defined pattern. The political influences are so numerous and so varied that their effect is kaleidoscopic. Sometimes they are so diametrically opposed that they tend to offset each other. Usually, however, either some one political interest is able to dominate or conflicting partisan interests are reconciled. The result is quickly reflected in leadership of poor quality, low standards of personnel management, inferior service, and a general decline in police prestige.

While the relationship between these causes and effects is widely recognized and as widely denounced, only a few police jurisdictions have succeeded in weakening the grip of political influence. The reasons for such failures are not difficult to find. They consist is a deeply imbedded distrust of police authority, in recurrent opposition to its vigorous exercise, and a determination that, whatever happens, the police shall never succeed to a position of actual civil control.

Such attitudes are probably inherent in the American concept of personal liberty, and represent a stubborn resistance to any precise delimitation of its sphere. The results in terms of criminal justice administration are, however, likely to be unfortunate. Since popular control is exercised through the medium of political party organizations, the private citizen who seeks to avoid the effect of police restrictions naturally turns to local party representatives for aid. No matter how meritorious his complaint may be, his motives in doing so are nearly always selfish. He wants something "fixed"—so it is fixed, and by a politician who distrusts abstract justice even more than does the private citizen. Justice under law proves to be too impersonal, too little concerned with individuals, too preoccupied with major social results, to lend itself to the multitude of petty adjustments which seem so necessary to our polyglot citizenship. Hence various means are found for assuring that police administrators, and our prosecutors, magistrates, and judges as well, shall be quickly responsive to both political and personal influences.

The Devious Path of Reform

Although in police matters it is not difficult to distinguish between the will of the electorate and that of the political machines, the latter have so effectively played upon the democratic prejudices of the public that the whole meaning of law enforcement has been thrown out of focus. In city after city and in state after state, it is literally true that the general public does not want law enforcement in the strict sense of the term. Thus a wide gulf appears between our democratic institutions and the administration of criminal justice. The instrumentalities of the law have been deliberately weakened in response to popular demand, and even law observance by the law-observing has suffered a severe decline. There are therefore the best of reasons for our high crime rates and for the unsatisfactory functioning of our agencies of public justice.

These do not constitute new problems. They were with us long before "crime waves" were discovered and exploited by a yellow press. There has been a whole series of police reforms, such as control by bipartisan, unipartisan, or nonpartisan administrative boards. Such as these rarely succeed in rising above partisanship. We have tenure of office acts and at times the most serious abuses of civil service control masquerading under the guise of a merit system. There are campaigns to "turn the rascals out," and other campaigns to put them in prison. What has been the net result of all these excursions and alarms? Most of them have proved futile and quite without effect upon the ills which they were intended to cure. As often as not, law enforcement reformers have succeeded only in replacing one set of corrupt or incompetent officials with another set of the same or similar stripe.

There has been a veritable revolution in the technique of law enforcement since the days when the first rumblings of the democratic upheaval were heard. Control over law enforcement agencies was then a relatively simple matter, because the official clothed with police powers usually acted as a separate and distinct instrumentality. He could raise "hue and cry" and then proceed to pursue and apprehend an offender by means which were easily comprehended and understood by all members of the community. If this lone operator lacked persistence, enthusiasm, or courage in performing his task, the fault stood out boldly and clearly for all to see.

Appraisal of the agencies of law enforcement is not now so simple. Police administration has become such a complex and technical calling that it is idle to expect popular education in civics to provide a satisfactory means of approach. The problems of law enforcement cannot be adequately dealt with in a penny press, however free, nor in a radio broadcast, because the interest of great masses of people can seemingly only be captured by superficial treatments or dramatized situations. Neither is calculated to clarify some of the most difficult questions of public management that have ever arisen. Yet the alternative, which involves a more or less complete disregard of public attitudes, is really no alternative at all.

Thus we are thrown back upon a reliance on the various means of public enlightenment, among which the press appears still to stand in the front rank. So far this great instrument has scarcely done its part. The most carefully formulated editorial policies, through which might be secured able discussions of police problems, are often offset by a news policy deliberately designed to appeal to the prejudices of the unschooled and the ignorant. Those who determine editorial policies themselves have been misled occasionally into condemning the police when they were right and praising them when they were wrong. So there are few influences at work for instruction of the public in the harsh realities of police duty and in the more or less objective standards of police service.

Police administration reacts strongly to such confusing counsels. Consistent performance is likely to be thrown to the winds, with each day's work done without much regard for the larger program. All ranks, from the highest to the lowest, become engaged in an effort to propitiate those influences having the greatest power to mete out immediate discipline. Meanwhile the police administrator who is subject to popular election or a short appointive term discovers that such devices readily lend themselves to strictly partisan ends. Moreover, the security of tenure accorded to the rank and file of police employees under familiar civil service systems does not necessarily restrict—on the contrary, it may even enhance—the less favorable features of popular political control. For if the police administrator enjoys less security than his subordinates, his powers are severely diminished. He is forced to resort to various expedients for placating not only his master, the public, but the members of his command. Much of his effort is thus directed at clinging to his precarious official rank, to softening the effect of his discipline, and to giving the public what it wants at the moment. Few men of outstanding executive capacity relish working under these conditions, and few such men are now attracted to high police command.

Police in Politics

Thus far we have considered only those political and other popular influences which are directed at the police. But the latter do not always play a passive role. On the contrary, they are often active agents in seeking preferment. The sheriff, township constable, or village marshal who is subject to popular election is naturally and necessarily in politics. But statutes allow it, and practical considerations require it. But appointed police chiefs, captains, lieutenants, sergeants, and so on down to recent recruits, also often invite and rely upon political assistance at every turn. It is sought as a means of securing appointment and promotion, as a shield against impending disciplinary action or the retaliation of the underworld, and as a means for securing or avoiding transfer of assignment. None of the safeguards and prohibitions usually contained in rules, regulations, and statutes have been effective in discouraging such practices, except for a few forces led by men who understood the savage threat implicit in all political influence. Hence the necessary basis for a mutually advantageous barter is provided. Politicians are able to secure privileges for themselves and protection for their friends, in return for aid and assistance extended to police.

The latter are accustomed to complain of the pressures applied to them, and to lay at the door of politics much of the responsibility for failure in law enforcement. There is foundation for the charge. But they are prone to forget that many police actively seek and gratefully accept advantages from political sources. They forget that if there were fewer police in politics, there would be less politics in police.

It seems inevitable that political considerations will continue to exercise a certain influence—and sometimes a preponderant influence—in the administration of police affairs. The American scheme of local government brings police well within the sphere of ward politics, and the very existence of some local political regimes depends upon police acquiescence or direct assistance. Thus the police administrator often finds himself at the focal point of influences which he cannot control without placing his own official position in jeopardy.

These conditions are already familiar enough to the American public. They have been the subject of so many exposures and denunciations that the public has abandoned hope of correcting the situation, and accepts them as a natural and inevitable part of the American system of government. It requires a particularly alarming set of facts to arouse civic indignation in such matters, and then the effect of the upheaval is likely to be dissipated in the forced retirement or prosecution of a few scapegoats and the substitution of new leaders temporarily enjoying popular confidence and trust. This reliance upon the efficacy of "the new broom" is likely to prove disappointing, however, since the old influences are left undisturbed.

Indeed, the results are positively bad in some cases. The rapid turnover of administrators is subversive of discipline, it prevents the development of a permanent corps of experienced leaders, and it discourages men of outstanding executive capacity from seeking a public career in police work. This is not to say that such men are not occasionally so attracted, or that they do not occasionally succeed in fighting their way up from the ranks to general command. Everyone enjoying a firsthand familiarity with American police forces knows that these things do happen, and that the level of police competence is sometimes much higher than the public is prepared to believe. Nevertheless, the generalization stands. Popular anxiety and distrust have blighted police administration at the top.

They have also served to impede the natural and normal development of police services in many other ways. Administrators find it difficult to enlist any large degree of popular support for or acquiescence in a number of minor regulations which are necessary to public order and safety. Active or even passive assistance to police in criminal matters is practically nonexistent in most jurisdictions. Police stations are frequently noisome holes not only because a poorly administered force is not successful at housekeeping, but also because of widespread indifference to the conditions under which policemen must work. Police equipment is sometimes kept in service long past the point where the need for replacement is indicated, because capital outlays for police purposes prove difficult to secure. Despite such unfavorable features the popular hope for better things is often reflected in high wage scales, generous retirement allowances, and adequate or superior facilities for transportation and communication or for the pursuit of various police techniques. On the whole, it is not men, money, and materials that American police chiefly lack, but a favorable climate in which to grow and develop.

Abuses of Authority

Really favorable conditions will never be provided so long as misuse of police authority continues to bulk large in the public mind. Notwithstanding the rapid extension of a policy of moderation in the exercise of law enforcement powers, the tide of general opinion still runs strongly against police. The reasons for this condition are easily identified. Universal use of the automobile invites an increasing volume of restrictions upon the motoring public, and the old easy division of the community into lawbreakers and law observers is thereby destroyed. Today all are lawbreakers, and a large and important minority are deliberate offenders. The imposition of fines and other penalties for traffic law infractions often leaves the violator unconvinced of the justice of such action, and his resentment is naturally directed against the arms of law enforcement. Administrators have striven mightily against this unfavorable trend in public opinion. Increasing emphasis is laid upon the need for civility and moderation in dealing with the traveling public. Sometimes these efforts go so far as virtually to prohibit the rank and file from actively enforcing the motor vehicles laws except in cases involving the most flagrant violations. Summonses have been substituted for arrests, and warnings for summonses, but public resentment continues unabated and even increases in bitterness.

Perhaps nothing short of some major change in the conditions of motor transport, which will make possible a simpler and more easily observed highway traffic code, can remove the basis for this unfavorable trend in public opinion. Meanwhile, however, there is another source of public dissatisfaction, concerning which the police have done almost nothing. Most police organizations are instructed and cautioned in the use of police weapons. Consequently it is only on rare occasions that any serious issue is drawn because of unjustified use of nightsticks or revolvers in subduing prisoners who resist arrest, or in suppressing disorders. Once a prisoner is safely deposited in a police lockup it might be presumed that he is secure against violence. Popular opinion is convinced, however, that "third degree" abuses are both universal and of common occurrence. There is sufficient factual basis for this opinion to assure its persistence. While the practice of police forces varies widely, even some of the most scrupulous administrators hold that under special circumstances the use of force, or the threat of force, in securing a confession is justified by the practical exigencies of police work. This in general represents the official attitude of the better police organizations. Untrained and inefficient police bodies employ the third degree with greater frequency, and there are those which rely upon it as an easy short cut to the successful investigation of cases involving familiar criminal characters.

The methods employed by police in extorting confessions need not concern us here. They have been repeatedly, and for the most part reliably, described by a number of observers, even to the most revolting detail. Police have made few efforts to defend themselves against such charges, and their defenses have seldom proved convincing to the general public. The upshot of the matter is that confessions are repudiated on the ground of duress, and juries acquit either because of inadequate investigation and faulty preparation of cases or in resentment arising from real or imagined police abuses.

It may be argued that an occasional failure to secure a conviction because of extorted confessions sometimes involves cases which in any event would have been lost on trial or on appeal, and that there remains a substantial proportion of difficult prosecutions which could never be won in any other way. This view puts the best possible front on the whole matter, though it overemphasizes the immediate advantages of a successful prosecution. It ignores entirely the continuing reproach to public justice that third-degree practices entail. Even a few well-authenticated cases can completely cover a police force with a cloud of suspicion. The secrecy necessarily surrounding police interrogation of suspects in itself serves to encourage a popular belief that such routine inquiries are generally marked by the use of illegal force. Supported by the already well-established distrust of police authority of any kind, these tentative beliefs quickly ripen into profound conviction. When that point is reached, as it often is, the police are obstructed by a forbidding front of popular resentment, and a reluctance to believe any police officer under oath. Thereafter the most carefully prepared prosecutions may fail because the testimony of police witnesses is either ignored or heavily discounted by trial juries. After all, juries are but small segments of the public at large, and they naturally reflect popular attitudes and prejudices.

Such distortions of the judicial process are of rare occurrence in other English-speaking countries, largely because responsible police authorities in them have learned to exercise restraint in the handling of prisoners The contrast between American and British police practice is in fact so striking as to lend force and significance to the humorous quip of an English chief constable who says that "if the members of an English force were assigned to police an American city, they would all be kidnaped within twenty-four hours; and if American police were transferred to an English jurisdiction, they would promptly be placed under arrest for abuses of police authority."[1]

Meanwhile our federal and state courts are becoming more and more incisive in their opinions concerning irregularities in the

[1] Personally communicated. The official in question desires to preserve anonymity, for obvious reasons.

exercise of police authority. These involve not only third-degree practices and extorted confessions, but also the procedures to be observed in executing search warrants, and the admissibility of evidence secured by "wire tapping." Police should take due note of these judicial expressions because they are likely to become more insistent as the years pass. They cannot be shrugged off on the ground that they have no practical application and do not recognize the difficulties involved in applying one standard of conduct to the many races and nationalities which crowd our great cities. Neither will complaints concerning the technicalities of the law advance the cause of police work. For it is through so-called technicalities that private rights are defined and enforced, and in any case the technicalities often rest not alone upon procedural law, but also upon basic constitutional guaranties of the most solemn and substantial character.

An experienced police administrator is sometimes so well versed in the policeman's art, and so familiar with the realities of policy duty, that he grows restive under the restrictions imposed by legislatures and courts, and even under those applied by the executive heads of the government which he serves. He becomes unduly conscious of his mastery of certain techniques—an expertness not shared by others who, from his standpoint, are laymen. While his position is understandable and is, indeed, one mark of the professional man, it cannot be too strongly emphasized that such narrowly conceived professional attitudes hold great dangers for the progress of police. For if police forces are more easily controlled in the exercise of entrusted powers by placing them under the leadership of men ignorant of the details of police practice, it is quite likely that such recourse will be had as frequently in the future as in the past. Yet the advance of police will continue to be impeded if they are thus subordinated to strange and changing disciplines. Their greatest opportunity during the years to come will consist in carefully observing private rights and thus winning and deserving the support of a public which, despite much evidence to the contrary, probably wishes to think well of its defending forces.

As yet there is little to indicate that police in the United States will firmly grasp this thorny question and dispose of it once and for all. Certain it is, however, that if police do not act, legislatures will do so, and that the restrictions thereby placed upon even a restrained use of preliminary interrogation may impose severe and unnecessary burdens upon effective law enforcement.

Progress in Law Enforcement

The foregoing pages have sought briefly to summarize the various strictures laid upon police whenever they become the subject of critical discussion. As already indicated, however, there is another aspect of police performance which, on general balance, is far more favorable. In criminal investigation, police are making important advances with the aid of new scientific techniques, although still notably weak in the exercise of administrative controls. Uniformed patrol, the core of successful police work, has been motorized to an extent far greater than is attempted in other lands, while foot patrol threatens to become a vanishing institution unless present trends in the unnecessary dispersion of man power are reversed. Facilities for traffic regulation are clearly the best in the world, though still notably lacking in uniformity and occasionally ill-designed for immediate needs. Material resources, in terms of transportation and communication, are so superior to those found elsewhere that the casual observer is in danger of being misled by them into the conclusion that American police have reached a commanding place in all other respects.

The truth is that much of the superiority cited above rests upon the acquisition of mechanical devices calculated to simplify, intensify, or otherwise improve the performance of policy duty. Such improvements in equipment are attributable chiefly to American manufacturing and sales organizations which have distributed their products far and wide, and to the willingness of some communities to pay well for anything holding promise for better police protection. The realization that good police service cannot be so easily purchased is slow to form.

Against this background of highlights and shadows, two features stand out in bold relief. One is the pervading influence of corruption. It afflicts all police forces—even the best of them—in some degree, and in a few instances has dominated police establishments for generations. The second prominent feature is in striking contrast. It represents the mighty and apparently irresistible surge of certain forces toward a new standard of administration and performance. During the past twenty years numerous American police agencies have made more rapid progress than have those of any other nation. They have accomplished this without the aid of unified direction, in the face of popular skepticism concerning both their motives and their objectives, and often despite stern political opposition.

During this period, in various parts of the country, a mere handful of able administrators has independently striven to place police service on a new basis. Though bearing the burden of an inglorious police past, they have made advances of the greatest importance. In this they have been supported by other administrators who, while possessing less native ability, are providing essential reinforcements for the new police front and flanks. Under such occasionally favorable auspices, a new type of recruit has been attracted to police service. Supplementing the police veterans who had never succumbed to abuses of long standing, they are now tipping the scales in favor of better police service. Thus an informed and vigorous leadership has gradually produced not only a new standard of management, but an increasing proportion of intelligent, trained, and hopeful members of the rank and file.

While such new and striking departures do not by any means solve the American police problem outright, they do hold real promise for the future. The years just ahead will provide an immediate test of the ability of American governments—national, state, and local—to continue to make the adjustments that will prove essential to an extension of the advances already made, and to the solution of new problems which even now are emerging. Improved personnel procedures, carefully adapted to the special needs of police, must be devised, and those already in operation must be more honestly and capably applied. Means must be found whereby a police force can produce its own future leaders with a greater degree of success than in the past. Such leadership must then be provided with the opportunity to lead. The areas of police administration must be re-examined in the light of modern conditions, but against a general background of established theories of local government. The present trend toward dispersion and wastage of patrol strength must be reversed. More effective administrative controls over criminal investigations must be established. The vexing problems represented by highway traffic congestion and highway accidents still await large-scale solutions. The alliances between politics, vice, and crime, which for so long have made war on police and public alike, must be dissolved. The police themselves must be removed from all suspicion of any part in such alliances. These and related questions often engage the attention of the governments and public of today. They will be the special concern of the administrator of tomorrow.

Nature of the Police Function

To the modern mind, the term "police"[2] connotes a body of civil officers charged with suppressing crimes and public disorders, and regulating the use of the highways. While this popular usage is substantially correct, it fails to recognize the additional and sometimes burdensome regulatory duties which police discharge. The historical setting of police has a special value in this connection, and it is worthy of note that in its early definitions, and also at various later stages of governmental development, the term has been employed to describe certain aspects of the control of sanitation or the suppression of political offenses, and has even been expanded to cover practically all forms of public regulation and domestic order. While it is now primarily used with reference to the maintenance of the peace and the protection of persons and property from the commission of unlawful acts, the police function as customarily administered is somewhat broader in its scope.

Thus, as to practically all types of licensed callings, the police are often charged with the preliminary inspection of premises and with investigations into the personal characters of licensees, and are sometimes required to make periodic reports to the licensing authorities concerning the manner in which the various licensed activities are conducted. When police perform such duties with reference to the licensing of private police and watchmen, operators of vehicles plying for hire, storage and cartage of explosives or other inherently dangerous substances, or the sale and possession of fire-

[2] The generic term "police" should not be confused with "police power," which is an idiom of constitutional law. According to the broad definition provided by Colonel George F. Chandler, "Police is the name given to the administrative powers of a unit of civilization, or to the agents used to enforce such powers." *The Policeman's Art,* p. xi. Raymond B. Fosdick's statement that "Today we mean by police the primary constitutional force for the protection of individuals in their legal rights," introduces a desirable emphasis into this general definition. *European Police Systems,* pp. 3-4.

arms, they operate within a fairly well-defined police sphere. They also act to prevent conditions threatening the public safety or morals —including traffic regulation, the maintenance of fire lines at the scene of a conflagration, and in some instances the exercise of certain limited powers of public censorship. This last causes police great difficulty because the public taste does not accept any single standard of decency, and the exceedingly wide range of entertainments and publications which must be regulated lies far beyond the cultural horizons of any bureaucracy that has yet been established. It is also an increasingly common practice for the police to extend emergency relief to the destitute during those hours when social welfare stations are not open to applicants.

These and various related duties less frequently exercised may be held to have a certain bearing upon the protective functions of police; but when the same theory is extended so as to include the inspection of elevators or buildings used as places of public assembly, it may fairly be questioned whether there are not some limits to its application. For soon or late the list of such duties becomes so lengthy and their performance so absorbing that the police force is literally dispersed and cannot be marshaled for any but the most urgent services relative to crime repression.

Such varied activities hold still further implications. When organized society sets up a police force, it is from motives of self-discipline. The civil enforcement body thus created must be clothed with broad powers and entrusted with the means to make them effective. This sometimes involves imposition of irritating restrictions upon the complete freedom of action of those who consider themselves to be law-abiding citizens. Under even the most favorable circumstances, there are many possible points of conflict between the public at large and its servants, the police. If the latter do not employ unduly harsh measures, and are moderately successful in the repression, detection, and investigation of offenses which were crimes at common law, they are generally accepted as the guardians of law and order and may win a measure of popular support.

The situation is otherwise, however, if the police are overburdened with many duties lying outside the proper sphere of criminal law enforcement. Here the interplay of two forces produces a condition that ultimately weakens, and may even destroy, police effectiveness. In the first place, the additional duties are often of such a minor regulatory nature that, while they rarely produce social benefits of an impressive character, nevertheless prove irritating to the sensibilities of people who believe they have a right to be let alone. Petty restrictions and complex codes thus fall into disrepute, and the police who administer them are confronted with the disagreeable task of "imposing" an unessential discipline upon a non-cooperative and resentful public. The unpopularity of the regulations soon is transferred to the police, thereby impairing the sources of public support which may turn impending success into dismal failure in the solution and prosecution of major crimes.

A second and equally grave problem arises from the fact that the police function may be progressively expanded without any compensating increase in numerical strength. If this resulted in an immediate lowering of police efficiency in all matters, both regulatory and criminal, there might be some hope that the relation of cause and effect would be recognized and the situation corrected. Unfortunately, however, human institutions do not seem to respond in any such prompt and positive way, particularly when the basic changes are gradual and spread over a long period of time. In some communities, new police activities—no matter how minor—receive more attention and attract the support of men, money, and materials more readily than long-established and basic activities not enjoying the attractions of novelty. The essential business of protecting life and property has thereby lost a part—and sometimes a considerable part—of the man power upon which it once relied.

Hence the scope of the police function is a question of the first magnitude. It not only affects the routine functioning of the force, but also profoundly influences that close adjustment of the police machine to the popular will without which no police body can ever succeed.

Nature of the Policeman's Art

The problems surrounding day-to-day operations are no less difficult than those which have thus far been considered. They are complicated, as we have seen, by public attitudes toward the police force as a whole, by popular confusion as to desirable objectives and the means for attaining them, and by the rather wide range of dissimilar duties sometimes imposed. All these factors have been roughly sketched against a general background of public policy and public administration. It remains to consider them in their natural setting—as viewed and applied by the police officer on his beat. Here one approaches close to the real crux of the matter, because it is the individual agent of law enforcement who usually determines how far popular attitudes shall control, to what degree official instructions shall be carried into effect, and what the net social result shall be. For when we equip a public servant with a gun, a club, a uniform, and a badge of ill-defined authority, we endow him with informal powers and duties akin to those of prosecutors, judges, juries, jailers, and executioners.

Thus all the devices for popular and administrative control —the enactments of legislative bodies, the aims of governmental executives, the hierarchies of structural organization, and the expenditure of great sums of public money upon men and equipment —all converge at last upon one focal point: the policeman. The manner in which he customarily reacts to the various stimuli applied to him therefore holds considerable importance for the realities of police service. To treat the individual policeman as a largely passive factor, who is moved hither and yon on the chessboard of police strategy, is a convenient and even necessary device for the purpose of generalized thinking and planning; but to complete and to execute such plans without considering the possibilities and the limitations of flesh and blood is to invite failure.

To some this emphasis upon the human side of police work may appear to be unnecessary, since it is the one aspect now thoroughly canvassed by press and radio, and presented each day to the public. Such treatments, however, are likely to depict the policeman as a fool, a knave, or a hero, and not as a man working for a living. The administrator, on the other hand, commonly thinks of him as human raw material that has been selected and molded so as to conform as closely as possible to current needs in police work. Yet as the patrolman walks his beat his mind does not persistently dwell upon the code of criminal procedure or the latest report on juvenile delinquency. If his thoughts turn to police work at all, they are likely to hit upon more commonplace aspects of the law and its enforcement. He may observe a multitude of violations, some relating to laws and ordinances which were never intended by the enactors to be enforced, others involving minor regulations of public order, the conduct of trades and callings having some color of public interest, or the use of private property. Their very number and variety are such that their requirements are largely unknown to the people to whom they apply. Hence violations are extremely common. The observing patrolman is thereby confronted with a dilemma. If warnings are issued to all such petty violators, they will not prove effective unless those who persist in their infractions are arrested or summoned; and if such letter-of-the-law enforcement is attempted, the patrolman will be so continuously engaged as a prosecuting witness before the courts that only a small proportion of his time will be devoted to patrolling his beat.

The policeman's art, then, consists in applying and enforcing a multitude of laws and ordinances in such degree or proportion and in such manner that the greatest degree of protection will be secured. The degree of enforcement and the method of application will vary with each neighborhood and community. There are no set rules, nor even general guides, to the policy to be applied. Each policeman must, in a sense, determine the standard to be set in the area for which he is responsible. Immediate superiors may be able to impress upon him some of the lessons of experience, but for the most part such experience must be his own. The course of his official action is the resultant of the various forces which play upon him. His official superiors are but one of many such influences. If his early training as a man and as a policeman has been faulty, he may take an unduly complaisant attitude toward certain offenses and offenders, particularly as familiarity with the seamy side of life is the policeman's lot, and this makes for tolerance. Thus he is a policy-forming police administrator in miniature, who operates beyond the scope of the usual devices for control. He makes and unmakes the fortunes of governmental executives and administrators, though rarely falling under the direct influence of the popular will. The only control to which he is subject is the discipline of his superiors. When that weakens, or is thwarted, the last vestige of control over this mighty atom of law enforcement disappears.

Hence the task of raising the level of police performance does not hinge upon the use of mechanical aids, as so many suppose. It depends upon sound organization and efficient procedures which are applied to—and by—alert and intelligent servants of the police organism. Since the human factor proves the most difficult to control and may actively resist all change, the process of raising the general level of police service sometimes proves to be a lengthy one. Even so, organization and administration will always be cardinal features of any police system.

Basic Outlines of American Police Systems

The general pattern of American police forces closely resembles that of our whole governmental system. That is to say, the federal, state, and local governments are all implemented with their own distinctive police services. To this broad generalization there are but few exceptions.

Under such a scheme of distribution, the police agencies of the federal government naturally exercise the widest territorial authority, although their powers and functions are circumscribed by the very nature of the federal union and by the familiar constitutional limitations upon federal powers. Except for the Federal Bureau of Investigation in the Department of Justice, all these national police units exercise only such police authority as is more or less directly related to the department of the national government to which each is attached. The nationwide police function is accordingly parceled out among the Treasury, Justice, and Post Office departments, sometimes with confusing results.

Police forces are maintained also by each of the several states. An increasing number of these perform general police duties throughout the length and breadth of their respective commonwealths, even though primary emphasis is placed upon rural protection. Many other state police units are restricted either by law or in practice to the regulation of traffic on state highways, while several still are of a rudimentary character.

It is at the local levels of government that the greatest variety of police units begins to appear. This is chiefly due to variety in the types of local governments themselves, to their overlapping jurisdictions and their occasionally complex interrelationships; but it is also attributable to the increasing tendency of local government units to set up rival police agencies—some of them with restricted police authority—within a single local area.

There is therefore no such thing in the United States as a police system, nor even a set of police systems within any reasonably accurate sense of the term. Our so-called systems are mere collections of police units having some similarity of authority, organization, or jurisdiction; but they lack any systematic relationship to each other. Some police forces trace their origins back to Anglo-Saxon institutions and persevere today chiefly as relics of the past, without any real current use or value. Others have come into existence as a consequence of the rise of great cities, and more recently in response to the challenge of organized crime or modern traffic hazards throughout wide rural areas. A few, including certain of the federal police agencies, have been created as mere convenient instrumentalities for the aid of other functions of government or because federal criminal jurisdiction had expanded to a point where specialized police appeared to be necessary.

From such complex relationships and disparate origins, our American police forces are descended. Clearly, they cannot all be treated in the same terms. Some differentiation is necessary. Since the more recent and more highly developed agencies have been influenced somewhat by the early police forms which have persisted down to the present day, it will contribute to an understanding of the entire structure if the progress of police development is traced through each stage and, as nearly as may be, in chronological sequence.

Coincident with this great variety and complexity, and largely as a result of it, the hierarchy of police establishments briefly described above involves a considerable degree of overlapping and duplication. There are at least five strata of police service. They conform in a general way to the major levels of government prevalent throughout most of the United States. Reduced to terms of governmental units and ranked in order of territorial extent they are as follows:

1. Police agencies of the federal government, particularly those now attached to the Treasury, Justice, and Post Office departments;

2. State police forces and criminal investigation agencies of fifty states;

3. Sheriffs and deputy sheriffs in over three thousand counties, plus a few county police forces which either duplicate the sheriff's police jurisdiction or virtually displace it;

4. The police of a thousand cities and over twenty thousand townships or New England towns, to which should be added an unknown number serving magisterial districts and county districts in the South and West;

5. The police of fifteen thousand villages, boroughs, and incorpo-

rated towns, together with a small number of forces serving public quasi corporations such as special or *ad hoc* districts.

However impressive this array may be, it does not completely reflect the full variety of American police. Hence there is no suitable niche in which to place the police force of the District of Columbia, nor such highly specialized agencies as the interstate bridge and tunnel police force of the Port of New York Authority, or the police department of the Massachusetts Metropolitan District Commission serving the parks and parkways of the Boston metropolitan area.[3] Such unique bodies defy inclusion in any but the most narrow categories.

There are other qualifying factors to be recognized, because the foregoing stratified summary oversimplifies the true situation. There is some overlapping of the police agencies of cities and townships, although the two types are listed above as though they were always coordinate bodies. On the other hand, there are many small townships, villages, boroughs, and unincorporated towns where no constables, marshals, or other local police officers are elected or appointed despite statutory requirements. Such lapses are due to a variety of causes. Either no one seeks election or appointment to the various posts, or appropriations for the support of local police are not made. The rise of state police and the recent appearance of a few organized county forces also are partly responsible. So there is a slight tendency toward police consolidations through the disintegration of some of the smaller and weaker units—a drift that will doubtless continue, even though it is unlikely to assume major proportions without positive statutory direction.

Finally there is duplication among police forces existing side by side at the one level of government. Such fragmentation of police authority is occasionally found in cities, towns, and counties, is quite common among the states, and is an outstanding characteristic of the rapidly proliferating federal forces.

By way of general summary, it is clear that there are about forty thousand separate and distinct public police agencies in the United States. The vast majority consist of one, two, or three men, who are employed on a part-time basis. Many of them are compensated solely

[3] For a description of the Metropolitan District Commission force, cf., *Report of the [Massachusetts] Special Commission on Taxation and Public Expenditures,* Part XIV (1938).

by fees, are selected without regard to physical or mental qualifications, are wholly untrained and largely unsupervised, are ill-equipped and undisciplined. At the other extreme stand the police of our great cities, a number of counties and states, and the federal government. These reflect the new influences now at work in behalf of crime prevention and the protection of life and property. Some show no evidence of ability to overcome the handicap of the ancient police tradition. Others have reached the point where they may be favorably compared with the best in the world today. Under such circumstances it is difficult to formulate a single set of broad generalizations that will prove both valid and useful.

Interrelations of Police Systems

The relationship between the varied types of police forces is difficult to explore in a systematic fashion. Partly it rests upon the personalities of the chief figures in the departments involved. As between forces in such specialized fields as narcotics suppression and liquor enforcement there is intense rivalry, based upon competition for informants and prestige. Numerous department heads imagine that inter-agency rivalry will develop a spirit of pride among their own subordinates: rivalry thus becoming a device for leadership. Despite department chiefs, however, a great amount of inter-agency cooperation occurs at the operating levels. State and local narcotics, liquor, and highway traffic men are frequently on the best of operating terms without the knowledge of their superior officers. A younger generation, whose members became familiar with the jaded techniques of unimaginative leaders during a great war, now serves in positions whereby, in their own quiet way, they can achieve high professional standards of cooperation.

Among neighboring municipal police forces there is even less reason for inter-agency rivalry, nor is the rivalry a serious problem as between municipal forces. A common bond between adjacent forces is frequently forged by the sharing of a police radio frequency, or by mutual monitoring of radio messages to assure operational cooperation in emergencies. In the crowded areas of the East and Midwest, where small police departments clustered about a central city are a rule, it is all but universal practice for the smaller departments to install adjacent to their radio dispatcher or desk officer a radio receiver (and sometimes a transmitter) to monitor the central city. Likewise radio receivers and perhaps transmitters are also installed to intercommunicate with nearby state police barracks. Thus, without the intervention of legislatures the police profession is establishing inter-agency cooperation in a practical manner and on a working level.

Police associations, which bring together policemen from neighboring towns for professional and recreational purposes, have no doubt aided in bringing agencies into cooperation. The common effort to achieve legislation favorable to the association objectives may develop into sincere cooperation in apprehending criminals.

Training programs and other services are now frequently offered to small departments by those in the larger cities. New York City has been outstanding in this respect: offering its facilities to any department in the New York metropolitan area.

State legislatures have entered into formal cooperative arrangements concerning arrests and fugitives from justice, and arrangements for interstate parole and probation supervision, and the federal government has sought to putty up the interstices of the penal law with various enactments enlarging the criminal jurisdiction of the federal government by defining new crimes and extending the definition of existing crimes.

Still, the germ for friction between enforcement agencies remains. Jurisdictions overlap in numerous cases, and these may be aggravated in investigations which bring together a combination of federal, state, and local enforcement agencies under the glare of national publicity and the desire for departmental or individual acclaim. This problem is so prevalent that it is difficult to visualize any satisfactory solution except upon the lines which the police of the nation are following. A common expedient to achieve a *modus vivendi* is for the officers of the higher (federal or state) level of government to carry through and complete police action in a case investigation or enforcement effort, but to yield publicity credit to the local police wherever the latter has the slightest claim to recognition: or even none at all. Thus the police themselves make workable a network of federal, state, and local enforcement efforts which cannot be justified or reconciled on the force of any principle of political science.

CHAPTER 2

THE CRIME PROBLEM

Our complex police system has grown with America, slowly evolving through three centuries of expanding governmental institutions. With a crime problem that became more and more baffling as our great urban centers developed, as wealth increased, and as new means of rapid transport leaped across the boundaries of local jurisdictions, additional police facilities have been provided for the control of criminal acts and for the enforcement of a multitude of minor regulations. Some concrete knowledge of the amount and distribution of crime, and of the means employed for its suppression, therefore should contribute to an understanding of the history of our police services, the extent to which they are adapted to current conditions, and the probable course of their future development.

Most systematic treatments of the police problem in America include an effort to compare our crime rates with those prevailing abroad. If these are well and carefully drawn, various qualifications and reservations must be made in order to allow for basic differences in crime reporting. Invariably, however, the conclusion is reached that crime in America—and particularly violent crime—overtops that of western Europe.

The present treatment will not further document the obvious. It is content to observe at the outset that American crime rates are higher than those of other nations; that experience both here and elsewhere indicates that they can be reduced by various governmental expedients; and that thus far the most effective measures for crime control have been applied by organized police forces employing the familiar devices of surveillance, investigation, and uniformed patrol.

Though American crime rates—and particularly those of our great cities—are much too high for social comfort, they do not of themselves establish a case for an underlying national inferiority in matters of law observance and enforcement. For they are neither distinctively American nor a special characteristic of our own times. During the brawling thirteenth century in England, we are told that "men were never secure in their houses and whole villages were often plundered by bands of robbers."[1] The criminal exploits of American gangsters, so widely acclaimed in our folklore, also had their counterparts in England during the nineteenth century, for

There were streets in Westminster, infested by gangs of desperate men, and so dangerous that no policeman dared venture there, unless accompanied by five or six of his comrades, for fear of being cut to pieces. These are not highly colored fairy tales, but actual facts as recounted in the Blue Books of the period; recounted moreover without exciting any particular notice at the time. In 1812, the crime of murder was so common, and so much on the increase, that a Parliamentary Committee was appointed to inquire as to the best means of combating the savage tendencies of the people. Offenses against property were even more prevalent than crimes of violence. . . .
Thieves and receivers, drivers of hackney coaches, and sometimes tollgate keepers, conspired together to rob the travelling public. . . . Still more serious were the conspiracies in which solicitors and police officers were concerned, which had for their object the levying of blackmail from bankers and others.[2]

That such conditions were not confined to the metropolis is attested by two distinguished English commentators, who declare that so late as the middle of the nineteenth century "these gangs of robbers and individual pilferers radiated into the country on all sides."[3] Thus it was not until quite recent years that England moved over into the ranks of the law enforcing and the law abiding, while the domestic peace and security of certain other nations have been effected only at the sacrifice of private and political rights and immunities. In the meantime Canada, which shares with the United States our North American civilization, is confronted by the fact

[1] W. L. M. Lee, *A History of Police in England*, p. 22.
[2] *Ibid.*, p. 199.
[3] Sidney and Beatrice Webb, *English Local Government*, p. 411. For a mid-eighteenth century comparison of crime and police in England and on the Continent, cf. W. H. Gillispie, "A Forgotten Police Reformer," in *The Police Journal* (London), Vol. XI (1938), No. 4, pp. 507-510.

that since 1900 its crime has increased three times more rapidly than has its population.

Such items drawn from foreign experience should not be allowed to obscure the fact that our own national history has been featured by crime waves. Men lived violently and died by violence in great numbers along the Penobscot and the Kennebec, in the logging camps of Michigan, on the Great Plains, throughout the vast empire that is Texas, among the river towns of the Mississippi, and in the mining settlements of the Far West, long before modern crime had pockmarked Chicago's boulevards with machine-gun fire, made San Francisco's waterfront a battleground for labor warfare, or taken over the purveying of costly vices on Miami's silver shore.

It is possible that such latter-day manifestations and many more like them in other communities both large and small may be nothing more than the last degraded form of a lusty manner of living which once marked the ever-advancing frontier. If this conclusion be correct, their final passing will be regretted by many law-abiding Americans who consider violent outbreaks to be an evil but necessary feature of a vigorous race. Meanwhile the civil disorder and corruption that attend such conditions make serious efforts at law enforcement a difficult and often a discouraging business.

I. THE VOLUME OF CRIME

Of the volume and distribution of criminal acts for the years prior to 1930 we know, almost literally, nothing. Since that date there are certain broad indices based upon the nationwide crime-reporting system represented by the *Uniform Crime Reports*. These have a direct bearing upon the scope and ramifications of the crime problem in America.[4]

On the basis of periodic crime returns from nearly all cities and a large part of the rural area, it is possible to estimate the nationwide totals for reportable offenses with a high degree of confidence. With larcenies over a million and a half annually, burglaries exceeding one half million, and auto thefts hovering around the three hundred thousand mark, these three major categories among them total two and a half million crimes annually. Homicide, rape, assaults with gun and knife, and robberies together account for about 190,000 additional crimes of truly major importance.

[4] For a description of the crime reporting system, see Chap. 9.

Staggering as these figures are, they do not include felonies and misdemeanors of both major and minor gravity which do not for various reasons fall within the "reportable" classifications. These represent such offenses as embezzlement, fraud, receiving stolen property, forgery, counterfeiting, violations of narcotic and liquor laws, arson, carrying concealed weapons, prostitution and other sex offenses, gambling, offenses against family and children, drunkenness, minor assaults, and disorderly conduct and vagrancy, not to mention the numerous categories represented by violations of the motor vehicle and highway laws, and a vast number of minor regulatory statutes and local ordinances. These last may reach high levels of frequency without affecting social organization in any material respect. They impose, it is true, heavy burdens upon police and other agencies of criminal justice, but few of them undermine the foundations of community life.

Trends in reportable offenses show considerable differences among the various crimes. Since extensive data first became available in 1930-1931, only the crime of murder has remained reasonably constant; rape, robbery, assault with a deadly weapon, larceny, burglary, and auto thefts are all increasing with time. Crimes in general were less frequent during World War II but all reportable offenses increased in frequency when the military forces returned from overseas. This last condition should not be interpreted as an unfavorable reflection upon the military establishment. Rather it was due to the return of those age groups having the greatest predisposition to crime, as will presently appear.

II. GEOGRAPHY AND CRIME

The geographical element is concerned with the relative frequency of urban and rural crimes, with crimes by groups of cities arranged according to size, and with the distribution of urban crimes by major geographic divisions. They will be considered in that order in the pages which follow.

Urban and Rural Crime

Urban crime rates are generally higher than those prevailing in rural areas. Sometimes the disparity is very wide, with the urban larcenies running as much as four times greater than the rural rate. The preponderance of urban crime is not difficult to understand.

The congested living space of cities, the virtual anonymity of a floating population, and the temptations offered by the display of valuable goods on every hand, all tend to higher crime hazards than are commonly encountered in the open countryside.

This preponderance of urban crime has been observed by many commentators both here and abroad[5] and although the factual bases for their conclusions do not lend themselves to close measurement, there seems sufficient reason to accept them at something like face value. But there is an increasing body of evidence accumulating in the United States indicative that a profound change in these relationships may be in progress.[6] For murder, manslaughter, negligent homicide (chiefly motor traffic fatalities) and rape, the rural crime rate of this country now equals the urban rate. As to all homicides, it actually exceeds the urban crime rate of the New England, middle Atlantic and north central states and shows such impressive advances for aggravated assault and burglary as greatly to reduce the former disparity. Such special indices raise the question whether rural crimes, reacting to urban influences such as new means of transport and consequent interchange of population have distributed far and wide, may not now be in process of attaining urban crime levels. Hence the new trend is in a sense an extension of a condition of long standing. In any case the frequency of rural crimes will bear close watching, since a persistent upswing will further challenge the traditional rural police system and perhaps open new and larger spheres of operation to the state police.

Urban Crime: by Groups of Cities

The sources thus far examined tend to indicate that, as a broad generalization distinguishing city from country, crime rates increase

---

[5] See Lombroso, *Crime: Its Causes and Remedies* (Boston, 1918), pp. 58-75, *passim;* Aschaffenburg, *Crime and Its Repression* (Boston, 1913), p. 62; *Criminal Statistics of Finland (Offenses Known to the Police),* Ministry of Justice, Helsingfors; W. L. Melville Lee, *A History of Police in England,* pp. 21-42, *passim;* Sidney and Beatrice Webb, *English Local Government,* pp. 407-411, *passim;* Glyde, *Localities of Crime in Suffolk,* in Journal of the Statistical Society of London, Vol. XIX (1856), pp. 104-106, *passim;* Pike, *A History of Crime in England* (1876), Vol. II, pp. 524, 526, 673; and Burchardt, *Kriminalität in Stadt und Land,* which surveys the available official sources.

[6] See for example Bettman, Jameson, Marshall and Miles, *Ohio Criminal Statistics* (1931); Smith, *Rural Crime Control* (1933), pp. 6-18; and particularly the *Uniform Crime Reports,* annual bulletins for the years beginning with 1944.

with density of population. The question then arises: does something like the same relationship hold with respect to groups of cities arranged according to size?

The *Uniform Crime Reports,* which are complete for all cities above 25,000 population, and in addition cover nearly all of the smaller cities, provide an emphatic answer to this question. When all urban places are arranged in six classified groups according to size, it becomes apparent that mere size does have a strong influence upon the crime rate. Cities of over 100,000 population have a clear preponderance in crime, while the small urban communities tend toward the more moderate levels which thus far have characterized rural life in America.

Urban Crime: by Geographic Divisions

Such comparisons are strictly of a general nature and do not hold true for all the cities concerned. Likewise their application is limited somewhat by the fact that geographical location has a bearing on the crime rate. Thus there is an interplay between location and size, with many other factors possibly involved, even though their effect is not immediately apparent.

In general, the broad band of states lying north of what is popularly conceived to be Mason and Dixon's line, and east of the Rocky Mountains, has much lower crime rates than the rest of the country. It is possible to arrange these divisions in some reasonably correct order of their crime rates, beginning with the regions having the lowest rate as follows:

1. The northeastern states (comprising the New England and Middle Atlantic divisions).
2. The north central states (comprising the east north central and west north central divisions).
3. The southern states comprising the South Atlantic, east south central and west south central divisions).
4. The far western states (comprising the mountain and Pacific divisions).

Traditionally the Deep South has been characterized by high crime rates in nearly all offense classifications. Though the South still experiences a high level of criminal activity the Pacific Coast now has assumed the position of being the most crime-ridden. This increase in crime in the West is in the face of high police pay scales, a large number of policemen per capita, and a concentration on the facilities for formal education in policing which overshadows any other section of the country. The causes of the premier role of the Pacific Coast as a crime center are shrouded in the conflicting forces at work in that area. An influx of persons of all ages and many races has perhaps overstressed police methods prescribed by another generation of police administrators.

III. THE TIME ELEMENT IN CRIME

Data concerning the commission of criminal acts may also be interpreted in terms of time; seasonal differences and distributions according to day of the week, or time of day. As to these elements, there is as yet no proof of a causal relationship between time and crime, although, as will shortly appear, certain crimes undergo marked fluctuations in frequency which are apparently in response to differences in time.

Crime by Month

For example, there is the effect of seasonal change as reflected in the crime rates of the several months. Figure I shows the per cent of monthly deviation from the annual average of certain crimes against the person for each of five consecutive years.[7] These graphs show that criminal homicides not arising out of negligence, and the related crimes grouped under the general descriptive title of "aggravated assault," fluctuate by about 30 per cent from the minimum in winter to the maximum in summer. Owing to the relatively small number of murders, the annual curves for this crime show certain wide divergences, without, however, destroying the general pattern based upon an increase during the summer months. Aggravated assaults, on the other hand, show a well-defined pattern year after year, while rape is subject to such violent fluctuation from month to month that it is only from the five-year average that any well-defined upward tendency during the summer months can be ascertained.

[7] Figures I and II are based upon returns from over 90 per cent of all cities in excess of 100,000 population, which have a combined population of more than 44,000,000. Rates for months of differing lengths have been equalized by employing daily rates for each month. See Chap. III for traffic accident fatalities.

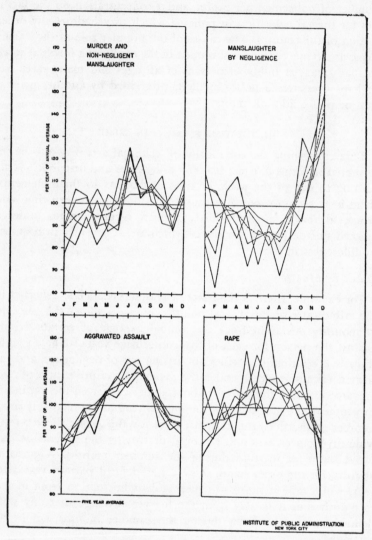

Figure I   Monthly distribution of crimes against the person, for each of five consecutive years, with five-year average.

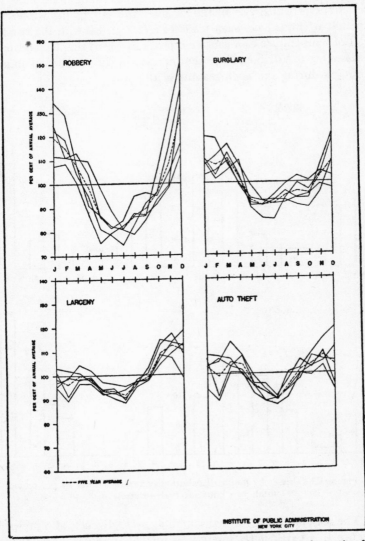

Figure II   Monthly distribution of crimes against property, for each of five consecutive years, with five-year average.

Of all the reportable offenses, these three crimes alone show seasonal curves which rise in the summer and fall in the winter. Although attempts have been made to associate this with the rise and fall of temperature as a causative factor, it seems simpler and more reasonable to attribute it to the increase in the number of human contacts during the open seasons of the year.

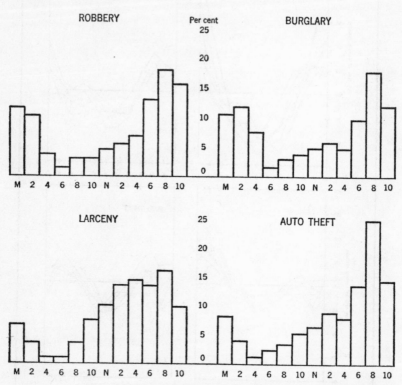

Figure III   Crimes by hours, distribution of certain crimes by per cent of total; two hour intervals—Detroit 1958.

The seasonal curve for manslaughter by negligence, also shown in Figure I, is particularly interesting in that it runs counter to that of the other crimes against the person. Still it must be remembered that this crime does not rest upon any element of actual malice or criminal intent. Practically all the crimes of this character arise out of the negligent operation of motor vehicles, and hence are more clearly related to the seasonal traffic accident curve than to crimes arising out of criminal interest and design. Fatal traffic accidents are most numerous during the autumn and early winter months, and it is to this fact that the monthly curve for negligent manslaughter may be most reasonably correlated.

Reportable crimes against property—robbery, burglary, larceny, and auto theft—show some tendency to increase during the winter and to decrease during the summer months, as shown in Figure III. As to these crimes, the repetition year after year of substantially identical curves is so marked as to lend special support to this conclusion, without relying upon the generalized curves for the entire five-year period. The seasonal swing is most pronounced in the case of robbery, which shows a 50 per cent fluctuation from minimum to maximum levels, but even as to the others it is sufficiently sharp to have some significance. It may be stated with a considerable degree of confidence that the variations in the length of days and nights with the changing seasons have a direct influence here, since the winter months provide more hours of darkness during which robberies, burglaries, and larcenies may be committed. This conclusion is heavily fortified by the facts adduced with reference to the distribution of crimes by time of day, treated at a later point in this chapter.

Crime Distribution by Day of Week

Organized data on the distribution of crimes by day of week are for the most part so inconsequential as not to warrant formal tabulation. When, however, these fragmentary sources are taken in conjunction with the reports of miscellaneous complaints, and with the results of more or less systematic observations by police and others, it appears that Friday and Saturday are often featured by the highest crime levels for such offenses as robbery, burglary, larceny, auto theft, aggravated assault, disorderly conduct, and public intoxication. Sometimes the spread between these two days and the balance of the week is not great, though on occasion it may rise as much as 50 per cent over the week's low point. But these general relationships appear to be so consistently maintained as to raise a strong presumption that the leisure generally enjoyed during week ends is conducive to the commission of certain offenses against persons and property. The presumption is also supported in some degree by the distribution of offenses during the leisure hours of the day, as described in the following section.

Although no data are available showing the effect of midweek holidays upon the incidence of crimes, the foregoing tentative conclusions suggest that these also may have relatively high levels. It therefore remains for police forces to analyze the rich supply of factual data already at their command, to the end that this available information may irrefutably substantiate the apparent distribution, or show how and to what extent the tentative conclusions here drawn must be qualified in the light of local conditions.

The all but universal acceptance of the five-day week by business and industry has been reflected in the peaks of police activity. Though Saturday and Sunday once were recognized as the most active days for police patrols, current experience in many cities would suggest that police activity rises throughout Friday afternoon and remains at a high rate until Saturday midnight or early Sunday morning. Sunday has become one of the least active days of the week for the police in many jurisdictions.

From the standpoint of police manpower requirements, the incidence of crime is not the only indicator of police activity. In some form or another virtually all police departments maintain a record of radio broadcasts and station assignments to all police vehicles. A few hours devoted to suitable tabulations of police assignments, roughly classified as to type of call, should be a revelation to many police administrators who believe that they have adequate patrol car coverage during predictable active days of the week.

Distribution of Crime by Hours

The hourly distribution of crimes against property in the city of Detroit, as shown in Figure III, is interesting chiefly because it serves to substantiate the hypothesis that leisure and darkness are factors influencing the commission of certain crimes. These graphic representations taken together include 29,000 crimes against property, as to which the hour of commission was approximately or definitely known. Of the four crimes included, the time of commission for robberies can be determined more frequently than for any of the others because the complainant is necessarily present when the crime is committed. But most burglaries, auto thefts, and other larcenies are committed by stealth, and as to these crimes a considerable proportion (sometimes running over 50 per cent in the case of burglaries) cannot be definitely fixed within any of the two-hour brackets upon which the compilations are based. Thus the profiles do not and cannot represent any fixed proportion of total crimes committed, since the time of commission for many crimes is unknown. They are merely general indicators of the hourly distribution, with the probabilities strongly favoring a more pronounced peak of crimes during the hours of darkness than is shown here: this for the reason that crimes committed during the daylight hours are more quickly discovered (and the hour of commission thereby definitely determined) in a larger proportion of instances than is possible for crimes committed at night.

The hourly distribution of crimes against the person does not easily lend itself to similar treatment, because the number of reported crimes is naturally much smaller than is the case with crimes against property, and the percentage distribution is thereby rendered less certain because of inadequate sampling. However, a tabulation of murders and aggravated assaults provides a profile which is somewhat similar to that for automobile thefts in Figure III. Sixteen per cent of these crimes against the person are committed during the extreme peak hours, from 10:00 P.M. to midnight; and 45 per cent during the high-level six-hour period between 8:00 P.M. and 2:00 A.M. During this maximum interval the level is more than four times that maintained between 4:00 A.M. and noon. Thus the patterns already established for crimes against property would appear to have a certain application to crimes against the person also. The nighttime hours when people are still awake and at leisure seem to offer the most favorable setting for their commission.

Just as the radio logs of assignments to patrol cars can aid in the identification of active days of the week, so also they can identify active hours for the police. The variety of demands upon the police service, as reflected in the radio call record, is astonishing. The vast majority of police services are not of a strictly criminal nature: fire calls, traffic congestion, aid to the sick, escorts, even taxi service for welfare recipients and other department employees. All of the police calls, as well as the normal meal periods, remove patrols from service for a greater or lesser period of time. Alert administrators will recognize that the average call, travel and report time considered, will remove a patrol from service for perhaps a half hour. A tabulation by area served may well reveal that at peak hours the police patrol to prevent crime is hopelessly hampered by the multitude of coincident assignments.

IV. CRIME AND THE CRIMINAL JUSTICE MACHINE

Offenses Cleared by Arrest

No satisfactory general measure of police activity and efficiency has ever been devised, and it seems at best doubtful whether one ever will be. Police activity is too pervasive and too varied to lend itself to close measurement. The best single index consists in the proportion of reported offenses for which persons have been arrested and formally charged. Thus if one person is arrested and charged with three locally reported offenses, three offenses would thereby be "cleared by arrest"; whereas if three persons are arrested and one or more is charged with committing the same reported offense, only one offense would thereby be "cleared by arrest."[8] Such data are not as yet reported by rural police agencies, but the record for over 1,800 American cities is now available.

Offense clearances follow certain well-defined patterns.[9] For example, police success is much greater with respect to crimes against the person (which constituted only about 5 per cent of the reportable offenses in cities) than is the case with the far more numerous crimes against property. While the relative gravity of crimes lies wholly within the realm of opinion, most people would probably agree that crimes against the person represent a more serious threat to civil peace and social order than do crimes against property. The police reflect this view and devote a relatively large part of their energies to the investigation of offenses against the person. They are greatly assisted in thus directing their efforts by the fact that these crimes are not relatively numerous. Such crimes lend themselves more readily to successful investigation because they are usually open and flagrant in character, and are committed in the presence of witnesses, including the complainant. Hence about 80 per cent of the reportable crimes against the person are cleared by police action. Homicides actually show the best results, with over 90 per cent cleared, while aggravated assault and rape commonly average from 10 to 15 points lower in the percentage scale.

[8] See footnotes 15 and 16, supra.
[9] For the regulations prescribed in reporting "offenses cleared by arrest," see Uniform Crime Reporting, Secs. 7, 61-67.

Most of the reportable crimes against property, on the other hand, are committed by stealth, and suspects must therefore be traced chiefly through the use and disposition of stolen property.

Robberies are cleared by arrest in about 40 per cent of all reported crimes, burglaries in from 25 to 30 per cent, auto thefts in 25 per cent, and miscellaneous larcenies, large and small, in from 15 to 20 per cent. Here it will be noted that best results are secured with respect to robberies, which permit some degree of identification of robbers by their victims. Yet by and large the record is not impressive, particularly as the most numerous crimes show the lowest clearance rates.

Such data as are available indicate that police generally do not meet with a greater degree of success in recovering stolen property than in apprehending and charging persons for its theft.[10]

The prospect for improvement in effecting arrests and recoveries for property crimes is somewhat confined within a vicious circle, for unless offenses decline in number the police will be overburdened in their investigation, whereas if offenders are not promptly arrested and convicted there is a lessened prospect of reducing the crime rate. That such baffling considerations are not wholly controlling is evidenced by the fact that crime rates do seem to decline in response to the operation of various social forces, including police, prosecutors, courts and jailers, among others. From this is derived the official and popular pressure to improve the criminal justice machine, in an effort to break through the vicious circle and start the crime rate spiraling downward.

Proportion of Defendants Convicted

Prosecutions and convictions in trial courts of general jurisdiction offer some measure of the effectiveness of this stage of the criminal justice process. The proportion of defendants who are convicted and sentenced varies with the type of crime. It generally ranges from 45 per cent to 65 per cent for crimes against the person (murder and manslaughter, assaults with a weapon, and rape), 75 to 80 per cent for robbery and burglary, auto theft, and miscellaneous larcenies.[11]

[10] Recoveries of stolen motor cars are at such a high rate as to constitute an outstanding exception.

[11] U. S. Bureau of the Census; *Judicial Criminal Statistics* (publication discontinued, 1945). See also, *Uniform Crime Reports*.

When the situation is viewed state by state, wide variations in policy and procedure are reflected in the percentage of convictions. Some states will convict only 60 per cent or 70 per cent of their major offenders and impose and execute rather heavy sentences upon them; in other states, where felons may readily plead guilty to a lesser offense, convictions may run over 90 per cent of the total, but with probation so freely used as to involve direct penalties for very few of the offenders passing through the judicial mill.

Thus it is apparent that there are many factors and conflicting influences to be considered in placing responsibility for ultimate results obtained by police, prosecutors and courts. The ratio of convictions for crimes against property is consistently higher than that for crimes against the person. In other words, prosecution is most successful in securing convictions for those crimes as to which the police encounter the greatest difficulty in making arrests, and it is least successful in the field where the police make their best showing. Indeed, if the record of the inferior courts which conduct the preliminary examinations of persons charged with felony and other grave offenses were included in the judicial dispositions, the record of such minor tribunals and of the trial courts, taken together, would appear even less favorable.[12]

While the situation is much too involved to permit broad generalizations as to responsibility, it is clear that the functioning of the judicial machine is far from perfect. Sometimes the degree of imperfection challenges attention. Thus the pioneer study of criminal justice in Missouri showed that less than 40 per cent of the felony cases originating with the issue of a warrant were prosecuted to a conviction,[13] while a similar inquiry in Illinois demonstrated that only 20 per cent of felony defendants were adjudged guilty.[14]

It is customary for prosecutors to complain that police arrest many persons against whom no valid charge can be laid and that as to others the police investigation is too inadequately performed to lay the groundwork for a successful prosecution. The police counter

[12] See, for example, Raymond Moley, *Tribunes of the People* (1932).
[13] C. E. Gehlke, "A Statistical Interpretation of the Criminal Process," in *The Missouri Crime Survey* (1926), p. 276.
[14] C. E. Gehlke, *Recorded Felonies: An Analysis and General Survey* in *The Illinois Crime Survey* (1929), p. 35.

with the criticism that magistrates, prosecutors, and trial judges are not sufficiently rigorous in their application of penal statutes to persons arrested, and that the community is thereby deprived of the protection and the assumed benefits of penal treatment for offenders. There are many commentaries in support of either or both of these positions, and while it is obviously impossible to strike a balance between them, the foregoing summaries indicate that there is still much room for possible improvement by each.

V. SOCIAL CHARACTERISTICS OF THE OFFENDER

So much has been written concerning the criminal offender—his antecedents, early life, mores, occupation, housing, anthropological and psychological characteristics, and the like—as to defy generalization in a broad survey such as is here attempted. Some of the researches in this ever-widening field of inquiry are still in the exploratory stage, and none has yet reached the point where definite conclusions can be drawn. Yet it may contribute somewhat to an understanding of police problems if the characteristics of offenders readily lending themselves to measurement are presented in summary form. Here the purpose will be confined to describing in general and objective terms the persons with whom the police are called upon to deal in the daily performance of their duties.

If the proportion of persons arrested and charged in American cities holds good for the country as a whole, somewhere near 30 per cent of the total population is annually arrested or is summoned and charged by the police. While charges of traffic and motor vehicle violations, drunkenness, and disorderly conduct account for about 95 per cent of these, the fact remains that in the course of a few years the police have occasion to charge practically every able-bodied adult with some offense of greater or less gravity.

Some limitation of the group passing through the hands of the police therefore seems necessary at the outset; for if all persons arrested or summoned were to be included, the result would come near to involving the entire community. Statutes and regulations carrying penal sanctions are now so numerous, and cover such a wide range of acts which are not crimes *per se,* that some of them are violated at some time by practically everyone.

Neither can the characteristics of persons who are confined in penal institutions be employed with much profit, since so many first offenders and others, particularly youthful criminals, are as a matter of public policy allowed to escape the rigors of penal servitude.

There remains the considerable bulk of information concerning certain characteristics of persons who have been arrested and fingerprinted and whose identification records have been deposited by some ten thousand federal, state, and local police units, with the national division of identification at Washington.[15] While police practices are not uniform in all respects, as a general rule only those persons are fingerprinted who have been charged with indictable offenses, or who because of previous criminal record are fingerprinted again regardless of the gravity of the offense currently charged. In any case, the relationships derived from this source are in general conformity with those indicated by records of arrests, convictions, and the like.[16] Thus the group which will now be brought under examination comes fairly close to representing what may be described as "the criminal class."

Sex and Age of Offenders

Although males and females in the United States are approximately equal in number, men provide by far the larger proportion of persons who are arrested and fingerprinted. Male offenders outnumber females in a ratio of twelve or thirteen to one. The two sexes do not show any extraordinary differences in the types of crime charged against them except such as are more or less naturally associated with sex differences. Thus rape, by its definition almost everywhere, is distinctly a male offense, and burglary shows a similar tendency, owing perhaps to the factor of strength and agility which enters into its commission.

The age groupings of offenders show a marked concentration during the earlier years of life. If the minor depredations committed by small children, for which no comprehensive data are available, be excluded and the comparison confined to groups over fifteen years of age, the criminal ages of man stand out in bold relief. In making such comparison it is necessary to take due account of the

[15] See the *Uniform Crime Reports*.
[16] See, for example, the careful study of Thorsten Sellin, *The Criminality of Youth—A Statistical Investigation* (American Law Institute, 1939); together with Supplement I thereto.

fact that the proportion of persons at different ages also varies some-what for the general population.

If the criminal propensity of each age group is thus reduced to specific rates it develops that the twelve-year period from age eighteen to age thirty marks the crest of criminal activity, with a bold peak between nineteen and twenty-five years of age, and a rapid falling off after age thirty-five. Owing to the fact that police are reluctant to fingerprint offenders below the age of eighteen years, and are often prohibited by the juvenile delinquency laws from fingerprinting offenders below the ages of eighteen, seventeen, or sixteen, as the case may be, there is a strong probability that the foregoing generalization reflects a lower crime rate for the fifteen to nineteen age bracket than prevails in actual fact. Even without allowance for this possible distortion, it is clear that high rates for burglary, auto theft, and other larcenies begin with the seventeen-year group.

In the course of an extensive inquiry into the ages of all persons arrested or committed on sentence in various jurisdictions for both major and minor offenses, Thorsten Sellin has observed that "the relative number of youths appears to be small in the case of assaults, embezzlement and fraud, violation of narcotic drug laws, liquor law violation, organized vice, nonsupport, drunken driving, disorderly conduct, drunkenness and gambling. In sex offenses other than rape and in vagrancy, the proportion seems small as well. On the other hand, about one-fourth of these dealt with for robbery were youths, and an even larger proportion of those arrested or committed for auto theft and burglary were youths. High proportions are also noted in larceny, receiving stolen property, rape, and the carrying of dangerous weapons. While youths do not dominate any large number of types of offenses, it is obvious that they figure greatly in the case of certain major crimes.[17]

While the peak age based on specific rates is twenty-two years, the raw figures annually compiled may sometimes run as much as four or five years lower. Many commentators have dwelt upon the fact that the modern criminal is young, and have drawn a gloomy picture of what the future holds. But this is by no means a recent development and there is some reason to believe that it has long been

[17] Sellin, *op. cit.*, p. 20.

associated with youth's physical vigor, leisure, and economic dependence.[18]

Nativity and Race

In a country such as the United States, which has been inundated by the greatest wave of migration in all history, any relationship between nativity, race, and criminality holds special interest. Much has been made of the fact that our people are not so homogeneous as those of other nations, and that our high crime rates may be largely attributable to this. Some go even further and lay our crime conditions at the door of foreign-born whites and of Negroes. Examination of the specific rates for the three major elements of our population only partially substantiates such statements.

The number of native whites, foreign-born whites, and Negroes who are arrested and fingerprinted, when taken in conjunction with the numbers of these respective groups in the general population, indicates that the specific rate for native whites is double, and the rate for Negroes six times that for foreign-born whites. The rather striking differences reflected by these ratios are not, however, by any means conclusive, since, as has just been shown, age and sex have a pronounced effect upon the incidence of crime.

A test of the validity of the foregoing ratios can be secured by reference to the age groupings of these several elements in the general population. For if any of them are relatively numerous between the ages of eighteen and thirty-five when crime rates are highest, or beyond age forty-five when crime rates are lowest, the conclusions to be drawn will be correspondingly affected.

Since the age distribution of native whites and Negroes is very similar, the higher incidence of crime among Negroes (as indicated by the proportion of persons arrested and fingerprinted) is established insofar as such compilations can establish it.

Foreign-born whites, however, have a quite different age distribu-

---

[18] Pike, *A History of Crime in England*, Vol. II, pp. 512-516, 668-670; Aschaffenburg, *Crime and Its Repression*, pp. 142 ff.; Lombroso, *Crime, Its Causes and Remedies*, pp. 179-180; Tarde, *Penal Philosophy*, pp. 310-311; Sutherland, *Principles of Criminology*, pp. 87-91; Gillin, *Criminology and Penology*, pp. 41-43. Among recent foreign sources, see Roesner, "Alter und Straffällinkeit," in *Handwörterbuch der Kriminologie*, 1:22-34 (1932); and others cited and summarized by Sellin in his report on *The Criminality of Youth—A Statistical Investigation*.

tion. Thus the possibility arises that the relatively low arrest rate for foreign-born whites is due, in part at least, to the fact that so many foreign-born whites fall within the higher age brackets where the arrest rate for the general population is lowest. With immigration at a low point for many years, this disproportionately large group above thirty-five years of age has for some time been growing even larger. Thus, no matter how grave the crime problem among the foreign-born may once have been, this group is of diminishing importance and, barring major changes of immigration policy, it is destined to drop to inconsequential levels.

Such attempts at refinement of apparent characteristics are interesting, and if confirmed when more extensive data become available may even prove to be significant. They should not, however, be permitted to obscure two bold and inescapable conclusions: (1) that the arrest rate for Negroes is incomparably the highest; (2) that the high level of criminal activity in this country is no longer directly due to the alien in our midst. Our crime record is now made in America—not overseas.

This much at least is true for the United States as a whole, though it must be remembered that in some of our cities the foreign-born still comprise one-third or more of the total population and hence constitute a special kind of crime problem from that fact alone. Furthermore, the foreign-born whites are not themselves by any means homogeneous, being composed of Canadians, Britons, Irishmen, western and eastern Europeans, Mediterraneans, and many others. Some of these have higher rates of criminality than the others and there are numerous fragmentary compilations indicating that they occasionally exceed the native white rate by a wide margin.[19] It is probably due to the high crime rates among such limited national groups that the widely held impression concerning foreign-born whites has been formed. Certainly it is not now correct for the group as a whole.

Even though the general rate among foreign-born whites is low, it does not follow that these low ratios apply to all offenses. On the contrary, there are indications that it consistently equals or slightly exceeds that of the native whites for assault and arson and for buy-

[19] See Sutherland, *Principles of Criminology,* pp. 112-115, for a summary of these studies.

ing, receiving, and possessing stolen property. Upon occasion the foreign-born rate may also show some excess with respect to criminal homicide, burglary, and the laws regulating intoxicants, gambling, and weapons.

Negroes also show strongly marked proclivities with respect to certain offenses. Although their rate is relatively high as to all crimes, it is especially so with respect to criminal homicide, assault, and the violation of laws regulating intoxicants, gambling, and weapons. It will be noted that this list bears a striking resemblance to that given above for the foreign-born.

One other major element in our population remains to be considered. It consists of the large and miscellaneous group that is native to these shores, but is descended either from foreign parentage (both parents born abroad) or from mixed parentage (one foreign-born and one native-born parent). Occasional reference is made to the fact that this group constitutes a special crime problem and that it is more inclined to criminality than any of the other groups which have been examined here.

No general data on arrests are as yet available for the native-born of foreign or mixed parentage and recourse must be had to comparisons based upon prison and reformatory records and various other fragments which are certainly not the best indices either of crime or of the distribution of criminals. On this point Sutherland summarizes the situation by observing that:

This excessive criminality of the second generation of immigrants has been generally recognized, although the statistical demonstration of the excess is perhaps not conclusive. Special studies have indicated that the delinquency rates of the second generation are comparatively low when an immigrant group first settles in a community and increase as contacts with the surrounding culture multiply. The rate remains low in these foreign colonies which are comparatively isolated from the surrounding culture. The rate is low in the heart of the colony but increases on the borderlines where the group comes into contact with other groups. Moreover the rates are comparatively low in the immigrant groups which have moved away from the areas of deterioration into the better residential neighborhoods. The statistics indicate, also, that the rates are comparatively high for the children in families in which the parents are not of the same nativity. These things point to a conclusion that the high rate of the second generation of immigrants is due to the contacts with delinquency in America and to the conflict of standards.[20]

Beyond this point it is not safe to go. All the statistical compilations concerning the relation between crime and race or nativity have produced only a welter of uncertainties on the biological factor in crime. Even the very high crime rate among Negroes, which seems well established in some communities, does not exist in others. In addition, the element of race prejudice as it affects the ratio of arrests must be considered,[21] together with the possibility that we are actually measuring not the racial factor but the effect of special economic conditions which influence the Negro in some parts of the United States.

Out of all this confusion one set of facts seems to be above question—namely, that Negroes contribute more than their share to the mass of people who fall afoul of the criminal law. The underlying causes for this condition we do not know. They may eventually be shown to have no bearing upon race or nativity. Yet police have reason to know and the data here briefly summarized tend to demonstrate that the presence of a large proportion of Negro, foreign-born, and foreign-parentage elements in the population of a community greatly increases both the size and the complexity of the crime problem.

Previous Criminal Record

A substantial proportion of the persons arrested and fingerprinted are identified as having been previously arrested and fingerprinted. This great body of recidivists now annually exceeds 60 per cent, with indications that the proportion will continue to increase for some years to come, owing to the fact that, as the identification files of

[20] E. H. Sutherland, op. cit., pp. 115-116. It is doubtful whether even this slightly unfavorable evidence against the second generation of immigrant stock has any validity. Cf. Sellin, Culture Conflict and Crime, pp. 78 ff.

[21] The arrest figures here under review do not on their face reflect any such prejudice. If racial prejudice entered into them in any marked degree, it is likely that the ratio of arrests for vagrancy and "suspicion" would be disproportionately high. But this is not the case—on the contrary, arrests on these charges tend to run proportionately lower for Negroes (and for foreign-born whites likewise) than they do for native whites. For a summary of other evidence tending to limit the value and qualify the meaning of arrest rates in relation to race, cf. The Annals, Vol. CXXXX, No. 229 (November, 1928), pp. 52-64.

arrested persons become more nearly complete, the proportion of identifications naturally increases.

Highest ratios of repeaters are registered for such crimes as violations of narcotic drug laws, forgery and counterfeiting, embezzlement and fraud, and robbery. These serve to give further definition to the nature of the crime problem in America, though they embrace a group which does not greatly exceed 50,000 offenders in any one year. Most of the total 500,000 known repeaters annually arrested and fingerprinted are distributed over the entire range of criminal offenses. These are a real challenge to our decentralized police system.

The Transient Criminal

Police have frequent occasion to remark that nonresidents constitute a substantial part of the daily totals of arrests. These observations have a direct bearing upon the crime problem, because offenders who are without local ties prove more difficult to locate and investigate.

It is probably true that a part of the high crime rates attaching to great urban centers is traceable to the population shift from farm to city that has been going on for several generations. Lack of specifically related data prevents close comparisons in the urban–rural setting. For the country as a whole there is some supporting evidence to be derived from the fact that less than one-fourth of our native population resides outside the state in which born, whereas one-half of those who are arrested and fingerprinted are taken into custody outside of the state of birth. This disparity is suggestive, but far from conclusive. More specific figures are needed which will permit comparisons on the basis of age groupings, for as already indicated, these are often decisive in determining the frequency of arrests. Another qualification may be traced to the indiscriminate "round-ups" conducted by some police forces, in the course of which all tramps, migratory workers, and other "floaters" are brought to the police net without too much regard for the substantiation of charges against them, plus the fact any offender is more likely to be taken into custody if he is far from his residential roots when police make contact with him.

VI. PROPERTY LOSSES AND RECOVERIES

The slogan "Crime Does Not Pay!" has been carried far and wide across the country. Its announced purpose is to convince the prospective offender that the rewards of crime are not sufficiently great to warrant the risk of imprisonment and other penalties. The data already presented tend to indicate that the risk of arrest, prosecution, and imprisonment is none too great even though it is unlikely that any but a small proportion of recidivists wholly escape the sanctions of the penal law in the long run.

Coincident with warnings of inadequate financial returns, however, gloomy estimates are made of the total cost of criminal operations. These may run as high as $15 billion annually. There is precious little factual basis for such impressively large figures. Nevertheless, they do serve to reopen the question whether crime is really so unremunerative as is sometimes assumed. On this score it is interesting and instructive to examine the average value of property stolen in connection with the commission of certain offenses and attempted offenses. Viewed over the years it is apparent that there has been a well-defined rising level of average value involved. Though this may merely be a reflection of monetary inflation, auto thefts do show an average value of over $1,000, robberies over $200, burglaries over $175 and miscellaneous larcenies over $70.

Law-abiding and self-supporting persons will not be greatly impressed by the size of these figures in dollars and cents, but it must be borne in mind that mere averages conceal cases involving much larger (as well as somewhat smaller) unlawful returns. The losses, furthermore, are based upon both completed crimes and attempts, with inclusion of the latter tending to reduce the average loss per successful operation. On the other hand, the amount of financial loss suffered as the result of crime often is not the measure of gain to the criminal. Certain types of stolen merchandise can be disposed of only through criminal receivers, or "fences," who take heavy toll for their services. Experience shows also that a considerable proportion of all stolen property is pledged or sold to pawnbrokers and secondhand dealers, and here again allowance must be made for reduced returns in appraising the net gain to the thief himself.

Over and above all such qualifications stands the fact that a disquieting proportion of those committing crimes against property are young persons who do not rob and steal for a steady income but for the opportunity to indulge in conspicuous spending. To such as these the average pecuniary returns of crime as indicated above doubtless appear more substantial than they are.

Worthy of passing mention here is the ratio of recoveries. Because of their high value, ease of identification and difficulties in concealment, stolen cars are regularly recovered in over nine-tenths of all auto thefts. This contrasts sharply with the small proportion cleared by arrest. But other types of property are restored to owners in less than one-fourth of all instances.

Thus on the basis of the summaries appearing throughout this chapter it may fairly be said that crime does pay—not well, nor without interruption, and not without occasional heavy penalties for failure—but moderately and with modest personal risks.

There are apparently many causes of crime and one of them arises from the inadequate protection afforded in the face of the greatest accumulation of wealth and the greatest popular taste for luxurious indulgence that the world has ever known. Some of the underlying causes of crime are not readily amenable to social treatment, but the prospect for criminal success is sufficient to stand as a continuing challenge to American communities—and to their police, prosecutors, judges, and jailers.

VII. CRIME AND THE POLICE PROBLEM

The foregoing generalizations really tell us little about crime and even less about the criminal. That is a fault inherent in all broad treatments: in their search for common denominators they necessarily ignore many special features that may have equal or even greater value in an understanding of causes and relationships. Progress in the identification of the causes of crime has thus far been slow, and while there are many hypotheses there are as yet no certainties. Pending the development of a wider and deeper knowledge of such basic factors, the incidence of crime and the superficial characteristics of the offender have a practical application to the realities of police protection and the control of criminal acts. The geographical distribution of reportable crimes, the relationship between the crime rate and the size of communities, the regular ebb and flow of the criminal tide with the seasons of the year, its rise and fall with the days of the week and the hours of the day, the varying success of police and prosecutors in bringing offenders to justice, the social characteristics of the offenders themselves, and the appraisal of crime as a gainful occupation—all these have a bearing upon the police problem, both from the standpoint of the public and from that of the officials charged with the complex tasks of police management.

The amazingly large proportion of the population annually charged with violation of penal statutes and ordinances holds grave implications for the future of our police systems. Some will strive to find in this high ratio evidence of the inherent criminal propensities of the American people. There seems, however, to be little in the figures themselves to substantiate this view. We have long since abandoned our hard-and-fast definitions of criminal conduct. We impose the sanctions of the penal law upon many who, while perhaps willful violators, are not by any stretch of the imagination criminals in the sense in which that term is generally and properly used. The complexities of modern life appear to have made it necessary to formulate a host of regulations of human affairs which can be enforced only by imposing various penalties for their infraction, and these are dealt with as crimes. But if we look behind such superficial indices to criminality we find that, as to the more common of the basic common-law crimes, only about 1 per cent of the population is annually involved. Control of such a small minority would not seem to be beyond the powers of the mighty governmental machine which has been erected by modern society.

Yet the large numbers of people who are formally charged with some violation—whether major or minor—when taken in conjunction with the much larger group of unknown proportions which is informally warned or reprimanded, constitute one of the most serious problems with which the police have to deal. Here the sheer weight of administrative routine entailed by all these charges and admonitions is a burden which the police find it difficult to carry. If they dealt with all minor infractions coming to their knowledge it is doubtful whether the police and judicial mechanisms could continue to function at all. Even under their more or less informal schemes for selective enforcement, police are confronted with problems for which no solutions have yet been devised. For if police are to use their powers against any large proportion of the people, those whose freedom of action has been restricted will hold grievances against them which surpass, in the bitterness engendered, any possible inconvenience such restriction may have caused. No matter how efficient a police force may be, and no matter how careful it is to observe civil liberties of long standing, it will always have to fight its way against an undercurrent of opposition and criticism from some of the very elements which it is paid to serve and protect, and to which it is in the last analysis responsible. This is the enduring problem of a police force in a democracy.

Other problems arise from the emergency character of most police services. Under badly organized systems this factor keeps a police force in a constant state of instability, with administrative superiors rushing hither and yon in an effort to keep abreast of the developments of the moment. The data here assembled indicate that such emergencies can be anticipated in some degree since it is possible to forecast with reasonable accuracy the time, place, and character of certain types of criminal acts. Detailed local studies of the incidence of crime, such as are presented above in a generalized way, hold real promise for a more systematic distribution and application of police resources and a more orderly execution of police duties.

This rather melancholy picture of the functioning of the police and judicial machine, of which the mere outlines have been sketched, will continue for many years to be a reproach to our system of criminal justice. The machine itself is still too complex to be responsive to even the most expert control. The causes of crime are still unidentified with any useful degree of precision. Our knowledge of the criminal is crude and rudimentary. So much needs to be done from day to day that the problem defies analysis in simple terms which can be readily apprehended by a public busily and necessarily concerned with its own affairs. Nevertheless, signs are not wanting that the functioning of police, prosecutors, judges, and jailers is in fact improving under the stimulus of popular disapproval of past and current failures. If this ameliorative process is continued and the gains already made are consolidated and extended, it is perhaps not too much to hope that the crime question may eventually take a secondary position among our national problems.

CHAPTER 3

THE TRAFFIC PROBLEM

Highway traffic regulation stems from two sets of factors. One set embraces the varied technologies clustering about the design and use of highways and motorcars. The other is concerned with questions of enforcement that involve scores of millions of operators and severely test the effectiveness of our police and judicial systems. Taken together these factors produce one of the largest public regulation problems of our time.

That America's share of the problem is incomparably the greatest in the world is almost self-evident, since we have three times as many motor vehicles as the combined total of all other nations. This extraordinary concentration has produced some extraordinary methods of control, with the numerous mechanical, electrical, and statutory devices here employed in the regulation of highway traffic finding no real counterparts elsewhere. It also compels an approach without much aid from foreign experience, while the rapidly expanding use of highways raises new and perplexing situations before tests of prevailing methods can be completed. Some traffic developments are of such recent origin that the accumulated experience and personal skills required for engineering tasks of first magnitude, are not yet equal to the demands made upon them.

The first successful demonstrations of a highway vehicle propelled by an internal combustion engine were conducted during the closing years of the last century. If anyone then was able to forecast the revolution in the conditions of urban and rural life that was implicit in these early efforts, his prescience went unregarded. The following decade marked the appearance of the motorcar as a familiar object, but it was not until the years immediately preceding the First World War that traffic congestion in urban centers was widely recognized as an urgent issue.

The abrupt manner in which that issue was drawn is indicated by the number of cars in operation at various times. The record starts with only four motor vehicles in the entire United States in 1895. By 1900 there were eight thousand, by 1910 nearly half a million, by 1920 nearly ten million, in 1930 over twenty-five million, and in 1940 over thirty million. While the years of World War II witnessed a moderate decline in motor vehicle registrations, the return to more normal conditions quickly restored the long-term upward trend, with postwar registrations crossing the sixty-five million mark for the first time. This impressive upswing in the number of motor vehicles has had a controlling influence upon the development of the traffic and accident problem. The full extent of that influence can scarcely be overestimated.

Better Cars and Better Highways

When the first cars made their appearance on the highways of this country, few of our three million miles of rural roads were hard-surfaced. Today almost half of the total is thus improved, and an increasing mileage is designed to permit the highest speeds of which stock cars are now capable. Meandering roads have been straightened and widened. Two-lane highways have been enlarged to accommodate three, four, six, and even eight lanes of traffic. Opposed streams of traffic are separated and defined by surface markings, and by concrete curbs or wide nontraffic strips. Electrically operated signal systems for highway intersections, once the exclusive concern of large cities, now feature not only the great rural thoroughfares, but are even encountered at village crossways. One-way streets, restricted-use avenues, and a bewildering variety of signs admonishing the motorist to stop or slow down, to avoid left turns or parking, to beware of steep grades, sharp curves, slippery road surfaces, and school crossings, and to observe quiet in passing hospitals—such as these have become common aids to traffic control everywhere. Many of the new highways are designed to accommodate large interurban buses, and the six, ten, and fourteen-wheeled trucks that day and night carry an increasing proportion of the nation's fast freight.

Like the new highways, our motorcars are designed for speed.

More than one-third of the traffic on expressways moves at speeds in excess of 50 miles an hour. Even on city streets a substantial component travels at rates that make a mockery of low-limit ordinances. These are but symptoms of a condition of long standing.

Since the early days of motoring, when most cars were operated under 20 miles per hour, the average top speeds of American stock cars in the low-price group have increased amazingly. As recently as 1927 this average was only 48 miles per hour. By 1932 it had risen to 70 miles, it exceeded 80 miles in 1934, and has since shown tendencies toward further increase.

Research and development have greatly increased attainable speeds not alone through the application of more and more mechanical power, but also through improved design and construction contributing to the essential safety of the rolling vehicle itself. Starting a half century ago as mere mechanized counterparts of the light horse-drawn carriages of that day, the motorcar has advanced through thousands upon thousands of structural and operating improvements. Driver guidance and control have been increased in numerous ways, braking power greatly enlarged and equalized, pneumatic tires are more secure from sudden deflation, headlight illumination is improved, and all car occupants are surrounded by steel surfaces and shatterproof glass.

Most such advances in design and construction were meaningless unless accompanied by higher operating speeds. Hence the whole logic of changes occurring not alone in the motor industry but on the ever-expanding network of express thoroughfares has led toward substantially higher average speeds, and vastly greater attainable speeds. Whether rightly or wrongly, many of those who are concerned with improving highway safety believe that speed represents the core of the accident problem. Thus far there is no evidence clearly establishing a causal relationship between speed and accidents, though it is obvious that speed aggravates the effects of collisions. Such uncertainty on a cardinal point greatly obscures the police view and unsettles a major segment of enforcement policy.

It is also disturbing to contemplate public attitudes of nonobservance where speed regulations are concerned. For the motorcar endows its operator with a sense of mastery over space and time that seems to afford extraordinary satisfaction to tens of millions of people. It is probably not too much to say that the mass of American citizens have a greater affection and regard for their automobiles than for their governments. Such imponderables promise to thwart all efforts to impose rigid speed controls.

Improving the Motorist by Regulation

No matter how great or how rapid the improvement in cars and highways, the motorist will always be a disturbing factor. To say that he operates his car at considerable peril to himself and to others is to state the obvious. So at every turn he is surrounded by governmental restrictions and limitations upon the manner of operation. Both in their variety and in the penalties imposed for infraction, they probably surpass any other form of public control over individual freedom of action.

The motorist is required to secure a license to operate, and to pass successfully practical tests in operation and the laws of the road. Physical and visual disabilities, or extreme youth or age, may disqualify him. In some states he is required to carry liability insurance to indemnify persons who suffer personal injuries or property damage at his hands. When he takes to the road, he is limited in the places where he may operate his car, even where he may stop it, in the length of time that he may leave it unattended on the highway, in the maximum speed (and sometimes also the minimum speed) that he is permitted to attain under varying conditions. Laws and regulations determine the manner in which he may pass moving or standing vehicles, and the manual signals he is to employ in signifying his intentions to slow down, turn, or bring his car to a stop. His use of headlights at night is closely defined. The warning horn with which his car is equipped must be used sparingly. In these and many other ways, government steps in to impose standards of conduct upon the motorist. To police is delegated the task of exacting compliance.

Full compliance, of course, is out of the question. Although prosecutions for motor vehicle and traffic offenses total each year more than one-half the number of motor vehicle operators, the actual but undisclosed number of violations must reach astronomical proportions. Thus the way is invitingly open toward an even greater degree of enforcement activity, with higher and ever higher totals of traffic citations, summonses, and arrests. The prospect should give us pause, lest our policies defeat our ends.

Some of the infractions are deliberate and arise from the belief in a certain segment of the motoring public that traffic laws and ordinances are unnecessarily restrictive. Other violations are unintentional, either because of ignorance of the regulations or because the latter are so varied and specific as to exceed the grasp or self-discipline of many operators. Most violations are not observed at all by enforcement officers and most of those that do come to the attention of police are ignored, tolerated, or condoned for various reasons. Even after the traffic offender has been summoned to appear before a magistrate, numerous devices come into play for disposing of his case without the formality of a judicial hearing.

It all adds up to a grand total of nonenforcement that is only remotely approached in other fields of criminal justice.

Unequal Enforcement Lowers Police Standards

The implications for police are disturbing. Any sharp rise in traffic enforcement would go far toward immobilizing the motorcar, and would surely diminish its social utility. Rapid personal transportation has become a major element in the national economy and substantial restriction would bring grave dislocations. The repercussions on police would be grave and immediate. But experience demonstrates that to tolerate widespread noncompliance is to invite administrative ills that ultimately attack the essential integrity of a police system.

This last danger is further aggravated by the fact that the traffic problem presents special hazards for enforcement policy. When police make an arrest for violation of the criminal code they usually can locate the aggrieved party and are alert in requiring him to make complaint and to swear out a warrant of arrest. The arresting officer thereby becomes a mere auxiliary part of the justice process. He can testify to what he knows without personal interest in or concern for the outcome, and can then pass along to the public prosecutor the chief responsibility for the manner of presenting the state's case.

The police situation is altogether different in the overwhelming majority of traffic cases. Here one generally finds no private complainants. If action is to be taken at all, it must be upon the initiative of a policeman. The discretionary element in enforcement thereby becomes decisive. The police officer can favor local offenders over those who are nonresidents, and vice versa. He can indulge racial, religious, political, fraternal, national, regional, and social prejudices almost at will. He can put a cash price on his nonenforcement with little danger of detection. When he does act, it is often because he personally feels impelled to do so; that is, because his own sense of justice or propriety has been offended. From this personal element in enforcement inevitably spring the harsh and overbearing attitudes and the abusive language so often attributed to traffic officers.

Police also occasionally contribute to unequal enforcement by "fixing" traffic violations. They may sell motorists admission tickets to benefit performances, or peddle associate memberships in police welfare associations. Police "courtesy cards" are losing their magic influence, though they are still with us. All these devices carry with them an implied immunity from traffic arrest or summons.

When the traffice violator appears in court to answer the charge against him, the arresting officer as likely as not is the only prosecuting agent who is present. A basic conflict thereupon develops between the role of the witness and that of prosecutor. The sworn obligation of the witness to tell the whole truth is impaired by the interest of the policeman who has initiated the action and now seeks to justify it before the court. Even when the traditionally disinterested status of the policeman is not thus affected, the offender, his family, and his friends are left unconvinced that such conflicting duties were actually performed with strict impartiality. The unfavorable effect upon popular attitudes and law observance can scarcely be overestimated.

Furthermore, the great bulk of traffic cases makes it impracticable to observe all of the safeguards that are provided for offenses of a graver nature. Juries are rarely impaneled. Often the justice is untrained in the law. The procedure is necessarily informal; the manner of the justice brusque and impatient. Judgments of guilty usually are reached in short order even though the sworn testimony of accuser and accused may be diametrically opposed. Such headlong dispositions are not confined to traffic cases, but are characteristic of them.

Unequal enforcement on a much larger scale appears when police administrators, harried by a public opinion that is aroused by the toll of highway accidents, seek to confine enforcement to the most hazardous thoroughfares or intersections, the most hazardous hours or days, or parking on the most congested thoroughfares. Reasonable though this approach may be as a means of securing quick results within a limited sphere of operation, downright necessary though it sometimes is as a practical matter, it represents an official abdication so far as the unemphasized locations, hours, or violations are concerned, and hence constitutes official toleration of all except the most pressing conditions. No matter how compelling the reasons for such policies, it is doubtful whether motorists and pedestrians can ever be educated, induced, or disciplined to better highway traffic habits by fast-and-loose enforcement. Hence the long outlook is unfavorable.

The Indices of Traffic Safety

Disconcerting as these features of traffic law administration may be, they are subordinated in public attention to a widespread anxiety concerning the extent and gravity of highway accidents. The trend has been so sharply upward for a half century as to produce widespread belief that efforts at control have thus far proved ineffective and that more radical methods must be employed in approaching the traffic problem. Hence almost any proposal for further traffic regulation receives an attentive hearing, while unequal enforcement is accepted without much concern for its effect upon individuals or the administration of criminal justice.

The number of highway accidents may be measured in various ways. Experience has shown that personal injury accidents, as well as those involving property damage alone, are too incompletely and too irregularly reported to offer a reliable yardstick that is equally applicable in all parts of the United States. While fatalities to motorists and pedestrians occur in only some 3 per cent of personal injury accidents on the highway, they are so uniformly reported as to provide a measure of superior reliability. Hence they are universally accepted and preferred as an index of traffic safety.[1]

From 1913, when the accident problem was just fairly emerging in its full nationwide proportions, to the eve of World War II in 1941, the number of motor vehicle fatalities increased almost ten-

[1] The National Safety Council's annual bulletin, *Accident Facts*, is replete with tabulations of highway fatalities.

fold, reaching the staggering annual total of 40,000 deaths in the latter year. This great upsurge was remarkably well maintained year by year throughout the period, and neither the gross figures nor the rate of increase provides any ground for complacency. It should be noted, however, that while the number of fatal accidents in relation to population shows a rising trend, the rate in terms of motor vehicles has decreased by 75 per cent since 1913. Since 1925 the ratio of deaths to vehicle miles has declined by more than one-half.

Our motor vehicle death rates in relation to population are naturally the highest in the world, but when comparison is made with other countries on the basis of numbers of motor vehicles the contrast is so striking as to challenge attention. Available prewar data indicate that the rate for the United States was from one-fourth to one-half of the rates then prevailing in Great Britain, Ireland, Sweden, Germany, Italy or Belgium, and that in a list of twenty nations for which such roughly comparable figures were available, this country had the third-best record. There is reason to believe that if the ranking could be made on the ratio of fatalities to vehicle miles our losses would prove to be the lowest in the entire world.

All this affords impressive evidence of the net results of the many engineering and enforcement measures that have been taken on behalf of highway safety. While it does not establish the value of any particular device, procedure or policy, it does lend confidence to a growing belief that our efforts to control the motorcar have succeeded in limiting the rise of highway accidents. The time is ripe to determine how and why such successes have been achieved.

The Age Factor in Traffic Accidents

Among the many characteristics of traffic accidents that have been laboriously compiled by students of the problem, several features invite emphasis here because of their bearing upon traffic law enforcement. The age distribution of persons involved in highway casualties offers a case in point.

As in criminal offenses, minors account for a disproportionately large share of motor vehicle accidents, with increasing age gradually reducing the ratio until age sixty is attained. At that point, however, the rate of involvement rises sharply, probably in response to visual and other defects commonly associated with advanced years. Since these data are the result of special studies that include the mileage driven by various age groups, they are accepted as indicating the need for special emphasis upon regulation of the youthful driver.

When the age distribution of all those killed in highway accidents is examined, somewhat similar results are observed. With the annual number of all motor vehicle deaths tripled during the thirty years following the close of World War I, it might be expected that all age groups would show some increase. Yet the challenging fact is that among children between the ages of five and fourteen years, the total number of fatalities has declined appreciably, particularly since 1927 the absolute decline is nearly one-half. That this amazing result could have been accomplished during a period when accident exposures, as measured by vehicle miles, were rising at a dizzy pace, goes far in supporting the assumption that safety lectures, by elementary school teachers, and police coverage of school crossings have served to control the accident rate among children of school age.

While these results are substantially verified when school-age fatalities in relation to the total number of school children are compared, such specific rates also disclose that fatal accidents among youths between fifteen and twenty-four years have more than doubled in thirty years. Here there is no blinking the fact that the agencies of safety education, highway protection, and law enforcement have thus far failed even to stem the unfavorable trend, much less reverse its direction. Until ways and means can be found for reducing fatalities among drivers, passengers, and pedestrians under twenty-five years of age, the outlook for highway safety is bound to be somewhat clouded.

A serious attempt to prevent traffic accidents among young drivers is being made through the high-school driver education program. Only a few states finance a part of the high-school driver training, though a study by the National Education Association suggests that the program has merit. A combination of classroom and behind-the-wheel-instruction, the program attempts to teach safe driving habits to students of driving age. Parents, of course, must bear the burden of instruction and supervision of high-school-age drivers, and their influence can be many times more potent than that of the public schools. Driving technique is the product of hundreds of thousands of miles of varied driving, and cannot be taught in a few classroom hours by the public schools. Parents can, if they will, instill courtesy, patience, and sober habits which may shield their offspring from suffering or from causing an injury while operating a vehicle.

The Time Factor in Traffic Accidents

Of more than passing interest is the influence exerted by the four seasons, the days of the week and hours of the day. These trace recurrent patterns. Since the seasons are directly related to the hours of daylight and darkness, it is natural that traffic deaths should somehow reflect that relationship. Nighttime fatalities are three times as numerous, in relation to vehicle miles, as those occurring by day. The seasonal cycle exercises a similar influence, with the highest death rates in terms of vehicle miles recorded during the winter months, and the lowest during the late spring and summer.

Traffic accident studies also disclose that the peak of fatalities occurs during the hours of dusk and early night, while the low point in the daily cycle is at or near daybreak. During the night hours the effects of decreased visual range, fatigue, intoxicants and reduced enforcement become apparent. Worthy of emphasis is the fact that between 5:30 P.M. and midnight, the percentage of pedestrian accidents is almost two-thirds higher than for nonpedestrians. Hence it may be argued that if this large evening component in the total fatality rate is to be reduced, a much more intensive control and general protective service for pedestrians will be required during the evening hours.

A well-defined cycle also is observed in the distribution of accidents by day of the week. Data for about two-thirds of the United States show a consistent week-end rise and midweek decline in motor vehicle deaths. Tuesday is the low point of the weekly curve, with a 25 per cent rise occurring in the course of the next three days, a doubling of Tuesday's rate on Saturday and Sunday, and a tapering off on Monday. While such daily changes are chiefly in response to similar variations in motor vehicle mileage, they suggest that there has been no compensating increase in the amount of police protection.

Geographical Distribution of Highway Fatalities

Fatal accidents show pronounced concentrations and dispersions by minor political divisions and by states. In any given year the death rate for traffic accidents, in relation to population, may be ten to twenty times as great in one city as in another, while numerous places under 50,000 population will have no fatalities at all. The variations in the death rate per 10,000 registered vehicles are less marked, though the highest local rates will occasionally be as much as ten times the lowest rate represented.

Such differences are in part due to the unsatisfactory bases available for computing the rates, since neither local population nor even local registrations bear a specific relationship to accident hazards that is at all comparable with that provided by motor vehicle mileage. In addition there are many local conditions arising out of street and highway plans, enforcement methods and policies, voluntary observance of regulations and the like, which can raise or depress the accident level.

Rate differentials among states and groups of cities are somewhat less marked than those noted for individual cities, because the variations among local political subdivisions may offset each other. Even so, it is clear that the larger cities tend toward slightly higher rates than those prevailing in smaller communities, and that the North Atlantic region has a substantially lower ratio of fatalities to vehicle miles than prevails in the rest of the country.

Accident distribution as between city and country can show sharp contrasts. Rural fatalities are twice as numerous as urban, and even when reduced to rates based on vehicle miles the spread is almost as great. Among probable contributing factors are the steadily increasing average speeds on improved rural highways, the higher prevalence of multiple fatalities in rural accidents and the more intensive enforcement of traffic controls that is applied in urban areas. Whether protection on rural highways can and will be improved by larger complements of state police is an issue that invites attentive consideration.

Toward Moderate and Equal Enforcement

The foregoing facts and conclusions relating to accidents represent only the more disturbing and highly publicized features of the highway traffic problem. Of increasing popular concern are the persistent and exasperating traffic delays that are due to narrow, winding, ill-paved, ill-lighted, or non-continuous street systems; to signal systems that are not adjusted to the actual flow of traffic; to overemphasized enforcement that slows traffic to a snail's pace; to unequal or ineffective enforcement at critical points; and to special types of congestion that arise when parking narrows the effective width of the highway. All of these represent failures by government to adapt its street plans, its off-highway parking facilities, or its enforcement policies to the special and changing requirements of the motor age. Such adaptations involve some admittedly large-scale programs which cannot be extemporized and quickly and cheaply put into effect. But too often the responses of government take the form of a counterattack upon the motor vehicle and its operator. Police spearhead the advance. They make "drives" on the enforcement of parking prohibitions or highway safety regulations. Traffic police conceal themselves in order to facilitate the entrapment of violators. The courts join in. Fines are substituted for warnings; jail sentences are imposed instead of fines. When the flurry of official activity is over, the standards of enforcement return to the old level. Since the conditions producing traffic congestion and highway accidents have not changed, there is no real improvement. But there remains a popular rancor against police that cannot easily be assuaged.

Some of the difficulties here listed seem to be inherent in this new field of public regulation; but others may yield to a more realistic code of highway deportment, or a more moderate, equal and uniform treatment of traffic law offenders. We are under no compulsion to step up the intensity of our enforcement efforts. It is even possible that we have already reached the point of diminishing returns from them.

Instead of increasing the degree of enforcement, we may need to moderate it, and to apply it on a more nearly equal basis to everybody everywhere, and thus open new avenues to public understanding and law observance.

Better and safer cars; improved motor equipment; highways designed for driving control; off-street parking facilities; school playgrounds and play-streets; traffic regulations, signals, signs, and markings in abundance; police supervision of the traffic flow—these and perhaps others probably have contributed their share to the most impressive speed-up-with-safety campaign of all time. Yet we still really don't know how it was done, except that we have tried everything that anyone could suggest, and impatiently increase the intensity of enforcement whenever things seem to go wrong.

All this serves to emphasize the vulnerable position of police in traffic control. Laws and ordinances provide them with no sure guide, since the scope of prohibited acts already is so comprehensive as to make literal compliance impossible. Enforcement policies are not confined to reasonably attainable ends. Emotional responses to the toll of accidents may increase the restrictions and the penalties, but they cannot reduce the losses. Only a better understanding of causative factors holds any real promise for the future. Out of such additional knowledge may come new safety measures or a new emphasis upon some of the more familiar approaches.

We have gone along for many years with conflicting views on these matters. Until the conflicts are removed, and until traffic safety engineers can more clearly identify causes in accidents, enforcement programs will continue to be confused and partly ineffective. Firm and ordered policies cannot be derived from the many uncertainties that beset us.

Meanwhile our motor traffic problems multiply the points of collision between police and public. There are lurking dangers here, because police exist for other and more exalted purposes of civilization. Unless policeman and citizen can reach some common ground of mutual respect and understanding, the many constructive influences now at work for better policing will be discounted in their effect, and perhaps wholly thwarted.

CHAPTER 4

RURAL AND SUBURBAN POLICE

Since practically all our police forces have developed from rudimentary origins, they are in the broad sense as old as the earliest English settlements in America. Viewed in the light of their historical development, it may even be contended that American police systems are the lineal descendants of the *vigiles* of the Emperor Augustus, and there are antiquarians who delight in tracing modern police institutions back to even more remote periods. Such excursions are often entertaining and serve as well to emphasize the patent fact that mankind constructs its new institutions from the ruins of the old, using the old materials insofar as they are serviceable. New materials are employed only as a matter of necessary invention.

The first police to appear in the American colonies were the sheriff and the constable. Neither office was native to our soil. They originated in England as substitutes for the Anglo-Saxon institution known as the frankpledge. It consisted in a mutual undertaking, by the members of each tithing, to apprehend and present for trial any members of the tithing who might commit an offense. Failure to seize the offender resulted in a levy of a fine upon the members of the group. The philosophy underlying this device for self-help in police protection is still strong in England, even though professional police forces have long since relieved the citizen of the actual performance of such duties.

English Patterns of the Shrievalty

So long as these principles of self-defense and group responsibility in law enforcement prevailed, no highly organized instrument for the maintenance of domestic tranquillity was likely to be developed.

The early sheriffs, and at a somewhat later date the constables also, held an important place in the scheme of national and local administration in England. There was a time when the sheriff exercised powers akin to those of a viceroy within the limits of his county. He received and interpreted the king's mandate not only in matters concerning civil order, but in military, fiscal, and judicial affairs as well. The whole plan of local government once centered upon this office. The Anglo-Saxon sheriff was in the full sense the king's steward. Not only was he the judicial president of the shire, and an administrator of the royal demesne, but also the chief executive arm of the law within his jurisdiction. The Conquest merely operated to strengthen still further the foundations upon which the sheriff's power rested and to reduce the whole scheme to a more systematic basis. Sheriffs were thereupon appointed from the second rank of the baronage and in a few cases the office seems to have become hereditary. As a rule, however, the Norman kings took care that the large powers exercised by the sheriff were employed for the ultimate benefit of the Crown. To this end the sheriff usually held his office at the king's pleasure, and enjoyed its profits only so long as the transactions were also profitable to the king.

Sheriffs enjoyed little popularity. Sometimes they bought their appointments from the Crown; often they were nonresidents of the counties which they served; nearly always they were primarily concerned with fattening their own purses. Acting in effect as royal prefects they could perpetrate the gravest abuses with impunity. Scandals multiplied. Sheriffs were repeatedly charged with inactivity in the pursuit and prosecution of criminal offenders, with peculations on a large scale, abuse of their powers to serve personal ends, falsification of election returns, and neglect to summon juries as a means of protecting favored defendants. Forgery and trickery marked their administration of office.

Within little more than a century after the Conquest, sheriffs were forbidden to act as justices in their own shires, a severe check was administered to their law enforcement powers through the creation of the cognate office of coroner, and they had already begun to act as assistants and bailiffs to the itinerant justices, rather than as colleagues and equals. Decline in the sheriffs' importance thereafter proceeded at an accelerated pace, their powers waning with the relaxing grip of the Crown. From time to time there were lapses into the old regime, when the sheriff reappeared as a kind of royal proconsul. During such intervals the sheriffs collected dues for the king, exercised an important judicial function in the sheriff's tourn, presided over the assembly of freeholders in the county court, pursued and apprehended malefactors, and upon the king's proclamation summoned the military forces in their respective counties. From their acts, no matter how oppressive, appeal lay only to the king, and it contributes somewhat to an understanding of the situation to recall that the Norman kings were often absent from England, and did not speak the language of the country.

Efforts accordingly were made to subject the office to local control and otherwise to restrict its influence. Just before his death Edward I conceded to the counties the right to select their sheriffs, but this power was quickly lost to the barons and Edward's successor promptly reasserted the ancient prerogative. So with the question of central control settled, the sheriff persisted as a kind of royal lieutenant. Such marked capacity for survival did not, however, protect the sheriffs from other losses. Magna Charta deprived them of many of their judicial powers, their accounts were made subject to annual audit, and their appointments limited to a single year. If, as is probable, it was intended that reappointment should thereby be forbidden, the expedient failed. Nonetheless, the work of, demolition and the leisurely processes of decay still went on for centuries. Glorious traditions clung to the office for many years, and the pretension to powers long lost was maintained until well into the nineteenth century. Then the petty civil jurisdiction which still adhered was swept away by statute, sheriffs were relieved of responsibility for the care and custody of prisoners, while the new system of highly organized borough and county police forces effectively blocked them off from exercise of their ancient police authority.

Hence there now remain only the duties to attend the judges, to summon juries, and to enforce civil judgments. Sheriffs are still selected by the Crown from lists submitted by the Chancellor of the Exchequer and the justices of King's Bench. Appointments are for one year, and service is both compulsory and unpaid. Undersheriffs do all of the work, with the traditional officer occupying a purely ceremonial place in the scheme of things. Maitland's description of the present-day sheriff as a "country gentleman, who (it may be much against his will) has been endowed for a single year with high rank," aptly describes the essential features of the present situation.

Development of the English Constable

Like the sheriff, the constable may be traced by direct line back to Anglo-Saxon institutions. His early history is similarly intertwined with military affairs, for after the Conquest the Norman marshals, predecessors of the modern constable, held positions of great dignity and were drawn for the most part from the baronage. As leaders of the king's army they seem to have exercised a certain jurisdiction over military offenders, particularly when the army was engaged on foreign soil, and therefore beyond the reach of the usual institutions of justice. The disturbed conditions attending the Wars of the Roses brought the constables further powers of summary justice, as in cases of treason and similar state crimes. They therefore offered a convenient means by which the English kings from time to time overrode the ordinary safeguards of English law. These special powers, originating in the "law marshal," were expanded until they came to represent what we now know as martial law.

During the reign of Edward I the hundreds were placed under the command of constables. These were required to supervise the armor and equipment of the men of the hundred who were employed both for military defense and for pursuing law violators. Every parish or township had its constable, and as the *posse comitatus,* or county militia, turned more and more to questions of defense, the constable was left to pursue felons alone. The ancient custom of "hue and cry," with the entire countryside up in arms and joining in the man hunt, lapsed into disuse. The civil police officer began to emerge.

It must be understood, however, that there was as yet no high degree of specialization. During the Middle Ages the constable was loaded down with a highly miscellaneous collection of duties, ranging all the way from collection of taxes to supervision of highways, with the magisterial function thrown in for good measure. The office soon became subject to election and was commonly conferred upon personages of local importance. The appearance of the justices of the peace quickly changed this trend. Their rise to power was effected at the expense not only of the constables, but of the sheriffs and coroners also. By the beginning of the sixteenth century they had secured control of the local police systems, and the constable was constrained to make arrests upon warrants issued by them. From being officers of wide discretion in conserving the public peace, the constables sank to the status of retainers to the justices. They did the difficult, burdensome, and dangerous work for the latter. The office of constable was no longer attractive. It had been deprived of civic and social prestige. It carried no compensation, the service was compulsory, and the duties onerous. Finally it became so unwelcome a distinction that incumbents were chosen "by house row," a kind of indiscriminate "rotation among occupiers." Under such circumstances frequent changes were a prime necessity, and hence the constable's term came to be limited to one year. Even so, many of those chosen sought to evade service, until the practice developed of permitting the elected incumbent to provide a substitute upon payment of a sum of from £5 to £10.

Throughout all these many years the police duties of the constables were combined with other administrative functions. The high constable of the hundred also served as tax collector until well into the nineteenth century, while the parish or petty constable, even after the loss of his judicial powers, continued to act as overseer of highways.

Thus at every turn the signs of disintegration manifest themselves. By a lengthy but consistent process the old power and glory once attaching to the office were gradually worn away. The middle years of the nineteenth century finally brought a crystallization of public opinion when Parliament in 1856 swept the entire traditional system into the discard and set up highly organized county constabularies in its stead.

Early American Police Forms

Such, in brief outline, are the English backgrounds of the sheriff and the constable. Their transfer to America was both easy and natural, though in the new environment both offices underwent some degree of adaptation. For one thing, central control of the sheriff and constable did not long survive on American soil. As representatives of the Crown, the colonial governors were so generally unpopular, and the large landowners whom they designated to office became so frequently involved in political scandals and peculations, that in most of the colonies the general outlines of local control were quickly impressed upon both offices. The marked trend toward popular election of local officers also had its effect upon the old traditions of the sheriff and the constable. On the other hand both offices have quite successfully resisted legislative efforts to reduce their functions and narrow the scope of their authority. Hence their American backgrounds stand in striking contrast with those in England. Thus the powers of the English sheriff were progressively trimmed down until they reached the disappearing point, with central controls vigorously and successfully defended. But in this country the powers and duties of rural sheriffs have been maintained with an impressive consistency, while the matter of control has been turned over to the county electorates. Similarly the American counterpart of the English constable still survives here, although his prototype finally disappeared in England almost a century ago. Transplantation appears to have endowed both offices with a vitality that carries them on despite political, social, and economic changes of first magnitude. But wherever the conditions of urban life appear, the sheriff and the constable either lose, or cease to perform, their police functions. Thus they tend more and more to be exclusively rural officers.

I. THE SHERIFF

The most striking characteristic of the American sheriff is his universality. Every state is divided into counties,[1] and every county has its sheriff. In all but a few instances the ancient peace powers of the office are still exercised in some degree. Popular election is the general rule.[2] Thus the sheriff is naturally and inevitably involved in partisan politics.

There are other and more serious complications. The official term is usually for two years, less commonly for four, and in a few cases for three years. Rotation in office, first established some centuries ago, is still widely recognized; most frequently by prohibiting the incumbent from succeeding himself, but occasionally also by limiting his tenure to two or three terms. The formal qualifications never reach beyond such elementary matters as age, residence, citizenship, and electoral status. Removals can be effected only for moral turpi-

---

[1] In Louisiana, the parish is the full equivalent of a county.

[2] In Rhode Island, the sheriffs are appointed by the governor, but possess only vestigial criminal law enforcement powers.

tude or official malfeasance, and then only by impeachment, or by executive action by the governor following a hearing, or (as is most common in New England and in the southern states) through action by the courts.

Such cumbersome devices for the selection and discipline of ministerial agents severely limit the police value of the sheriff. They are supplemented by other unfavorable features surrounding the office. Being but a political bird of passage, the sheriff naturally clings to his private occupation, if any. He may be a farmer, a miner, a carpenter, a blacksmith, or a butcher.[3] Rarely does he possess prior police experience. Even though he does possess it, or acquires something akin to it during a rather brief official tenure, his duties cover such a wide range as necessarily to involve further diffusion of his activity and interest. Everywhere in the United States the sheriff is charged with the service of civil process and with custody of the county jail. In parts of the South and Southwest he is also the tax collector, and in some southern states he acts as public administrator for the property of persons who die intestate leaving no readily identifiable heirs. The unsound and often iniquitous fee system under which the sheriff usually derives all or a part of his compensation operates to divert his attention to the more lucrative tasks, often to the neglect of the primary duty of law enforcement.

The Compensation of Sheriffs

Subject to certain qualifications later to be described, the sheriff relies heavily upon the fees he receives for the performance of nearly every official act. He receives so much for serving a summons, so much for a warrant of arrest, or for a subpoena, a writ of attachment, or other process. When he locks a prisoner in a cell he receives a fee for it. When he summons a jury he receives another.

Prisoners must be fed. The sheriff feeds them. Either by statute or by local ordinance, the scale for table board at the county jail is fixed in a formal schedule. If the sheriff can keep his prisoners alive and reasonably healthy for less—and apparently he always can—the difference between the actual cost and the lawful allowance belongs to him.

[3] See, for example, the summary of sheriffs' occupations provided by Raymond Moley in *The Missouri Crime Survey*, p. 65.

In one county a reliable investigation indicated that the cost of feeding a prisoner was eight cents a day while the sheriff received forty-five. In many counties the sheriff is permitted, either directly or through concessionaires, to sell special articles of food, tobacco or other "luxuries" to the prisoners. He is thus permitted to starve them to the point where they or their friends purchase food to supplement the daily ration. He thus enjoys the extraordinary privilege of reaping a profit not only from starvation but from the relief of starvation.[4]

Wherever the sheriff's income is brought under close scrutiny, it develops that the feeding of prisoners is an important source of profit, and sometimes the chief source. In the larger counties, and particularly in those containing populous cities, the sheriffs' civil process fees may run to fantastic amounts. The total compensation ranges all the way from $1,200 per annum in the smaller rural areas to $100,000 in a great metropolitan center. Thus the sheriff is sometimes found to be the best paid administrative officer of the county, and one who not infrequently enjoys a public income far in excess of that of the county judiciary.

Even the fixed salary, without supplementary fees, is generally equal to, or higher than, that accorded to professional police administrators. In the more populous counties these fixed salaries range to $25,000 per annum. The small rural counties provide a more modest scale of fixed compensation, which usually runs from $2,000 per annum. Sometimes this fixed scale is determined by state law, and may take the form, as in Ohio, of a definitely prescribed ratio to county population.

To the basic salary of the sheriff, and the various fees and profits already described, are added one or more of the following perquisites and emoluments: food and lodging for the sheriff and his family, mileage allowances for his own automobile when engaged in the public service, and interest on cash balances entrusted to his care. Thus the grand total of the sheriff's compensation varies widely from county to county, and may bear no necessary relation to the responsibilities of his task or to the taxable wealth or population of the county which he serves.

4 Moley, "The Sheriff and the Constable," *The Annals,* Vol. CXLVI, No. 235, p. 31.

Performance of Police Duties

All this stands in striking contrast to the popular image of the sheriff. That image is cast in heroic mold. It is the result of certain vivid though fleeting impressions of a day now long past. In these the shrievalty is associated with a glorious tradition.

Despite the intervening centuries, the early English sheriff still stands out bold and clear. He is the "great man" of the county who, though he may not walk with kings, is a trusted lieutenant of the sovereign in the practical aspects of local government. Most of his official duties are performed by subordinates who do not hesitate at irregular and even corrupt practices for the benefit of the king's purse, or that of the sheriff, or their own. The titular holder of the office is often a nonresident of the county, but anyone may catch a glimpse of the sheriff himself when the royal judges visit the county for the assizes. For on that occasion the sheriff must be on hand at all costs. Official etiquette demands it. His is the duty and the privilege to "attend the judges," which he does by lavish entertainment. At the opening of the sessions the sheriff affects a considerable display. He and his chief aides are richly turned out for the occasion, while his retainers, sometimes numbering a hundred or more, surround him in ordered and colorful ranks. This official pomp and display survived all the vicissitudes of the office itself, and is still occasionally re-enacted at the assizes, on but a slightly diminished scale. The glamour of the English sheriff as a personage of high though temporary official rank still lingers.

The early American sheriff, particularly during the colonial period, proves somewhat more difficult to visualize. Under the relatively simple conditions of colonial life, even the great man of the county was not likely to cut an impressive figure. Regal display did not flourish, though the real swing toward democratic simplicity had not yet begun. But at all events it is certain that the colonial sheriff was a landed proprietor, and that the shrievalty brought him much honor and some profit.

Then, as the frontier moves westward, a novel kind of sheriff appears in an epic setting. The day of the tribesman on the prairie is interrupted by the appearance of the white settlers in their covered wagons. Just as the intruders come to rest and establish their first communities, two figures of heroic proportions arrive upon the scene. They are the town marshal and the county sheriff, and their exploits as empire builders sometimes rank with those of the cattle kings and the railroad magnates.

The western sheriff holds the stage for a generation or more. For the first time in history, and perhaps the last, he is personally active in law enforcement. His duties as an executive arm of the courts or as a fiscal and general administrator are completely subordinated to the more exciting business of rounding up cattle thieves, leading a mounted posse in pursuit of desperadoes, or engaging in gunplay with tough characters. It would be satisfying to know whether the frontier sheriff actually did succeed in quieting his turbulent fellow citizens or whether the growth of wealth and population, and the vastly changed social conditions attending this development, alone operated to suppress the high-spirited practices of the early settlements. In any case, here is the golden age of the sheriff as a peace officer. When it passes, the sheriff of the West becomes almost indistinguishable from his counterparts of the older East and South. Still the glamour lingers on, and the sheriff of the present day, who performs his prosaic functions in a group of prosaic communities, is often envisaged in the popular mind against this composite background of high official rank, vigorous action, and personal glory.

There is, of course, little or nothing in current experience to support this view. On the contrary, factual findings and official judgments in state after state are against it. Even before the advent of state police in New Jersey, sixteen of the twenty-one sheriffs admitted that they did not take seriously their statutory duty to apprehend criminals. More than half of the whole number confined themselves to care of the jail and its inmates, and to service of civil process. Some of them even expressed surprise that they should be expected to assume any responsibility for crime repression. The sheriff of a large and important rural county stated that "in all my experience with the sheriff's office for the last twelve years, the sheriff has never been called upon to apprehend a criminal." Another emphasized a general and understandable difficulty when he complained: "How can you expect me to apprehend criminals and take care of this jail at the same time?" In still a third county the function of arresting criminals had lapsed to such an extent that the sheriff did not seem to be aware of its existence. He declared quite frankly that "the sheriff is not supposed to perform police work except in case of a riot."[5]

In Kentucky a state commission appointed to investigate state and county government returned a finding that the chief interest of the sheriff lay in the collection of taxes.[6] In Delaware a similar inquiry indicated that the prime functions of the sheriff are the execution of civil process and the administration of the election laws;[7] in Illinois, "serving writs and orders of courts, caring for prisoners, custody of the jail, and in some cases the collection of taxes, are the chief duties."[8] Inquiry among sixty-one sheriffs there indicated that "in most cases the deputy sheriffs devote not more than one-half of their time to criminal work, and that in a number of counties, little or no time is so spent. . . . There are a few counties which provide no regular deputies at all. Most of the others have but one deputy sheriff, and a mere handful provide for more than four. . . . Viewed as a police agency, the office is little more than a monument to an historic past."[9] In Missouri a governor declared the sheriffs to be abject failures since, being generally untrained in their work and locally elected, they "share the common desire of mankind to offend none of their constituents."[10] Two years after this official judgment a general survey of the office concluded that "the average [Missouri] sheriff considers it his general duty to investigate crimes, but unless rather extraordinary circumstances surround the particular offense, he does not act."[11] In Connecticut, where English traditions and forms are highly regarded, the conclusion has been expressed that "the office of sheriff is the highest paid, most ornamental, and least needed office in the state."[12]

In the old South, a Virginia survey of county government summarized the situation as follows:

[5] State Research, a supplement to New Jersey, Vol. IV, No. 4 (1916), p. iv.

[6] Efficiency Commission of Kentucky, The Government of Kentucky (1924), Vol. I, p. 575.

[7] C. C. Maxey, County Administration, p. 25.

[8] W. F. Dodd, Government in Illinois, p. 219.

[9] Bruce Smith, Rural Police Protection, in Illinois Crime Survey (1927), pp. 338-339.

[10] Governor Hyde, Biennial Message to the 52nd General Assembly, 1923.

[11] Raymond Moley, The Sheriff and the Coroner, Missouri Crime Survey, p. 70.

[12] A. M. Mathewson, The County System of Connecticut (1917), p. 6.

There is ample evidence that the criminal aspect of the sheriff's work is of secondary importance in the eyes of most of the incumbents of the sheriff's office. The rather extensive range of his other duties naturally serves to divert his attention from the police function. The practical operation of the fee system is to direct the sheriff's attention chiefly to the management of the county jail, from the operation of which he receives the larger part of his compensation.[13]

From North Carolina, where the sheriff's failure as a police officer is unusually striking, comes the following incisive comment:

It might be supposed that the sheriff would be a satisfactory peace officer in the case of local offenders and petty offenses, but unfortunately he is no more efficient in this field than in combating professional crime. The reasons, however, are different. He cannot out-maneuver professional criminals because he lacks training and facilities. He does not suppress the lawlessness and crime of the community because he lacks the inclination. The sheriff secures his office by popular election and he does not like to offend a voter if it can be helped. . . . There is another reason why many of the sheriffs are weak as police officers. They are elected for another purpose. The office is attractive because of the generous commission paid for collecting taxes. Many who have no interest in or capacity for police work are thus elected to the office.[14]

In the border states, where vigorous police action was once a characteristic of the sheriff's office, there are extensive and disquieting changes. Some years ago the governor of New Mexico asserted that "it is a well-known fact that the sheriffs of the various counties, even on a fee basis, are not always diligent in pursuing and capturing criminals,"[15] and in the neighboring state of Texas, the following naïve statement by a sheriff who was quickly overwhelmed by the disorderly elements attracted by the discovery of oil, serves to illustrate a condition likely to arise when nonprofessional police are faced with a novel problem. "Well," testified this officer, "we just woke one morning and found the crowd here; that is to say, the oil boom came all at once. We were officers without experience and

---

[13] New York Bureau of Municipal Research, *County Government in Virginia* (1928), p. 51.

[14] Wager, *County Government in North Carolina*, p. 270.

[15] Governor McDonald, *Annual Message to the Legislature*, 1912.

hardly knew what to do, and I suppose the crooks were smart and experienced, and saw the situation and took advantage of it."[16]

Failure to act promptly appears to be a fairly common occurrence. A well-qualified commentator on rural administration in Texas declares that "the sheriff has so many other functions to perform that his police activities are limited to organizing the pursuit of criminals, frequently many hours after the crime has been committed."[17]

Montana also once bred sheriffs on whom memory still lingers, but its crime commission has declared that "the sheriff system is admittedly inefficient. It is a combination civil and criminal office, dealing with a wide variety of matters and the man in charge is a political officer, subject to the vagaries and whims of political campaigns every two years. . . . There are at times veritable reigns of terror along our main automobile highways due to the influx of desperate and experienced criminals who commit many crimes of violence and are beyond detention and detection before the forces of law can get into operation. Our inexperienced and untrained county sheriffs and deputies are ill-prepared to combat such situations."[18]

These and other complaints have been leveled against the shrievalty in California. A commentator on the situation in that state observes that "The sheriff, often elected for his lodge-room popularity, although completely ignorant of modern police methods, was often so anxious to make political capital by solving a great crime that he would not divide the credit by calling any of [the] efficient state agencies to assist him in doing so."[19]

Future of the Shrievalty

Despite the impressive bulk and quality of the evidence piling up against the sheriff as a peace officer, efforts to salvage the office continue. Sheriffs' deputies are increasingly employed for regular patrol work; they are provided with expensive means of transportation and communication; rudimentary training programs are in-

---

[16] Ex parte deposition of Jim Wasson, sheriff of Freestone County, Texas. Report of the adjutant general on *State Ranger and Martial Law Activities of the National Guard*, 1921-1922, pp. 14-15.

[17] H. G. James, *County Government in Texas*, p. 82.

[18] Report of the Montana State Crime Commission, 1930, p. 93.

[19] W. A. Beasly, "California Unifies Enforcement Agencies to Fight Crime," in *American Bar Association Journal*, Vol. 20 (1934), p. 758.

augurated, and crime-reporting systems established. The nature, extent, and significance of these innovations will be more extensively treated in connection with county police systems.

In the vast majority of American counties the sheriff system has already collapsed. The reasons for this failure are partly historical, since the office has been declining in effectiveness and in popular esteem for centuries. A multitude of economic, social, and political factors has also been introduced during recent decades, and these have hastened the process of degeneration.

In a day of highly developed police techniques, elected police administrators are an anachronism.[20] This, combined with short terms and rotation in office, effectively closes all promising avenues for eventual improvement. So it is difficult to see any real prospect, however remote, that the trend of centuries will be reversed. The long descending curve marking the decline in the shrievalty's prestige promises to remain unbroken.

II. THE RURAL CONSTABLE

Next in order of universality is the office of constable. Its history may be traced by direct line back to Anglo-Saxon times. The Normans imposed upon the office various duties relating to the militia and martial law, and for some time clothed it with great official dignity. There followed several hundred years of decline, and by the beginning of the sixteenth century little was left of the constable's powers but tax collection, highway supervision, and maintenance of the peace. Even this rather modest residuum was exercised under the control of the local justices. Thus the transfer to America was effected at a time when the constable had already reached a state of minor importance. In England the office continued to decline both in power and in prestige, until it was swept away in the legislation of 1856 which established the county constabularies. In America, however, the process of disintegration, though continuing without abatement down to the present day, has rarely resulted in statutory extinction.

On the contrary there are more separate and distinct police units constructed around the office of constable than around any other type. Twenty-one states accord it formal constitutional recognition.

[20] In this connection it may be noted that the constitutions of thirty-eight states prohibit the appointment of sheriffs.

Since all of these are in the South and West, where the distinction between constitutional and statutory subject matter is none too strictly drawn, it is doubtful whether the constitutional status of the office holds any special significance. The constitutional provisions relate to such matters as official term (ranging from one to four years); to the method of election or appointment; and in the case of four states, to the method of removal. The Kentucky constitution alone specifies any formal qualifications for the office, by requiring that a constable must be a citizen of Kentucky, at least twenty-four years of age, with an established residence in the state for two years, and for one year in the county in which he is to serve.

Practically all the New England towns, and the townships, judicial townships, magisterial districts or county districts into which counties in other parts of the country are divided for purposes of rudimentary local administration, are provided by statute with one or more constables. In some instances, however, constables are not elected because it proves impossible to find anyone to accept the office. It holds neither honor nor dignity, owing to a fee system that is often unsupported by fixed remuneration of any kind, and little hope of other reward.

Selection and Duties of Constables

Popular election is by far the most common method of selection. Outstanding exceptions are to be noted in Maryland, where designations are made by the county commissioners; in New York and Rhode Island, where the town boards exercise this power; in South Carolina, where local justices appoint; and in Delaware, where the governor and senate appoint for two of the three counties, and the levy court (county board) appoints in the third. In many instances the constable is not only charged with maintaining the peace and serving civil process for the local courts, but may also be the tax collector and perhaps even the poundkeeper. Combination of fiscal duties with the police function is common in New England and throughout the central states. To them are sometimes added other activities, such as issuing the call or notice of local elections. All this, of course, is in addition to long-standing powers relating to the execution of civil process for local courts of inferior jurisdiction.

In New York a general examination of the services rendered by constables in fifty rural counties shows that they displayed no activity as to criminal matters in forty-one counties, that some measure of activity was observed in four counties, and that in only five counties, or 10 per cent of the total examined, were constables deemed by the sheriffs to have any substantial value as peace officers.

A more intensive study of 906 constables in 11 counties in the western portion of the same state likewise shows that even if their work as servers of civil process be included as a measure of activity, anywhere from 10 per cent to 73 per cent performed no public duties of any kind, at any time. Taking this rather large and representative group as a whole, it appears that almost 40 per cent are wholly inactive. In the course of some scores of personal interviews the same statement was repeated over and over again; namely, that the constable while occasionally serving the peace justice in civil matters, never under any circumstances made an arrest or served any form of criminal process. Even in Monroe County, where many constables are on a salaried basis, and hence might be expected to perform some measure of public work, the ratio of activity did not rise above the general average for those on a fee basis.

The situation in Pennsylvania is only slightly more favorable to the constable. Of 1,330 officers examined by field investigators, or reported upon by local justices, only about 27 per cent were shown to be entirely inactive. Yet this is in some degree offset by the further findings that of those who showed some form of activity two-thirds devoted less than 10 per cent of their official attention to criminal work.

Likewise in New Jersey, of 217 constables examined or reported upon, it appears that not more than 70 per cent showed any form of official activity. Here again, however, 70 per cent of the so-called "active" group devoted less than 10 per cent of their attention to work involving criminal jurisdiction.[21]

Constables' Private Occupations and Public Fees

Whatever the scope of his activities, the rural constable is almost never a full-time public officer. Hence it is necessary for him to have some private means of support, the nature of which may have a definite bearing upon his availability for both routine and emergency services of a public nature.

[21] Data collected from sheriffs, justices, and constables in New York, Pennsylvania, and New Jersey.

The revolution in the conditions of rural life has profoundly affected the means of livelihood for many rural dwellers. Though once predominantly concerned with agriculture and directly related callings, they now pursue occupations of an urban character. It follows that many such are of a nature inconsistent with the public duties of a constable, and that their pursuit in connection with the exacting work of crime repression, and the service of civil and criminal process, may in many instances prove difficult or impossible.

In order to lay a factual basis for any conclusions on this point, the interviews conducted in Pennsylvania and New Jersey, with constables and other local justice officials, and the reports received from them, included a statement of the constables' civil occupations. As might have been anticipated, the latter covered a wide range. The total of 1,327 Pennsylvania constables from whom such data were secured showed that 76 distinct occupations were represented, including one who was described by a peace justice as a "racketeer" and another (a woman) who confessed to being a "housewife." The larger occupation groups, in order of size, were as follows: laborers, 295; farmers, 265; no occupation other than constable service, including 40 who described themselves as "retired," 162; miners, 93; railroad workers, 55; mill hands, 46; painters, 43; watchmen, 34; truck drivers and draymen, 33; carpenters, 30; merchants, 22; clerks, 20; blacksmiths, 18; mechanics, 10. The balance, constituting 15 per cent of the total, were distributed over the remaining four-fifths of the occupational list. These last, however, were in themselves notable in some degree since they included such widely divergent callings as butchers and auctioneers, florists and opticians, cattle dealers and mail carriers, landscapers and icemen, schoolteachers and glass blowers.

A similar analysis of 112 constables in New Jersey showed 43 occupations represented, of which the following proved most numerous: no occupation other than police, including three who were "retired," 22; laborers, 16; farmers, 12; carpenters, 8; truck drivers, 5. The balance, constituting 44 per cent of the total, were distributed over the remaining seven-eighths of the occupational classes.

Thus in both states it appears that many of the incumbents of the office of constable belonged to one of three major groups: (1) those having no other employment; (2) laborers; (3) farmers. Of the first class it may be said that direct observation indicated that they were of advanced years and, therefore, not well fitted for the rigors of police service; the laborers generally lacked the intelligence and educational background to equip them for responsible public service; and the farmers represented so many diverse characteristics that no generalizations with respect to their personal qualifications and capacity could be made.

Of the remaining occupational classes enough has probably been said to indicate their highly varied character. Still it should be noted that few of them were engaged in employments that left them free to meet sudden and irregular demands upon their time and attention. Gas and electric meter inspectors, truck, bus, and cab drivers, mail carriers, railroad employees, furniture movers, collectors, icemen, milkmen, plumbers, carpenters, masons, linemen, miners, salesmen, telephone operators, and many others of similar character were engaged in callings involving an occupational discipline inconsistent with the demands of constable duty or were carried so far afield by their daily tasks as not to be constantly available for public service in their own communities. In fact, everything surrounding the constables' occupations served still further to support and justify the general view concerning their exceedingly limited use and value as police, or as servants of the local courts.

Another feature worthy of emphasis is that these rural constables are drawn from much the same occupations and classes as are the police of the larger cities both here and abroad. But the parallel stops abruptly right there. For while the professional policeman is selected according to certain standards of age, physique, weight, height, health, character, education, and intelligence; is raised by successive stages of training from the status of good human raw material until he becomes a drilled and instructed arm of the law; and is subjected to corps discipline in some degree; the rural constable remains primarily a member of his occupational group. He commands none of the techniques in which the policeman is trained; is selected by popular vote or casual appointment, without reference to any standard but residence and citizenship; is untrained, unsupervised, and entirely undisciplined. Thus none of the distinguishing marks of the modern policeman can be identified in the rural constable, and any identity of the occupational and social groups from which they both happen to spring thus has no significance.

With few and unimportant exceptions the rural constable receives his sole compensation from fees based entirely upon the service performed. Owing to this fact the office is far less lucrative than the shrievalty, which ordinarily offers a fixed cash salary, with fees, perquisites, and miscellaneous emoluments piled one upon another, until the total sometimes reaches a rather impressive figure. It is not so with the constable; his compensation for the occasional public services he is called upon to perform almost never represents more than a small fraction of his private income, no matter how modest that may be. This means that in fact, as well as in theory, the rural constable is strictly a part-time official, who is often elected against his will, and who occasionally declines to take the qualifying oath because of his reluctance to serve. It also means that he receives no compensation for doing protective police work, for crime prevention, or for performing the difficult, dangerous, or unpleasant services often entailed in policing.

Efforts to Abolish the Office

In state after state the evidence accumulates that the constable has outlived his usefulness, that his law enforcement activities have lapsed, and that the time has come when he can be abolished without any concern about the effect such action would have upon the administration of justice. In fact, one may search the published sources and interview hundreds of state, county, and township functionaries without encountering more than an occasional halfhearted endorsement of the constable system. Its few defenders are more concerned about the trend away from local self-government which such proposals suggest, than with any conviction that the constable can be revived as a positive factor in law enforcement. Yet even here the case for retention is none too impressive, since the rural constable does not partake of a representative character, but is merely an untrained and minor functionary. Thus, if the office is to be retained it can only be on the ground that it has become a symbol of local self-government, and as such should not be disturbed under any circumstances.

In suburban townships surrounding some of the great cities on the eastern seaboard the ancient office has already been destroyed. In most instances regularly organized town police are substituted. Thus a new type of police agency has come into existence which promises in time to acquire some importance in the larger and rapidly growing towns. Inevitably it also will strive to entrench itself so that it may successfully resist later attacks upon its own existence. Such attacks may come from without as part of a general movement toward the integration of small police forces. Nor are signs wanting that there will be dissatisfaction with the new setup among local taxpayers, since township police have invariably proved more costly than the part-time constables they displace. Problems of township financing produced by the depression years forced the abandonment of these newly organized police agencies in a few instances, with the result that the task of protecting such areas has been turned back to the state police, though now relieved of the complexities formerly imposed by the mere existence of the traditional office of constable.

It is too early to forecast whether such occasional retracing of steps is destined to provide a general program for the future. On the basis of past and present experience with the part-time township constable, however, it is difficult to see how the office can survive much longer. The infusion of urban culture into rural life, with all that this revolutionary change implies, seems certain to destroy the office, but whether the state police will continue to be drawn into the administrative vacuum thus produced, or whether the rural constable will be replaced by another local police agency, is as yet far from clear.

III. VILLAGE CONSTABLES AND MARSHALS

The foregoing observations on the offices of sheriff and rural constable indicate that neither of them was primarily devised for what we now know as police work and that neither office has shown capacity to adapt itself to prevailing conditions.

There is little that distinguishes the village constable, marshal, or policeman from these rural counterparts. Like them, the police agencies of the villages, boroughs, incorporated towns, and other small municipalities are usually brought into existence in response to some local need having only a remote connection with crime control. Nowadays the pressure for their creation is more likely to rise from a need for traffic regulation in a congested business area or on streets adjacent to schools. But since state laws contemplate the establishment of village police forces, the members of which are clothed with the general powers of peace officers, these rudimentary agencies easily spring into existence. Whatever the reasons for their creation they are ultimately drawn into the criminal work by which modern police are distinguished. If the communities they serve are destined for rapid growth, one may observe within the span of a few years the transition of a rural police agency into an urban police force. Casual, part-time, and nonprofessional police service is succeeded by full-time police officers who are uniformed, career-minded, and subject to some degree of supervision and control by higher command. Electrical and mechanical means for traffic regulation are installed at street intersections; motor patrols are instituted; radio broadcast facilities are provided in many instances; teletype receivers are installed, and promotional and retirement systems established. In these and other respects the village force takes on the superficial characteristics of the police of a much larger urban center.

Compensation of Village Police

Most of these improvements involve increased costs, not alone for equipment and technical assistance, but also in terms of annual salaries for the rank and file. Even in the smaller villages making no effort along the lines just indicated, the fee-compensated constable is rapidly disappearing and full-time village police who work on fixed salary scales are being substituted. In some instances such changes are due to a conscious desire in the community to relieve both itself and its rudimentary police force of the effects of part-time police services that are rendered only when the prospect of an official fee makes such services profitable. Often, however, the departure from fees to salaries stems from a need for protective and regulative services at traffic intersections which must be covered regularly and systematically and without the stimulating or deterrent effects of cash reward upon the official action taken. Once launched upon this course, villages come to realize that police service is not cheap after all. Their salary scales are profoundly influenced by those of nearby cities; disability and superannuation retirement systems are agitated and adopted, and thus they find themselves burdened with new and unanticipated items of expenditure.

Adaptability to Modern Conditions

Some local forces undergo no such metamorphosis. They continue, decade after decade, almost untouched by the revolutionary influences that are making and remaking our modern police systems. It is not at all uncommon to find the fee-compensated office of village constable or town marshal remaining vacant for extended periods. The comments of local authorities in the rural portions of Missouri are fairly descriptive of this situation. A town official in Butler County declares that "we have no marshal and cannot get one. No one will accept the office." The mayor of another small community in Holt County reports that "we have elected a marshal at each city election, but none would qualify." A city clerk located in New Madrid County seeks to explain the lack of local police protection by stating that "the marshal moved away, and no successor has since been elected or appointed." From nearby Scott County comes the observation that "at times a marshal is appointed." In these instances village police continue to resemble the rural constables and can easily be dismissed from further consideration so far as their importance as factors in crime control is concerned.

It is not so easy to dismiss the protection problems of more than 15,000 incorporated places having less than 10,000 inhabitants, and a total population of more than 20 million. They cannot support much more than an average of one policeman apiece without substantially exceeding the per capita cost of police protection for all but the very largest cities. Thus do the village police quickly recede into the background of rural life.

Yet even when they are caught up in the rush and growth of urbanism their importance to the present and future of police development is not greatly increased. At the best they continue to be responsible for the protection of narrowly limited areas, and of relatively small quotas of people and property; they cannot expand the police resources which science places at their command without assuming overhead and equipment costs which are prohibitively large; the specialized techniques they seek to master are given little opportunity for exercise in a small community where crimes of a major character are necessarily of rare occurrence; and they cannot themselves provide formal training even for their own recruits, much less give their experienced members advanced instruction in the policeman's art.

Though the village police must of necessity rely upon larger departments for many services, still many are attempting to achieve a professional stature. Through training conducted by state police or FBI instructors the rudiments of the policeman's art are being taught in many small forces. In addition, many of the younger village police have had the advantage of military training as military police or shore patrol.

As to the role of the village police, clearly there must be wide variations in the quality of performance. The background, training, and personality of the individual officer establish the character of the force. Numerous small municipalities utilize their village police as a watchman and traffic control group, placing some reliance upon state police or a larger municipal force to perform difficult or costly services. Though small village forces may never be viewed as holding large potentialities and importance for our far-flung network of police systems, yet with intelligent administration they can serve a real need. No state police force in the nation can assign the manpower to provide concentrated watchman service and traffic enforcement which at least some villages desire and for which they are willing to pay.

Village police forces promise to survive as separate entities for some time. All of them are aided by the stubborn "home rule" sentiments of even the smallest municipalities and by the widespread fear of prejudice or neglect by administrative officers who are not their immediate neighbors.

If the village forces are ultimately abandoned and the task of local policing is turned over to units covering larger areas—as has already happened in a few instances—it will probably be because the per capita costs of modern police protection, when conducted on a small scale, reach high levels. That problem has not yet arisen in aggravated form, except in the suburban areas surrounding large cities, but the indications are that it will eventually appear throughout the country generally. In other words, as village police acquire more and more of the characteristics of the modern police force, their costs rise disproportionately high, and it is this factor, of unfathomed future importance, which may eventually bring about their destruction and the substitution of other police forms.

IV. COUNTY POLICE FORCES

Additional evidence of the impending collapse of the sheriff-constable system is provided by the establishment and progressive expansion of county police forces. They often find their origin in the sheriff's office, with the occasional appointment of a deputy to serve as a uniformed patrolman. The transition from this point to a more or less highly organized county police system may be a matter of slow growth in some instances, while in others it is accomplished at a single stroke. As a result, the term "county police" embraces agencies of such dissimilar character as to carry with it no clear or precise definition. Before any appraisal of these new departures in police administration can be attempted, it becomes necessary to describe various county forces which will in some fair degree be typical of all the rest.

Such an undertaking invites an attempt at classification at the outset, though it should be emphasized that this can represent nothing more than an aid to description, and does not rest upon any systematic conception or theory which has guided the development of county police.

Sheriffs' Highway Patrols

Perhaps the simplest form of organized county constabulary consists in a uniformed highway patrol functioning as an integral part of the sheriff's office. This type may be found operating in the rural and semirural portions of Hamilton County, Ohio, which surround the city of Cincinnati; in Monroe County, New York, for service in the vicinity of Rochester; in Oakland County, Michigan, and in Mobile County, Alabama. The "special police" maintained by Norfolk County, Virginia, are of the same general type. Similarly in Cook County, Illinois, the suburban routes tributary to the city of Chicago are patrolled by 150 highway police who operate as an integral part of the sheriff's office.

More ambitious is the scheme developed and put into effect in Los Angeles County, California. The latter embraces a population of over a million in its unincorporated sections, which are policed by deputy sheriffs and a county constabulary operating from a number of local stations. Modern means of police communication are employed, and extensive criminal records, identification systems, and a laboratory of police science are maintained. The total numerical strength of this county police unit, which is directly administered by the sheriff, is in excess of 2,100 including patrolmen, detectives, policewomen, staff services, and supervisory personnel. In its formal aspects, this force is one of the most highly developed county police agencies to be found in the United States.

A comparatively recent development in Los Angeles County is the leasing of sheriffs' patrols to seventeen incorporated municipalities. Towns which have not the population to justify a full service police department of their own are contracting with the sheriff's office for one or more radio car patrols at the cost of men, equipment, and overhead. These patrols are fitted into, and supervised by, the sheriff's organization and are concerned primarily with the motorized watchman service of the towns. Here, as in a few other counties, the sheriff, although an elective officer, has achieved sufficient continuity in office to build and develop a patrol force.

By force of character and devotion to duty a few of the nation's sheriffs have developed patrols as effective and as professional as many municipal departments which are headed by appointed police chiefs. In fact, the latitude traditionally permitted an elective official in budget and personnel matters makes possible, though it does not assure, the highest standards of police service.

The outstanding feature of the county forces falling within the foregoing category is the administrative control exercised by the sheriff. This fact sharply distinguishes them from an equally large and rather miscellaneous class directed and supervised by public authorities other than the sheriff.

Independent County Police

Thus the legislative creation of special police forces for several of the larger counties of South Carolina provides in some instances for appointment and control by the county board, while in others the appointments are made by the governor upon the recommendation of the members of the general assembly from the county in question. Under the latter plan the local members of the state legislature virtually constitute a police board, and exercise a varying and uncertain degree of control over the administration of the county police force. Neither method, however, appears to have produced in South Carolina standards of police service which are appreciably in advance of those developed under the sheriff-constable system.

Likewise, one may find in Kentucky various county police patrols which are largely or wholly independent of the sheriff's office. In Campbell and Kenton counties the sheriff and his aides are virtually relieved of police duty. Campbell County maintains a small patrol force, the members of which are appointed by the county judge for one year. Motor patrols are conducted throughout the three eight-hour tours of duty. The situation in Kenton County is similar, except that the county patrolmen, though designated as "deputy sheriffs," are nevertheless appointed by the county judge and perform their duties primarily under his supervision.

Arlington County in Virginia also vests county police appointments in the judge of the circuit court, although administration of the force is a responsibility of the county manager. In this instance the transfer of the county force from the control of the sheriff was due to the influence of county politics upon that office, and hence upon the police force subordinated to it.

Nassau County, New York, maintains the largest county police unit that is operated independently of the sheriff's office. This county, adjacent to New York City, partakes of both an urban and a rural character. It embraces 10 cities and villages with populations ranging between 5,000 and 25,000 and 56 smaller municipalities. The total population of the county exceeds a million inhabitants. Prior to the establishment of the Nassau County Police in 1925, the usual pattern of the sheriff-constable system, supplemented by some thirty-odd city and village police forces, and supplemented still further by a small detachment of state police and a few prosecutor's detectives, provided a highly miscellaneous and generally inadequate police service.

The advent of the county police force brought extensive changes. The sheriff's office was relieved, in effect, of all responsibility for police duty. The town constables, long dormant, ceased even the pretense of activity. The state police detachment was withdrawn except for patrols on state parkways traversing the county. The new county police force, starting with only 50 officers and men, rapidly increased its numbers to a total over 2,000. A part of this increase is due to the fact that the county police, originally constituted for the protection of unincorporated territory, is authorized to extend its jurisdiction through a process of merger with village forces. So far only about half the villages have joined the county police system. Those which have joined were for the most part incorporated after the county police force was established. Villages antedating the county force have tenaciously clung to their local arrangements.[22]

[22] For a proposal to consolidate the county and local police forces, cf. National Municipal League, *The Government of Nassau County*, pp. 21-30.

The Nassau County police force maintains a wide range of facilities. These include an identification bureau, crime laboratory, motorboats and airplanes, about three hundred motor vehicles, and the latest in radio, teletype, and other communication equipment.

Parkway Police

A third type of county police force has some of the structural characteristics we have just been considering. It is most frequently found in the counties surrounding great metropolitan areas, and consists of a highway police agency charged primarily with traffic regulation on county parkways and boulevards. Such units are administered by the county park board or other special authorities, and conduct their work entirely outside the sphere of the sheriff-constable system.

Sometimes the duplication of these new county police agencies reaches impressive proportions. Thus in Hudson County, New Jersey, which comprises a large group of urban and suburban communities, there are

in addition to municipal police departments . . . three county police organizations performing special police duty in restricted areas. The Hudson County police department performs traffic duty on most of the state highways within the county, and upon certain county highways. This department patrols 34.7 miles of highways and mans 19 crossing posts, operating in ten municipalities. . . . The Hudson County boulevard police department performs exactly the same kind of police service upon the Hudson County boulevard having a total length of 19.75 miles. . . . The Hudson County park commission, having control of seven county parks, employs special police as park guards.[23]

Similarly, the Westchester County (New York) Parkway Police, a force of about 150 men, divides with the state police responsibility for patrol of the state and county parkways within the county.[24] These bisect the normal police areas of a score or more of cities, towns, and villages. Thus there is occasional administrative friction that is traceable in part to the overlapping jurisdictions.

[23] Commission to Investigate County and Municipal Taxation and Expenditures, State of New Jersey, *Local Police Protection Services and Costs*, pp. 21, 22.
[24] Institute of Public Administration, *Report on Police Administration in Westchester County*, pp. 1-13.

From their very nature such police situations arise only in the large and rather thickly settled suburban areas, and do not represent what in any fair sense may be described as rudimentary police forces. Their chief interest in the present discussion revolves about the significant fact that their management has not been lodged in the hands of the sheriff, but has been entrusted to public agencies of more recent origin.

Prosecutor's Detectives

The fourth type of county police agency partakes of an entirely different character from the others. It owes its existence to the very special place occupied by the prosecutor in the American scheme of justice. In county after county, and in state after state, the prosecutor exercises a large influence upon police operations. He usually takes office with a more or less clearly defined popular mandate. It may involve the rigid enforcement of all laws, the rigid enforcement of some laws, or an attitude of tolerance toward statutory regulations which do not happen to fit the tastes and customs of the local electorate. Since the prosecutor virtually holds the key to the criminal courts, and can in large measure determine the what, when, and how of their functioning, there is a continuing disposition to arm him with such police instrumentalities as will make his program of enforcement more effective. This tendency is materially strengthened by the fact that sheriffs and constables are rarely criminal investigators, have little or no knowledge of the value of evidence, and hence are of uncertain value to the prosecutor either in the early or the late stages of a criminal investigation. Prosecutors have therefore been impelled to employ private detectives as a supplement to the regular police resources of the county.

Such special aides are never numerous in counties of a pronounced rural character and are often engaged on a temporary basis, as need for their assistance arises. In the larger counties prosecutors command the services of a permanent body of investigators, and in counties containing great urban centers it is customary for the prosecutor to demand, and to receive, the exclusive services and assistance of some scores of the regular police of the nucleus city. While such as these remain on the city payroll, their direction and discipline are transferred to the prosecutor who may employ them on either original or supplementary investigations, may organize them into raiding squads, and with them may even "invade" the city from which they are drawn, for the purpose of general law enforcement therein. By such means the police establishment of a given city may be split into two parts, with responsibility for their direction so completely diffused that they become, in effect, not merely separate but rival organizations. All this despite the fact that they are in contemplation of law, and in their financial support, still one single police force.

County "Vigilantes"

The fifth general type was developed chiefly in certain states of the Midwest in the late 1920's, but is already becoming extinct. The "county auxiliary protective units," or "vigilantes," which were organized through the initiative of the American Bankers Association, and certain of the state associations affiliated with it, represented a quasi-public effort to secure a larger degree of police protection for rural banks. In Illinois, Indiana, Iowa, and Kansas anywhere from one-half to nine-tenths of the counties were systematically organized for special protection, with the ratio in Michigan and Wisconsin materially smaller. Some three hundred counties distributed over these six states thereby acquired emergency police forces.

The plan of organization everywhere was much the same. Local banks pledged financial assistance and support to the volunteer bank guards who were recruited in each county. The sheriff appointed each bank guard as a deputy and the Bankers Association provided the latter with firearms, ammunition, and a liability insurance policy to indemnify the sheriff against loss due to the acts of such deputy. The county force either served directly under the orders of the sheriff or under one of their own number who was selected by the sheriff as "county chief."

In its actual operation the plan was simple enough. Each volunteer bank guard was notified through the exchange telephone operator whenever a burglary or robbery attack was launched against a local bank, and was directed to take some general or specific action with reference to the protection of the bank or the pursuit and apprehension of the offenders.

Similar associations of volunteer rural police, organized for protection against horse and cattle thieves, flourished in various parts of the country during the nineteenth century. At no time, however, did they enjoy the consistent financial support which has been extended to the bank-guard units, and most of them have accordingly disappeared or lapsed into inactivity. The system of volunteer bank guards has itself now disappeared, largely because the new state police have taken over their functions. Although the whole scheme was rather rudimentary in its conception, and utterly failed to provide either protective patrols or any procedure for systematic criminal investigation, the provision of armed manpower and assurance of hot pursuit which the plan afforded stands in striking contrast with the dilatory and uncertain performance characterizing the sheriff-constable system. Indeed, during the years when the bank guards flourished there was some evidence that the mere existence of a band of these volunteer police operated as a deterrent upon bank robbers and burglars.[25] In recognition of this fact, the underwriters and the Bankers Association developed a standard organization for bank-guard units which, when adhered to by the banks of any given community, entitled the latter to a 10 per cent discount on their specific burglary and robbery insurance premiums.

This evidence of interest on the part of the underwriters has a special significance. For it should be noted in passing that a similar program, when followed by the fire underwriters, exercised a profound influence upon the functioning of volunteer fire companies and expedited the transition to professional and governmentally maintained fire forces. So it appears probable that these latest examples of volunteer police will likewise be completely displaced in the course of time.

The County as a Police Unit

Most of the efforts thus far made to revive the waning prospects of local police in rural districts have revolved about the county as a police unit. Yet it may fairly be questioned whether the county represents a satisfactory basis for any large plans for rural police reorganization. With a few exceptions to be found along the Atlantic seaboard, county boundaries were determined in the first instance by considerations of convenience in reaching the county courthouse. It was a matter measured in terms of hours and minutes of traveling time, and did not, of course, bear any necessary relation to the

[25] See, for example, *The Illinois Crime Survey*, pp. 342-343.

density of population, its geographic and social distribution, or the economic resources of the area and its ability to support essential agencies of government. The failures and shortcomings of county administration have now brought these considerations to the front and have resulted in a new search for the social and economic bases of local government in general.[26]

Any review of the regional problem will inevitably involve some consideration of the fundamental facts and principles upon which local police administration, both urban and rural, should rest. Of utmost importance is the fact that our whole scheme of police organization is largely based upon the concept of local autonomy and control. This has resulted, as we have seen, in extensive duplication of police agencies. When the sheriff-constable system has broken down, new police units have been added without any real concurrent effort aimed at the integration of police strength. The fact that adding together several inadequate police forces does not solve the police problem was not recognized until the new units had come into being and were well entrenched politically.

The disappointments and failures attending this course have been most obvious in metropolitan areas embracing rural and semirural territory as well as a central nucleus of highly urban character. For any effort to determine the region for police administration is quite likely to end by vaulting over municipal and county boundaries, and sometimes state lines. Thus, in the region surrounding Cincinnati, it was found that the urban influence affected parts of Ohio and Kentucky, that it extended throughout six counties, which in turn embraced 51 townships and 13 magisterial districts, with 12 cities and 65 villages superimposed upon them.[27] Each of these governmental units maintained a police establishment of some character. All told, there was a total of 147 police agencies, each independent of the others and all of them overlapping in some degree. The six counties comprising the police region were distributed over 2,000 square miles of compact territory and included a total population of over 1,000,000 inhabitants.

[26] Cf., for example, *Factors Bearing on the Zoning of New York State for Local Government; Memorandum to the New York State Commission for the Revision of the Tax Laws,* by the Institute of Public Administration, New York, 1932.

[27] Bruce Smith, *A Regional Police Plan for Cincinnati and Its Environs; passim.*

Wide variations prevailed with respect to the numerical strength, organization, and character of the agencies affording police protection. Many of the villages and townships (or magisterial districts) had maintained only the popularly elected and part-time constables and marshals of the type described above.

Although it was found possible to set up a cooperative program which included central facilities for training, identification, crime records, pawnshop control, and radio and teletype communication, with the outlying areas committed to a systematic supervision of certain control points on highways and other transportation lines, there were no practicable means by which the police strength of the region could be consolidated. The essential character of the sheriff-constable system persisted and materially weakened the corrective influence of any cooperative program.

The example thus drawn from the Cincinnati region is generally typical of the situation as it exists in our other metropolitan areas. All of them are featured by a multiplication of police agencies. Within a radius of 15 miles of Boston Common, there are 40 cities and towns, each with its own police system, with the entire region crisscrossed by the parkway patrols of the Metropolitan District Commission. As Leonard Harrison summarizes it: "There are, therefore, forty independent police departments, forty chiefs of police, forty administrative heads including police commissioners, directors of public safety, and boards of selectmen, and forty different policies governing police work. This is home rule with a vengeance."[28]

Within the 50-mile radius which defines metropolitan Chicago are 350 police forces, municipal, county, and state, most of them holding no promise of adaptibility to the crime problems of an heterogeneous community of more than five million population.[29]

In the much more numerous police regions not centering on a large urban district the outlook is even less favorable. For in such as these the sum total of miscellaneous police resources is not supported by a large neighboring police force, nor does one find the

[28] Leonard V. Harrison, *Police Administration in Boston*, pp. 158 ff. Cf., also, *Report of the Special Commission on Taxation and Public Expenditures*, Part XIV; *The Police Department of the Metropolitan District Commission* (1938).

[29] Merriam, Parratt, and Lepawsky, *Government of the Metropolitan Region of Chicago*, pp. 86-89; Bruce Smith, *Chicago Police Problems, An Approach to Their Solution*, pp. 10-11.

wide variety of staff services which are proving so essential to systematic police protection.

An overwhelming proportion of the nation's area, and a substantial minority of its population, are accorded only so much and such a quality of police protection as the sheriff-constable system can bestow.

This brings us to the possibility that police service can be effectively consolidated within county lines, as suggested by the efforts already made to set up county police forces outside the sphere and control of the sheriff's office. Although developments thus far give no sure indication that such consolidations will be effected, success in Great Britain with the county constabulary plan invites consideration of its adaptability to American conditions.[30]

It must be conceded at the outset that the local government situations of the two countries offer little of a parallel character. There is no avoiding the fact that the English situation is in certain respects more favorable than that prevailing in the United States. The density of population, over 17 times that of this country, naturally results in more compact communities, a preponderance of large corporate entities, and correspondingly greater resources for police support. In England, the urban population now exceeds 80 per cent of the total while that of the United States is less than 40 per cent.

Such considerations serve to emphasize the wide differences that underlie the English and American problems, and to raise serious questions concerning the adaptability on a large scale of county constabulary systems to the conditions prevailing in this country.

Other doubts arise when the population distribution by counties is considered. Our 3,053 counties average slightly less than 40,000 population. Yet "nearly a fourth of all counties have less than 10,000 inhabitants, nearly a third range from 10,000 to 20,000, and over a fourth range between 20,000 and 40,000. In other words, four-fifths of all counties have less than the average population. The median county has 17,000 inhabitants, and the largest single group of counties (543) ranges from 10,000 to 15,000 population."[31]

Such summaries serve to clarify some of the fundamental aspects of the American rural police problem in its nationwide aspects. It

[30] For a general treatment of county constabularies in England, see Smith, *Rural Crime Control*, pp. 114-117, 120-123.

[31] William Anderson, *The Units of Government in the United States*, p. 17.

is apparent from them that even with the integration of all municipal, town, and county police agencies, lying within the boundaries of the individual counties, only a mere handful of counties would be of sufficient size and possess sufficient resources to maintain modern police units so staffed and equipped as to meet the exacting police requirements of the present day. In those sections where urban areas set down in a general rural setting are not found at all, the prospect for adequately financed and effective county constabularies is highly unfavorable.

V. THE PROBLEM OF SMALL POLICE JURISDICTIONS

When public agencies for protection falter in discharge of their duties recourse is had to extralegal, and sometimes illegal, methods. Such action is usually delayed until all hope is past that the regularly constituted officers can perform the functions entrusted to them. Thus the middle of the eighteenth century marked the almost complete collapse of the parish constable system in England, attended by the conditions already described.[32] Rural crime flourished to such an extent that the thin pretense of a police system based upon selection by lot or by "house row" could no longer be maintained. So there sprang up all over England a multitude of voluntary associations which made it their business to pursue, apprehend, and prosecute offenders. In many instances they engaged paid employees who were sworn in as constables. For a century and more, private interests continued to combat conditions which had overwhelmed the archaic scheme of rural justice. Of the success which met their efforts we have no reliable knowledge, but it may be significant that voluntary associations continued to be numerous until well into the nineteenth century, and disappeared only upon the establishment of an organized and trained constabulary for every county in England.

This country has likewise had recourse to various expedients for local self-protection. As the outer line of settlements was pushed farther and farther west, the suppression of disorder became "one of the most difficult problems that arose under the decentralized system of American local government . . . and from a very early period the frontiersmen exercised a self-assumed criminal jurisdiction which was commonly sustained by the common consent of the

[32] *Supra,* pp. 31, 32.

neighborhood immediately concerned."[33]

When the most aggravated conditions have arisen, featured by the general collapse of law enforcement and overwhelming courts and prosecutors as well as sheriffs and constables, the abuses of privately administered justice have become far more serious than the failures attributed to public agencies.[34] At such times lynch law has stalked through the land. Its heavy hand has been felt not merely in the old South, where racial fears and antipathies held sway, but in the industrial East, on the Great Plains, and along the Pacific Coast. The disturbing rise in attacks upon rural· banks, a striking feature of our crime record during the last two decades, has also been attended by a revival of protective groups which are strongly reminiscent of the vigilance committees of a bygone day. These and similar expedients have been employed as substitutes for public police protection.[35]

It may be argued that the solution of our rural police problems should be sought in the strengthening of the local agencies of justice, on the theory that it is sometimes more important for the physician to know all about the patient than to know all about the disease with which he is afflicted. There is a certain element of truth in this view, and one which might possibly be employed in the reconstruction of our rural police system. In its most perfect form such a plan would involve reconstructing the ancient Anglo-Saxon institutions of the frankpledge and the tithing. If that were practicable in any reasonable degree under our modern conditions it would represent a highly satisfactory solution. The burdensome public costs of police protection would be eliminated at one stroke, and the compulsory association of all citizens for observance and enforcement within each group might quickly restore law-abiding tendencies in communities which now lack them.

Yet it is clear that the time for such devices has long since passed. The frankpledge and the tithing were probably not an invention of those seeking a higher degree of police protection; more likely were they the result of an actual interdependence of all members of the community in matters public and private, social and eco-

[33] Williams, *History of the San Francisco Committee of Vigilance of 1851*, p. 31.
[34] Cf. J. P. Shalloo, *Private Police*, American Academy of Political and Social Science, Monograph 1 (1933).
[35] *Supra*, pp. 116-118.

nomic. Many things have since occurred to revise this interdependence so that it covers not only much larger groups of individuals, but draws together those who are separated by great distances, and whose relations with each other do not include all possible social and economic contacts, but are confined to one or two special common interests. In other words, the social group is no longer a small, self-sufficient community, which can be counted and delimited, but an uncertain and shifting relationship of individuals that defies close governmental adjustment. Lacking the aid which definite social groups could lend to a scheme requiring mutual police protection, it is difficult to see how any mere rearrangement of the sheriff-constable system could produce a really constructive result.

There are also other angles of approach to the problem. One of them consists in the creation of new general and special police agencies designed to supplement the work of the older, traditional forms. Application of this method sometimes results in the superposition of one force on another until the whole mechanism of protection becomes burdened by unnecessary complexity. Our rural communities, particularly those which have begun to feel the influence of modern crime, are featured by police resources and facilities of almost tropical luxuriance and variety. In addition to the long-familiar sheriff-constable system, there may be several uniformed deputy sheriffs and township police patrolling the more frequented highways; civil defense volunteers; a number of state highway police patrols; state liquor law enforcement officers; game wardens; prosecutors' detectives, and other police agencies of less frequent occurrence.

It is apparent that such multiplication of police units has been derived from the inadequacy of each unit standing alone. It does not follow, however, that their individual weaknesses and structural defects as protective agencies tend to make their reform or consolidation a simple matter. On the contrary, the complex political relationships arising out of all this confusion of jurisdictions are calculated to add to their powers of resistance against any material change in existing arrangements. One cannot readily disentangle and rearrange them by any general program, because the pattern in each community differs from all the others in some degree, and to undertake the task of systematic revision in each local area involves endless perplexities in thousands of jurisdictions.

There remains the possibility of radically revising the whole local police system, but a program of such magnitude cannot be easily launched, and only under the most pressing circumstances can it be carried to a successful conclusion. Even its barest outlines are determined not only by the inadequacies of the rudimentary police systems, but by the nature and backgrounds of the police systems of cities and states, and even those of the federal government itself. These matters are the concern of the chapters which immediately follow.

VI. THE PROBLEM OF VOLUNTEER POLICEMEN

During World War II citizens in the suburbs and in the cities were encouraged to join various civilian defense units in the name of national security. Oriented to provide a quick-functioning civilian organization to assist the established units of government in the event of an enemy attack upon the homeland, the civilian defense agencies still received only lukewarm support from the public. At the end of the war, interest in many of the civilian defense activities dropped to the vanishing point, except among the professional staffs of civil defense agencies: public relations men and retired military officers. One aspect of the civilian defense effort, however, still thrives in many cities and suburban communities: the auxiliary police.

In 1959 there were 388,000 persons throughout the country listed as members of the auxiliary police of civil defense. An unknown fraction, however, can be relied upon to participate in training exercises or be considered active. These training exercises may consist of the viewing of training films, lectures, or applied police work with or without the company of professional police officers. Civil defense auxiliary police have been used at one time or another to control pedestrian traffic at church crossings, direct the parking of cars at shopping centers, patrol congested areas on foot, or to accompany professional policemen on radio car patrol. As to the arming of these auxiliary police there is no pattern: some carry a pistol when on a training exercise, others a night stick, and still others are unarmed.

The reasons for joining the auxiliary police no doubt are various. The service is without pay, and on a volunteer basis. Patriotism may actuate some volunteers, but it is likely that others join as police "buffs" to "know" policemen, to have an occasional "night out," and in some instances as a basis for applying for a permit to carry a pistol.

While on training duty auxiliary policemen exercise the powers of a policeman: they may arrest persons, they may use force, and they may assert authority. The frightening aspect of the auxiliary police is the general lack of character investigation. While professional policemen are normally subjected to an investigation of their past to assure that they at least are not Communists or criminals, the auxiliary policeman is subjected to no such test in the vast majority of municipalities. In some cities, individual auxiliary policemen are known to have criminal records of a serious nature, yet they are retained in the unit and are permitted to exercise police authority.

It is probable that virtually every police chief in the nation would gladly rid himself of responsibility or contact with the civil defense auxiliary police. Yet the fear of the unfavorable publicity which would attend any concerted effort to divorce the police from any civil defense organization is no doubt a deterrent to positive police action, and a life-preserving shield for the civil defense auxiliary police.

CHAPTER 5

URBAN POLICE

The line of demarcation between the police forces of the larger villages and those of the smaller cities is indistinct. As indicated in the preceding chapter, the larger village forces come to acquire many of the characteristics and attributes of urban police, and a few of them are actually better manned, better equipped, and better administered than those of the smaller cities. Yet there comes a point in the growth of most communities when their police defenses are improved and enlarged out of all proportion to the increase of population. However ill-defined this critical stage may be, it marks the point of departure into new and more complex urban problems of great variety, among them being the social and administrative questions associated with crime and police. Here we approach close to the core of what is popularly believed to be the American police problem; for it is chiefly in our cities, and particularly in the great cities, that this problem is encountered in its most aggravated form. In a highly urbanized setting, with its clash of racial and alien interests, devious political methods, baffling labor problems and the like, popular government and law enforcement often seem to work at cross-purposes. The results are common knowledge. Whatever the causes for this collision of democratic processes and high standards of criminal justice administration, there can be no doubt of its grave potentialities

Early Municipal Police Development

If the early days of our municipal police were marked by distinguished achievement, the historians of the time failed to note it. There is, however, some evidence that policing the lusty, growing cities of America was once a task which attracted chiefly the shiftless, the incompetent, and the ignorant; citizens contemplated the members of the city watch with uneasiness and distrust, while scandals reaching from the top to bottom of police establishments were of frequent occurrence. During the first half of the nineteenth century there was increasing concern with problems of police organization, with the distribution of patrols and the selection of watchmen. Yet there is no evidence that these stirrings toward improved patterns were in any wise affected by the far-reaching plans proposed for metropolitan London by Dr. Patrick Colquhoun[1] in 1796, and put into effect more than thirty years later by Robert Peel. On the contrary, most efforts toward improvement were frittered away on relatively trifling matters or through an overcautious approach to questions demanding vigorous treatment. Separate police were organized for day and for night duty; similar distinctions were introduced for each of the wards of some cities; watchmen were elected by popular vote; and multiform methods were employed which it was hoped would in some manner solve the never-ending problem of popular control without arousing popular distrust of armed and disciplined police forces. American cities literally ran riot in their experimental devices. There followed a hurried effort to consolidate the forces which had been organized by wards or other minor areas, to break down the puerile distinction between day and night watches, and thus to present a more solid front to violent disorders.[2]

Then came attacks from other angles. Rotation in office enjoyed so much popular favor that police posts of both high and low degree were constantly changing hands, with political fixers determining the price and conditions of each change. So the struggle toward police improvement continued, with the reformers generally a bit confused and divided as to ways and means for achieving even the simplest objectives. Police training was as yet unthought of; police techniques were largely confined to various methods for wielding a night stick; and criminal investigations were conducted without the aid of modern science. The whole police question simply churned about in the public mind and eventually became identified with

[1] Colquhoun, *A Treatise on the Police of the Metropolis* (London, 1796).

[2] For a well-documented account of this period in police development, see Fosdick, *American Police Systems*, pp. 58-73.

the corruption and degradation of the city politics and local governments of the period. Despite many recent advances in the art of police administration, the development of a multitude of useful police techniques, and the enthusiasm and idealism of a new order of policeman, the American police problem continues to be synonymous with nineteenth-century municipal corruption. Still more years must come and go before this lengthening shadow finally recedes into its obscure and inglorious past.

Numerical Strength

Cities represent the core of our problem in another respect, because their police establishments, taken together, constitute by far the largest body of professional police in the United States. Other highly developed forces maintained by some of the states, and by the federal government, have made contributions of the greatest significance to the maintenance of the peace and the protection of persons and property, but their total manpower is not impressive when compared with that of similar agencies maintained by a thousand cities great and small.

The so-called urban area of the United States, which includes places having over 2,500 population, embraces a total of about 70,000,000 people who are protected by 135,000 policemen. Two-thirds of these are in cities over 250,000 population. The largest single force is, of course, that of New York City, where a body of close to 24,000 men is maintained. The scale-down in size is, however, rapid from this peak, and dwindles away to the disappearing point in the great bulk of the smallest municipalities.

Perhaps the best general view of police quotas is provided by the ratios they bear to the local population served. If comparisons are made on this basis, it becomes clear that the size of the city not only bears a direct relationship to that of the police force but, as might also be anticipated, the larger the city the larger is the ratio of police to population.

For cities over 250,000 population an average of about two and one-half police department employees per thousand of population is maintained; in cities between 50,000 and 250,000 the ratio drops to one and two-thirds employees; in cities from 25,000 to 50,000, the average is also one and two-thirds, while in the highly miscellaneous group of small cities and large villages one and one-half police employees per thousand inhabitants is the average level.

The foregoing figures do not include the independent park police forces maintained in or by some of our largest cities. In particular instances these may increase the municipal police strength by 10 to 15 per cent. Nor do they include the private watchmen, special police, and commercial and industrial guards maintained to a varying extent in all of the more important centers. Such as these are supported from private funds, but may be subject to state or local regulation. They perform within a restricted area, and often on private property, the usual functions of a uniformed and armed police body.

It must also be remembered that these averages conceal many marked deviations. Thus, in the largest population group (cities having over 250,000 inhabitants), some cities will have a ratio four times greater than others. In the smallest communities they involve a spread, in extreme cases, of as much as 3,000 per cent even as between places of comparable size and location. It being impossible to explain or to justify such wide variations by any differences in the police problems involved, they can safely be dismissed as being the result of other factors having no direct relationship to police work or public needs, or to a disposition by certain small communities to abdicate the field of law enforcement almost entirely, and to turn it over to state police. There are, in fact, a number of isolated cases that show a tendency in this direction.

With respect to the regional distribution of police quotas, few safe conclusions can be drawn. The uneven regional distribution of the larger communities, where quotas are in general relatively high, exercises a preponderant influence. Hence the regions with the heaviest concentrations of large cities will have the higher ratios of police to population. If this special influence be eliminated, and the regional comparisons are confined to cities of small to moderate size, the South Atlantic and the Pacific regions show the highest quotas.

Finally, the point should be stressed that even the clearest of the relationships shown above do not in any sense imply that the police ratios represent desirable objectives. Necessary or desirable police strength for any given city cannot be determined by any such convenient and simple method. It can be computed or estimated only with the aid of extensive knowledge of many demographic factors, and a firsthand acquaintance with local geography and similar physical elements, some of which do not lend themselves to direct measurement.

One other feature requires emphasis. It is that five-sixths of our cities and towns fall within the population group below 25,000 inhabitants. These 2,200 places are therefore far more characteristic of the American police setup than are the larger communities. Yet the average strength of the police forces which they maintain is only eight men per municipality. When such meager manpower is divided into three eight-hour shifts and due allowance is made for rest days, vacations, sick leaves, special details, and many other homely realities of police management and distribution, the essential weakness of our police defenses becomes clear. For one is tempted to lay down the positive declaration that, man for man, no small force can ever be as effective in protection, investigation, and apprehension as a large and widely ranging police body. Such a broad generalization is obviously open to attack through concrete examples to the contrary, but the basic soundness of the observation still remains. So until some effective and practical means can be found for consolidating the numerical strength of small police units, thereby reducing the number of independent police forces, our police defenses will continue to be structurally weak.

Salary Scales of Patrolmen

Table I establishes a fairly well-defined relationship between size of city and minimum and maximum salaries for patrolmen; that is to say, the larger the city, the higher are the police salary scales. From the standpoint of geographic distribution, the highest brackets are to be found in the Middle Atlantic, New England, and Pacific states, and along the Great Lakes, while the lowest scales are quite definitely located in the South Atlantic and South Central areas. Thus, as to both size of city and geographic location, there is at least a superficial relationship between police salaries and the cost and standard of living.

A geographical comparison of police salaries with the distribution of per capita incomes likewise shows a striking correlation. Here the West Coast, Middle Atlantic, and New England states lead by a wide margin both as to police salaries and per capita incomes; while in the South Atlantic and South Central states,

TABLE I*

RANGE OF ENTRANCE AND MAXIMUM SALARIES FOR PATROLMEN 1960

	Pop. Group	Cities Rep.	Lowest	Lower Quartile	Median	Upper Quartile	Highest
Entrance salary of patrolmen	Over 500,000	12	$3,780	$4,410	$4,700	$5,127	$6,228
	250,000 to 500,000	17	3,913	4,165	4,500	5,205	6,396
	100,000 to 250,000	41	2,576	3,812	4,241	4,609	6,060
	50,000 to 100,000	90	2,100	3,887	4,340	4,881	6,180
	25,000 to 50,000	208	3,000	3,818	4,251	4,718	5,988
	10,000 to 25,000	419	2,664	3,500	4,030	4,560	7,488†
Maximum salary of patrolmen	Over 500,000	12	4,680	5,207	5,719	6,018	6,828
	250,000 to 500,000	17	4,320	4,998	5,574	5,934	6,828
	100,000 to 250,000	41	3,780	4,605	5,096	5,356	6,900
	500,000 to 100,000	90	2,100	4,320	4,819	5,452	6,984
	25,000 to 50,000	208	3,216	4,305	4,800	5,555	6,900
	10,000 to 25,000	419	2,700	3,958	4,540	5,250	8,760†

* From the *Municipal Year Book*, 1960.
† Anchorage, Alaska.

where per capita incomes are lowest, police salaries are also at the bottom of the scale.

Hence the policeman's economic position, in relation to that of the general population, seems to be approximately the same in all sections of the country. Despite many departures in individual cities, the bald fact stands out that American cities generally compensate police in proportion to the community's capacity to pay.

Police salaries are relatively stable. Yet the long-term trend of police salaries has been definitely upward, and in certain cases sharply so. While the economic depression, first felt in 1930, finally forced some arbitrary reductions in police salaries, they were temporary in their effect. Among the larger cities, where police salaries reach the highest average levels, there was a slight net increase even during the depression period 1929-1937; but this did not hold good for cities of more moderate size.

Also significant is the marked upswing in police salaries since World War II. In the smaller cities where police salaries are lowest, this increase exceeded 100 per cent between 1941 and 1958 with the larger places showing similar readjustments that were almost as great.

Obvious, too, is the long-term trend toward greater uniformity in police salaries, even though the scales of very small and very large cities still offer some striking contrasts.

Salary Scales for Superior Grades

Less satisfactory conclusions can be drawn with respect to the compensation accorded to the higher police ranks. Although there is rather strict adherence to the obvious need for discriminating between the numerous levels of rank found in most police hierarchies, the salary spread between different ranks may be, and often is, as little as 3 or 4 per cent of the base pay of a patrolman, and may bear little or no relation either to the responsibilities such as superior rank entails or to the pay scales for generally comparable civilian posts. This is not a fault peculiar to police administration, and it is doubtful whether it will ever be corrected with reference to the police alone. Salary standardization almost necessarily implies the use of a broad personnel base, which may mean the entire personnel of the government concerned.

The responsibilities of police leadership vary so widely as between very large and very small communities that no direct comparisons of the cost of such leadership to the community can lead to profitable observations. If New York City pays its police commissioner $25,000 a year, whereas the police chief of a small city receives less than a patrolman in one of the larger centers, no conclusion can be drawn except that such differences are inherent in the nature of the job and the salary standards of two widely differing communities. Average pay scales for superior ranks also tend to increase with the size of the city.

Finally it should be noted that the wealthier or more progressive communities, however small, sometimes raise the compensation of the police chief to a point substantially above the prevailing level for towns of comparable size and location. Such communities are reaching far beyond their own limited borders in the search for superior capacity in police management This represents one of the significant shifts in the police scene of today, and its possible influence upon the police future of America invites optimistic speculation.

Fixing the Level of Police Salaries

Determination of police salary scales, like fixing police quotas, should not be allowed to revolve around uncertain and inconclusive factors. American cities must face the fact that police compensation scales are part and parcel of the wage level of each community, and that police forces are in direct competition with commerce and industry in seeking to attract capable and reliable man power. Comparisons with the salary scales of other cities, therefore, do not rest upon any relationship of local value.

Police authorities and other municipal officers should ask themselves three questions in determining police salary scales:

1. What kind and quality of police recruits is it desired to attract?
2. What salary is necessary to attract them?
3. Can the community afford to offer salaries at the level indicated?

If this course be followed, it may involve collecting data which are not easily secured, but which once in hand will have some direct bearing upon the local situation. The results in some instances may be surprising because it may be found that, although a high standard for police recruits is determined upon, it nevertheless may not be necessary to raise the salary scales at all. This condition is most likely to prevail in communities where police service is held in high esteem, where partisan influences are relatively weak or the merit basis of police employment is generally satisfactory. Policies with respect to hours of duty, rest days, vacations, sick leave, promotional opportunities, and retirement provisions are also important factors in determining the kind of human raw material that aspires to police service. These and related subjects will be reviewed at a later point in the present chapter.

Municipal Police Costs

Closely allied to police quotas and salaries is the matter of police costs. Since 85 per cent of the total expenditures for police protection are allocated to salaries and wages, the number of police and the salary scales that apply to them go far to determine the total outlay. Contributing to the rise in police costs have been the increased complements of men who are actively engaged in street traffic regulation. Finally, American police forces have turned more and more to mechanization in performing routine police tasks, though without imposing technological unemployment in perceptible degree. In any case the cost of motorized patrols and the new communication systems has been only a minor factor in the rise of police expenditures, for the reasons stated above.

Yet police have not been especially favored in the matter of financial support because per capita police costs for operation and maintenance have risen in strict conformity with those of the general departments of city government. This raises some doubt concerning the influence of unfavorable public attitudes toward the police, and suggests that the spending moods of city governments have carried along police budgets to high levels as a matter of course and without much discrimination. Also worthy of passing notice is the fact that police costs show a tendency to vary directly with the size of the city. This is a reflection of two other features; namely, that the ratios of police to population and police salaries show the same tendency. Taken together they naturally determine the level of police expenditures.

The conclusion seems inescapable that the police of our cities have not by any means fared badly in attracting financial support. They have done well by comparison with their chief rivals for popular approval. They have enjoyed substantial increases in pay scales and in securing ways and means for employing additional personnel and purchasing new equipment. During the depression years, the restriction of their resources was less severe than in the case of comparable city activities. Following World War II per capita expenditures for police protection rapidly rose to new high levels.

Distribution of Effective Strength

With the great bulk of police funds being expended chiefly for man power, the distribution of the rank and file becomes a matter of some moment. While there are no sure rules for distributing police effectives, and no formulae for determining the ratios applicable to each service or activity, a few generalizations do have theoretical bearing and some degree of practical application.

As a general rule the smaller the city the greater is the proportion of effective strength assigned to the office of the chief administrative officer, and to various types of desk duty; and that as the size of the city increases, the proportion of police employees assigned to miscellaneous services also increases.[3] In any given situation, this last may be quite as important as the first-named feature because it tends to offset the advantages otherwise accruing from large-scale operation. That the advantages of mere size may sometimes be substantial is indicated by the increasing proportion of captains, lieutenants, and sergeants employed in the management of the smaller police forces of our cities.

Of similar import is the fact that, as the size of the city increases, the proportion of "civilian" employees in the police force also

TABLE II

Nonpolice Employees

Population Groups		Per Cent "Civilian" Personnel
2,465 cities under	10,000 population	6.8
795 cities from	10,000 to 25,000 population	5.1
275 cities from	25,000 to 50,000 population	7.4
128 cities from	50,000 to 100,000 population	8.7
65 cities from	100,000 to 250,000 population	12.5
41 cities over	250,000 population	8.6
Average, all cities	....	8.3

tends to increase. The ratios for cities of varying size appear in Table II.

[3] The "miscellaneous" services referred to include such items as the inspection of licenses, pawnshops, elevators, buildings, and automobiles; assignments with the health department, the courts, or at the city pound; a multitude of trades and callings involved in building and equipment maintenance; and such specialists as crime-prevention officers, matrons, police surgeons, and the like.

With the increasing emphasis upon professional standards in police work, it is only reasonable to expect that whenever police forces require the services of skilled accountants, stenographers, clerks, or mechanics, these will be employed on the basis of their several skills, and not sought among the rank and file of police who are recruited with reference to quite different standards. Thus far, only about 8 per cent of all employees of city police forces fall into this special "civilian" category, although it is significant that the proportion is increasing rapidly in the smaller places.

Police Equipment

Man for man, American city police forces have more mechanical aids and other equipment at their command than those of any other nation. This is not to suggest that the confident claims of those who sell police equipment, or the optimistic hopes of those who buy it, are often realized. Indeed, many urban police forces in this country are actually burdened with equipment. Traffic signals are installed at street intersections that do not require regulation or cannot be controlled by anything short of the physical presence of a uniformed patrolman. Parking meters line the street curbs of cities large and small. Expensive call-box systems, designed for a day when radio communication to motor patrols was unknown, are operated on a decentralized basis through district stations, where an undue amount of manpower is absorbed in receiving routine patrol reports. Teletype systems are installed without regard to their specific local value as supplementary recording devices; and signal switchboards are provided with multicolored panels and decorative schemes of illumination which delight the eye of the beholder without contributing anything of value to the grim business of police protection. Ingenious contrivances have in truth become a special kind of police problem, both because they are costly and also because they serve to distract the attention of administrators and public alike away from those primary considerations of organization, personnel, and procedure upon which successful police operations ultimately depend.

A case in point concerns machine records installed in recent years: the recording of information on punch cards. On the face of it, machine records appear ultramodern to the observer unfamiliar with either police records or machine methods of record keeping. Ostensibly machine records offer quick and thorough records searches at the flick of a switch. If the police desire the name of a criminal based upon a verbal description, it would at first glance seem the machine records would be an aid.

Analysis, however, will demonstrate that machine records are neither useful nor economical in any except the largest of police departments, and even in these there is room to doubt their usefulness. The rental on equipment for even a fairly small installation for machine records will cost about $5,000 a year, and more ambitious installations are more expensive. The manpower required to operate a machine records system is often numerically as great as would be required to maintain useful police records by hand tally. Even these cost factors might be disregarded if machine records were really more effective. In practice they are not.

San Francisco maintains machine records on offenses, occurrences, and persons arrested. In the course of a survey in 1957 it developed that the machine records had never been used by anyone in the department to locate a criminal, nor did any of the section chiefs in the detective division believe that it could be done. The reasons for the failure of machine records in police work are: their inflexible nature, once information has been recorded on a punch card; unreliability of information (such as descriptions) in the most vital matters; too common characteristics (such as blue eyes, blond hair, and medium build) which produce so many matches that they are worthless. As applied to crime report preparation, or accident report analysis, machines cannot select the significant or unusual so often recorded when hand tally and normal clerical methods are utilized.

Yet certain types of basic equipment, when carefully selected for their practical application in police work, may yield good results. During recent years the advent of the automobile (which is necessarily expensive) and the police radio (which is relatively cheap) have acquired particular importance because taken together they make possible a reasonable degree of protection even though the manpower may be inadequate. Indeed, few cities over 10,000 population are not adequately motorized, and nearly all possess facilities for receiving radio broadcasts in patrol cars. Of a total of almost 14,500 police cars operated in these cities 80 per cent are radio equipped, as are over 40 per cent of the 4,500 motorcycles.

Such impressive fleets of motor vehicles have generally been acquired because they represent the cheapest form of police protection. By means of radio broadcasts of alarms and instructions to police cars it is possible to use the crews of the latter in a dual capacity, both for patrol purposes and for quick response in emergencies. This avoids the duplication of manpower and equipment which was involved before police radio systems became available—a duplication then considered to be unduly expensive by all but the largest cities

The Question of Uniformed Patrol

All such considerations are in a sense merely preliminary to the large and ever-increasing problem of the uniformed patrolman and the best means of employing his services in crime repression. The proportion of police engaged in uniformed patrol duty is only slightly more than half the urban police strength. The ratio has been falling for some time, owing to the increasing demands of new responsibilities, particularly street traffic regulation, and the operation, maintenance, and repair of a multitude of mechanical and electrical gadgets. While foot patrols constitute under one-third of the police strength, they must be divided into three shifts or platoons under prevailing eight-hour-day arrangements This brings the actual proportion of the force engaged in foot patrol duty down to a point where the overhead, miscellaneous, and indoor assignments may be actually larger, at a given time, than the patrol assignments. The situation is further aggravated by the fact that the foot patrol force is a kind of reservoir of manpower. Each day this reservoir is heavily tapped in order to provide replacements for those assigned to other divisions of the force, or who are off duty as the result of vacations, rest days, special leave, suspension, illness, injury, and other causes. Such losses generally range between 40 per cent and 60 per cent of the total manpower. Clearly the foot patrol strength is wholly inadequate to provide replacements for the entire force, though this is occasionally attempted. Cities thereby are confronted with a situation that threatens the virtual elimination of foot patrolmen.

While motor patrols have served to fill in the gaps left in the foot patrol defenses, too few maintain the same intimate contact with the law-abiding citizen or with other sources of criminal information. Motorization actually reduces the number of patrols whenever the number of men assigned to each car is increased from one man (as is the case in some cities) up to two, three, four, or even five men. The crews of three, four, or five men per car are in no sense typical of, or even primarily intended for, the business of routine patrol. But two-men crews are common, owing to a widely held belief that these are necessary for adequate defense of the crews themselves. The same argument was advanced for many years on behalf of foot patrols in pairs, yet these have gradually been abandoned.

Already one observes a trend away from the exclusive use of either one-man or multiple crews, and strongly toward the use of both complements in a clear majority of American cities. This is a healthy sign, because it represents a trial-and-error approach to the question, with some effort to adapt the size of the crew to the specific area to be patrolled.

Ever-increasing demands for police service, coupled with a decline in available manpower, continues the trend away from foot patrolmen in favor of radio cars. Proper training and supervision, leading to effective radio car patrol, can make this necessary change in method a desirable change. In too many municipalities foot beats have been unchanged for twenty or thirty years. The common pattern was to annex to a small business area a much larger residential area to be assigned to foot patrol. Thus foot patrol manpower continues to be wasted by dispersion in areas better patrolled by radio-equipped autos. Concentrated areas of police hazard require foot patrol, often more than they now receive; but more adequate foot patrols can be achieved only by recognizing the capability as well as the limitations of the patrol car.

The motorized patrol has a higher potential of effectiveness than has the foot patrol, and is correspondingly more difficult to conduct. It has been said that at least five years of experience are necessary to train a radio car patrolman, though of course some men are not competent after twenty or thirty years of police experience. There certainly has been a tendency for radio car patrolmen to rely too heavily upon their radios to notify them of calls for police assistance, the remaining time on patrol being consumed in aimless driving. In a few cities such as Richmond, Virginia, and Salt Lake City, Utah, at least some of the men assigned to radio cars are conducting highly effective motorized patrols. Through familiarity with the patrol sector, and close observation, these patrolmen are especially effective against burglaries, robberies, stolen autos, and traffic violations. By conscious informant development, by friendly chats with residents and businessmen, by leaving the vehicle briefly to patrol special hazards on foot, the best radio car operators are of greater effect than many foot patrolmen in the same area would be. At the same time, while patrolling for the traditional police patrol objectives, radio car patrolmen are available to respond to a radio message to any point in or near their patrol sector.

A frequent analysis of patrol needs is required in every department. This analysis need not involve a complex of statistics; in fact statistics improperly used may becloud the issue. Each department does need a frequent reappraisal of police hazards, and what type of patrol (if any) can meet the hazards. Without formulas, without punch cards and machine records, almost any district captain (or police chief in a smaller town) should be able to pinpoint at any moment in time where his hazards are. If the hazards are sufficiently concentrated to be effectively patrolled on foot, and if they are such as can be dealt with by a foot patrolman, then a need is established, at least for the moment. The alert police administrator bears in mind, however, that economy of manpower is a part of his duty to the public and to his profession. Too many men, wastefully employed, invite a lower recruit standard and may prohibit high professional police salaries.

Certain of the larger forces also suffer avoidable losses of effective manpower through maintaining unnecessary district stations or from operating the patrol wagons which are a common appurtenance of them. Many police districts were perhaps necessary before modern means of transport brought their revolutionary changes. Changed also are the conditions of service that once attached to the horse-drawn patrol wagon. Motorized police vans, some working on regular schedules for the distribution of prisoners, others held in reserve for emergency "pickup" service, can effect major economies if properly employed. These matters receive considerable attention in a number of cities, some of which drastically reduce their plant and equipment with beneficial results.[4] Such developments pro-

---

[4] Police district consolidations have reduced the number of district stations in Chicago, Pittsburgh, Cincinnati, Cleveland, Louisville, Rochester, New Orleans, Boston, Syracuse, St. Louis, Utica, Providence, Norfolk, and New York City.

vide significant evidence of a recognition that manpower is the most important single factor in law enforcement.[5]

Meanwhile, the new means for quickly mobilizing the entire police strength have removed the need for large police stations. When a certain proportion of the force was required to act as an off-duty reserve, extensive dormitory space, large squad rooms, and recreation facilities were essential features of police stations. Two- and three-story district stations were provided, each with a small adjacent stable and a shed for the horse-drawn patrol wagon. Today police stations require merely one or two offices of moderate size, a communications and records center, a squad room with lockers, perhaps a small cell block, and ample storage space for motor vehicles. The necessary cubic footage is thus sharply reduced and with it the cost of construction. Yet despite such favorable changes, great monumental stations in brick, limestone, and granite continue to be constructed, sometimes at staggering cost.[6]

Police Costs vs. Community Needs

The main outlines thus far traced have been concerned with the ability of police units to attract and hold the financial support of their respective city governments, and to indicate a few of the specific ways in which the men, money, and materials thus made available may be applied more effectively. Here the varying fortunes of

[5] This subject has also received recent attention abroad. With reference to England and Wales, Colonel Frank Brook declares that "there are . . . instances where divisions could be merged and where subdivisions and sections should be made more appropriate commands. In some cases where this has not been done it is mainly a matter of local sentiment, and while I am reluctant to decry local pride, this should not be allowed in these difficult days of policing to stand in the way of progress and sound police organization. . . . I am satisfied that in some instances divisions, subdivisions, and sections can be extended, for means of mobility and telephonic communications have had the effect of shortening distances." *Reports of His Majesty's Inspectors of Constabulary*, 1938, p. 6.

Among the most interesting English developments during the past two decades are the sector plan of patrol, evolved for the urban districts of Hertfordshire by the late Lieutenant Colonel Alfred Law, Chief Constable of Hertfordshire; and the decentralized system of patrol supervision devised by Chief Constable Frederick J. Crawley of Newcastle-upon-Tyne. The Crawley plan has been widely adopted throughout Great Britain. Cf.: F. J. Crawley, "Decentralization and the Police Box System," in *The Police Journal* (London), Vol. I (1928), No. 1, pp. 118-127; Alfred Law, *Police Systems in Urban Districts* (1923) and "Police Patrol Systems," in *The Police Journal*, Vol. II (1929), No. 2, pp. 280-293.

[6] When the New York City Police Department dedicated its Newtown precinct station in the Borough of Queens in December, 1939, the cost was announced at $650,000.

police management in some hundreds of widely scattered cities render any close and definite appraisal of administrative efficiency quite impossible. However, a few broad generalizations can be made without undue distortion of the patterns applying to a given community at a given moment.

Waiving all questions of uneconomical operation resulting from poor business methods, random purchasing, and inadequate property and fiscal controls—since these are common faults of governments in general rather than of police forces as such—the almost palpable fact remains that city police forces waste a part, and sometimes a considerable part, of their available manpower on:

1. Performance of unnecessary or so-called "public relations" assignments.
2. Distribution of uniformed patrols and of investigating and traffic units, without regard to established need.
3. Lax supervision of day-to-day operations, and failure to control malingering by men on disability or light duty rolls.
4. An inability or unwillingness, or both, to retire aged police officers to the pension rolls by executive order, and without regard to the inclinations of the incumbent.

The results are reflected in unduly large police costs for the amount and quality of public service that are rendered.

Few municipal police forces are even approximately free from the kind of waste described above. In some instances such faults are so pronounced as virtually to destroy the effectiveness of the police organism. Sometimes their origins are to be found in incompetent administrative leadership. But often they are the direct result of outworn methods and procedures that become fixed and crystallized by mere lapse of time, and may survive even a vigorous administrative housecleaning long enough to carry over safely into a successor regime, when the largely futile process of piecemeal reorganization is repeated.

Such maladjustments exist in their most pronounced form in the larger cities, where problems of large-scale administration are most difficult; but they arise also in even the smallest police forces, because in them the more intimate association of officers and men quickly levels the barriers of official rank and overwhelms an impersonal discipline.

In common with practically all other governmental agencies, municipal police administrators have been active in their efforts to secure ever larger public appropriations for their activities. The considerable degree of success attending such efforts has already been described. It is reflected in the steady rise not only of police expenditures as a whole, but also in the increases effected in the number of police and in the salary scales applying to them. Such advances have generally been secured without the aid of objective standards with which to measure local police needs. Demands upon the public purse are made through arguments and demonstrations having little basis in fact. If the crime rate is high, it is contended that larger police quotas will lower it; if low, then more police are needed to keep it low. If local police salaries can be shown to be low in comparison with those of selected cities, the comparison is vigorously employed on behalf of higher scales.

These devices, and others of a similar character, do not advance the cause of better police administration. Even though additional manpower may be secured through them, it does not follow that the increase is necessary or that the new effective strength will be effectively employed; and a mere increase in salary scales that is unsupported by improved procedures for recruiting, training, promoting, and disciplining the rank and file may only result in increased costs, without any compensating factor in the form of better police personnel.

Such conditions invite efforts at correction, though it appears unlikely that any large advances will be made in the measurement of police needs for some time to come. As will be shown in the succeeding section, police personnel is largely engaged in patrol, investigation, and traffic regulation, but without the objective standards by which the need for applying police manpower to these activities can be measured. The whole question resides in the realm of expert opinion as applied to specific situations, and even assuming that the expert is himself unbiased and objective in his approach, experience has amply demonstrated the difficulties to be encountered in translating the technical bases of his judgment into terms readily apprehended by budget officers, city councilmen, civic leaders, and the public generally.

Police are agreed that uniformed patrols discourage the commission of certain types of criminal acts, but even this elementary proposition lacks scientific demonstration. So until we have a whole series of controlled experiments which show with some degree of conclusiveness the effect of uniformed patrols upon the crime rate, and the point where additional patrol strength results in diminishing returns, police service not only in America but elsewhere throughout the world will continue to hinge upon expert opinion, while governing bodies and the taxpaying public will be handicapped in appraising demands for additional expenditures in this highly important field of police protection.

Meanwhile, it may be questioned whether the patrol resources of American cities are being used to the best advantage. Though extensive compilations are lacking for foot patrols, it is a matter of general observation that these are usually distributed on an equal, or nearly equal, basis throughout the twenty-four hours of the day, despite the fact that the crime curve shows a marked peak between 6:00 P.M. and 2:00 A.M. One reason for this condition is that police have many functions other than those relating to crime repression, and that distributions must be made with reference to the whole task rather than to a part of it. Even so, wherever the problem is systematically reappraised, foot patrols are increased in some degree during the late evening and early morning hours.

Use of uniformed police in street traffic regulation and control raises other questions for which there are as yet no answers. In an effort to reduce the toll of traffic accidents, American cities have spent large sums of money on various types of signs and signals. These have been produced in great variety and with considerable mechanical and electrical ingenuity. They have been adopted and installed upon the representation and in the belief that not only would they reduce the number of traffic deaths and injuries, but would render unnecessary the use of ever-larger complements of traffic police on main traffic arteries and at street intersections. Neither of these anticipated results has been realized anywhere in any convincing degree. Yet the traffic accident problem is not by its nature so many-sided and baffling as that of crime control, and should lend itself to some kind of solution by the application of engineering principles to specific situations.[7]

The third major police activity absorbing the energies of large

[7] An impressive beginning has been made by the Bureau of Highway Traffic at Yale University.

quotas of manpower is criminal investigation. Here also is continuing need for careful analysis of results in terms of manpower employed. Like the traffic problem just described, there are no large obstacles to something like real measurement of the interaction of police activity and the successful conduct of criminal investigations. It is not an inherently difficult matter to classify criminal investigations so that the more simple inquiries can be conducted by the uniformed force, reserving for the detective force only those requiring the special aptitudes and opportunities of "plain-clothes" investigators. These in turn can be measured in terms of time expended, and the whole question thereby reduced to a simple approximation. If such devices are supplemented by service ratings of individual detectives to the end that only those shall be employed in specialized criminal investigation as are demonstrably fitted for it, the need for objective standards in determining manpower quotas should be fully satisfied.

By far the vast majority of police departments recognize criminal investigators with special rank and pay, within or without the civil service tenure. There is in consequence a steady pressure by department personnel and politicians to increase the manpower assigned to the detective division above that required for investigation assignment. To occupy the efforts of detectives usefully many administrators assign them to cruise the city as plain-clothes patrols, accepting investigations too difficult or lengthy for the uniformed force, and thus serving as a bridge between the uniformed force and the detective squad investigators. Cruising detectives are often effective: they constitute an arm which can be utilized on investigations or used as patrol emphasis in hazardous areas. As with all specialized units, provision should be made for the supervision of cruising detectives, else their patrols and their investigations deteriorate in quality. The primary need for cruising detectives is during the peak hours of criminal activity: often from about six in the evening until two the following morning.

The achievement of manpower economy will continue to wait upon the development of police administrators, and particularly detective administrators, who possess and exercise an active interest in the problems of management. Our cities attract and train many capable detectives, but thus far they have not often developed competent directors of criminal investigation.

Police Protection in City Parks

The preceding chapter dealing with rural, suburban, and other transitional police forces, also noted the appearance of park and parkway police as occasional agencies of county governments. Such as these are recent developments which may not be able to resist for long the apparent trend toward police consolidation in suburban areas. Some of our larger cities also maintain specialized park police units which for several decades have enjoyed an independent existence under the guidance of the local park authorities. While these park police were created in the first instance for the protection of public property, their law-enforcing powers often match those of more general police agencies. As a matter of practical necessity they are charged not only with the protection of park property, but also with the safety of visitors to the parks. Hence they find themselves involved in the enforcements of traffic laws and ordinances, and in the investigation of robberies, auto thefts, and a wide range of other offenses against persons and property. In the regulation of traffic the park force may follow methods widely differing from those of the surrounding city force, thereby creating confusion among the motoring public. In criminal investigations practically all its work must be performed outside the park jurisdiction and within the normal sphere of the rival city force. Wholehearted cooperation is seldom extended by the latter under such circumstances. Yet whatever the faults inherent in the arrangement, there is much factual support for the complaint of park administrators that municipal police do not allot sufficient numbers of men on park assignments to assure the protection of park property.

Thus new problems of conflicting jurisdiction and duplication of the police function arise on every hand. Chicago, to take an extreme example, struggled along for many years with no less than nine park police forces, comprising some 800 park policemen. Some express thoroughfares came under the control of as many as four separate and distinct police systems. Uniform traffic enforcement was impossible. These park thoroughfares cut across the city police jurisdiction from every angle. Many of them were business streets lined with banks, shops, and other major crime hazards. Yet from the police standpoint they were in a kind of twilight zone. The park police were virtually negligible instruments in crime repression,

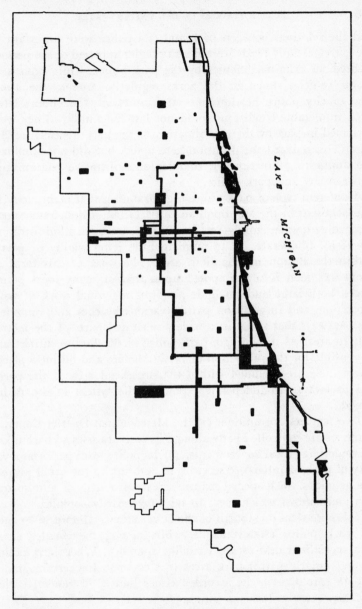

Figure IV Independent park police areas and thoroughfares are superimposed upon the jurisdiction of the Chicago Police Department.

and the relations between park and city police were uncertain in the extreme. Only rarely were the city police apprized of the persons wanted for criminal offenses by the park police, while reports of motor vehicles stolen in the parks regularly came to the attention of city police headquarters at least twenty-four hours late.[8] Such intolerable conditions could not last indefinitely. They were corrected in part by the consolidation of the park districts in Chicago. This reduced the diffusion here noted, but did not eliminate the duplicating functions or complex administrative relationships between city and park police.

A different type of park police organization is that maintained in Massachusetts by the Metropolitan District Commission, a state body charged with water supply, sewage disposal, and park administration functions. It operates in 43 municipalities lying wholly or partly within the Boston metropolitan area. The work of this force of about 225 men is superimposed upon that of many local police forces, both large and small. It performs the usual work of park protection, and in addition patrols various beaches and meandering parkways that reach into widely separated parts of the metropolitan area. As in Chicago, park police in the Boston district are responsible for the protection of private homes and business places where these are included within the superficial area of the parks and parkways. An independent police radio system is also maintained.

Two features are unique: (1) the Metropolitan District Commission is a state-controlled body, though its costs are assessed back upon the underlying local governments; (2) its police force performs a variety of park maintenance services, in addition to the usual protective activities. Such special features create problems of administration and control which seem to be unnecessarily complex.[9]

Not more than one-fourth of the larger cities maintain independent park police establishments, while among the smaller cities such specialized devices are virtually unknown. Where city police forces regularly patrol park areas it is common for certain grades of park employees to be accorded either limited or general police

[8] *Chicago Police Problems*, pp. 163-165.

[9] For a detailed and critical description of the Boston problem, cf. Commonwealth of Massachusetts, *Report of the Special Commission on Taxation and Public Expenditures; Part XIV, The Police Department of the Metropolitan District Commission* (House No. 1714, April, 1938).

powers, although experience shows that these are rarely exercised. Apparently there is no middle ground in such matters; either the city police must be entrusted exclusively with the task of park protection, or park authorities must assume it in all of its ramifications.

In most instances where county park systems are maintained, the policing is done by county park agencies, rather than police of the county's various municipalities. With the exception of these metropolitan park systems, it appears probable that independent park police forces will eventually be absorbed into the city police jurisdictions upon which they are now superimposed. But until this happens some of our largest cities will continue to struggle with problems of overlapping police agencies that are not very different from those of rapidly growing suburban areas.

Merit Systems

Practically all the leading municipal police forces of the country are now subject to the control of either state or municipal civil service commissions. In some of the larger cities, such as Detroit and St. Louis, where efforts have been made to bar such extradepartmental controls, the results in terms of honest and effective personnel management certainly have not been inferior to those achieved in most of the civil-service-controlled forces. On the other hand, it must be conceded that rarely is either type of merit system pursued with any marked degree of enthusiasm in our large police forces. Routine examination of applicants, the deadening influence of fixed official hierarchies, and tenure-of-office acts that place police employees beyond the reach of all ordinary disciplinary measures, have operated to reduce both the present and the future effectiveness of many police units.

All told, civil service commissions control the police forces of about three-fourths of our cities, and the proportion is rising. Thus the time is not far distant which shall see the last of the independent police merit systems reduced to a numerically negligible factor. Thereafter the future of municipal police service will be in the hands of state or local civil service commissions, operating without competition as to methods or results from police forces lying outside such controls, and without much prospect of a return to administrative independence in personnel matters.

Based upon the past record of civil service control—the political pandering, the personal corruption, and the bureaucratic rigidity so commonly noted among its characteristics—there is little in the prospect to lend hope for better things in municipal police administration. Two possibilities, however, will always be present: (1) a reform in the civil service regime, such as is taking place in a few centers; (2) an increasing disposition on the part of police administrators to lead the way toward new personnel selection techniques that square with the realities of police duty.[10] While the evidence of such impending changes in attitude and functioning is none too impressive, it seems safe to conclude that, whatever the future of our municipal police forces, the civil service system will exercise a great influence for better or for worse.

If one is to be guided by results rather than academic argument, it would appear that the best personnel administration is achieved by civil service commissions which are organically close to the police department. State-administered civil service control, as exemplified in Massachusetts, has yielded the least desirable results in terms of personnel selection, promotion, and discipline. In contrast, local civil service, aided in technical matters by the state Civil Service Commission, has produced superior results in New York State; while purely local civil service control as in Virginia has produced several outstanding police departments. That local personnel control may be abused is apparent, but here it is aided by technically qualified personnel administrators as in New York State, the flexibility attained has more than compensated for theoretical weaknesses.

Recruitment

Regardless of the methods employed for controlling the management of municipal police personnel, the ways and means for selecting recruits fall into easily defined patterns. These are concerned with such formal matters as citizenship and local residence, as well as with the more substantial questions revolving about the police aspirant's health, physique, age, character, education, and intelligence.

Full citizenship status is so nearly universal as a prerequisite and

[10] Donald C. Stone, *Recruitment of Policemen* (*Bulletins on Police Problems,* No. 1, International Association of Chiefs of Police, 1938), for excellent summary treatments of such techniques; also Richard L. Holcomb, *Selection of Police Officers* (Bureau of Public Affairs, State University of Iowa, 1946).

bears so directly upon the demands of law enforcement as to present no difficult problems. It is otherwise, however, with respect to local residence. Either by state law or by local ordinance, 90 per cent of our cities require municipal police recruits to be local residents. The required period may be as short as six months, or as long as ten years, with one- and two-year residence requirements predominating. Two arguments are adduced in behalf of this rule. It is defended because (1) it guarantees that locally recruited police shall be familiar with local geography, government, and problems, and (2) it simplifies the task of conducting character investigations into the past records of police applicants.

Opposed to this practice is the view that appointments to local police service should be open to citizens everywhere, or at most restricted to residents of the state in which the appointment is to be made. The argument is advanced that the field of choice should not be arbitrarily limited and that undue familiarity with certain types of local conditions may be a positive handicap to an honest exercise of police powers by the police recruit. As to the difficulties to be encountered in conducting the character investigations of nonresident applicants, it may be noted that investigation of even local applicants has rarely been vigorously performed.

The formal arguments pro and con might be viewed as leaving the whole issue of local residence undecided were it not for the fact that state and federal police regularly draw their recruits from wide areas without difficulty and with some advantage, while local police forces in many other parts of the world often prefer nonresident recruits because they have no local political or social ties.

American cities have made such great advances in raising health and physical standards for police recruits that it may appear ungracious to emphasize those things still remaining to be done. Yet a few communities are still dependent upon the judgment of the applicant's own physician, and do not require an independent check by a police surgeon or other representative of the public interest.

The minimum height requirements range between 5 feet 7 inches and 5 feet 10 inches, with a tendency toward the lower end of this scale. The permissible range of weight for a given height is also generously broad in many cases, resulting within a few years in overweight policemen who are partially incapacitated by that fact.

Police and civil service authorities should not be content merely to attract a fair average of the general population to police service. Unless the physical standards of the service are substantially higher than average, they may just as well be abandoned.

Requirements as to age at the time of recruitment vary widely. The minimum age ranges between 21 and 28 years, with 60 per cent adhering to the lower of these figures and nearly all keeping the lower limit to 25 years or less. Permissible maximum ages show a far wider range. In some cities no person over 26 years of age may be recruited for police service, while in others one may enter the service at any age up to 60 years. Eight cities impose no upper limit whatever. More than half the cities fix the maximum entrance age at 35, and in some of the largest urban centers—for example, in New York, Chicago, Detroit, and Los Angeles—the maximum is from 28 to 30 years.

In view of the general adoption of security of tenure for police, and the widely prevalent arrangements for retirement pensions, it is difficult to see how American cities can much longer permit the recruitment of aged or aging police applicants. Aside from the pressures supplied by retirement provisions stands the bold fact that the better municipal forces are seeking to recruit young, hopeful, and ambitious men rather than the unemployed and the unemployable. Past laxity in these respects is a reproach not only to the police administrators who tolerated them, but to the civil service commissions which were content to test and certify whatever human raw material happened to present itself for appointment. And, while the situation is now changing for the better, it is significant that the initial drive for improvement comes quite as frequently from police as from civil service administrators.

Few municipal forces have as yet devoted enough attention to the character investigation of applicants. Civil service routines often merely require that the applicant provide character vouchers, or "references," which are accepted without further question. Police sometimes supplement such elementary arrangements with an investigation of their own, though without much hope of affecting the result unless some positive disqualifying feature—such as conviction of crime—is discovered. The fingerprinting of all applicants and a check of the federal and state clearinghouses for identification have proved a useful device to this end. Rarely, however, does one find either civil service commissions or police staffs actively engaged in testing the applicants' past by every available means. When such tests are applied the results are clearly evident not only in the police force as a whole, but in the public esteem which it enjoys.

Most of the recruiting effort is expended in preparing and applying tests that are presumably concerned with the police applicant's mental qualifications. Here one finds so much confusion of objective, such uncertain distinctions between formal education and intelligence, and so little reliable knowledge concerning the nature of police aptitude, that progress at best has been slow, and there is as yet no convincing evidence that we have progressed at all.

Much is made of the fact that the formal education of police recruits, which rarely exceeded six years of schooling two generations back, now averages around eleven to twelve years. This change, however, merely reflects the increasing standards imposed by compulsory education laws, plus certain features serving to make police service more attractive to high-school graduates and to those with one or more years of higher education. About one-half of our cities now require police applicants to be high-school graduates.

Few police forces have moved out from under the shadow of the old, cut-and-dried civil service examinations for patrolmen, of tests primarily concerned with spelling, elementary arithmetic, and familiarity with a few legal definitions and points of local geography. Now at last we are beginning to employ the intelligence tests, the psychological test, and the police aptitude test, though still without much knowledge of their validity when judged by police criteria.[11] Nevertheless, the inclination to experiment is gaining ground, and it is not too much to hope that this will ultimately produce techniques for the selection of police which will be far superior to the crude and unsatisfactory devices now generally employed.

Probation and Training

Once the recruit is appointed, the question of his preparation for active police work becomes one of prime importance. Prior to 1920

[11] Cf. Searles and Leonard, *Experiments in the Mental Testing of Detroit Policemen* (1936); also E. M. Martin, "An Aptitude Test for Policemen," in *Journal of Criminal Law and Criminology*, Vol. XIV, No. 3 (November, 1923), pp. 376-404, and the *General Adaptability Test*, developed by L. J. O'Rourke, Director of Personnel Research, U.S. Civil Service Commission (1934).

the formal training facilities for police were so rare that their influence upon the great mass of recruits was negligible.[12] Now all cities over 500,000 population, together with a few score of smaller cities, have their own training establishments. While the quality of these is exceedingly uneven, and with all but a few is distinctly inferior, due allowance should be made for the veritable revolution in police attitudes which had to be effected before even a start at police training could be made. That revolution is now complete, with the result that practically all municipal police recruits are subjected to training in local, zone, or state schools for periods ranging from a few days to several months.

Eventually the recruit is assigned to active duty and the real test of his aptitude for police work begins. This initial period should be a critical one both for the recruit and for the force in which he serves, because errors in the selection process can be corrected by dismissing the inept recruit in the early stages of his service and before he has acquired the extraordinary protection thrown about him by tenure-of-office acts.

The probationary period during which the recruit is thus subject to informal dismissal varies widely in American cities. In some it is as little as two weeks and may run as high as three years, with about one-fifth of all cities providing no probationary period at all. Almost half the cities subject the police recruit to a probationary period of six months[13] with the larger urban centers in general imposing longer probationary periods than the small places.

While much remains to be done to improve civil service law and regulations with respect to police probation, the whole problem will remain unchanged until municipal police administrators more frequently exercise the powers of dismissal now lodged with them. Until this is done, little sympathy need be accorded the police chief who complains that he does not possess sufficient power to discipline the rank and file; for even when the chief's powers in this respect are complete and unrestricted during the probationary pe-

---

[12] Notable, however, were the early training programs of the Pennsylvania State Police, the New York City Police Department, the Detroit Police Department, and the New York State Police, which served to lay down many of the lines of instruction now generally followed elsewhere.

See Chap. 9 for a discussion of the general training facilities for police.

[13] In England and Wales, the probationary period for police is two years; in Scotland, one year.

riod, almost never are they exercised, with the result that the errors arising out of inadequate selection processes quickly come under the full protection of civil service laws and regulations.

Whatever the ultimate status of the policeman may be, whether he serves under the protection of civil service laws or tenure-of-office acts, or at the will of a superior, it is clear that completion of the training course for recruits and the modicum of experience acquired during a probationary period still fall far short of desirable objectives in professional police training. Additional practical experience can be acquired through mere lapse of time in police service, but supplementary theoretical training in various police specialties can be secured only through formal schooling. The progress made by municipal police forces in this respect is not impressive in either bulk or quality. Indeed, the advanced training resources offered by the New York Police Academy are so varied as to stand in a class by themselves.[14] Such facilities are out of the reach of the great mass of American cities and must be produced, if at all, by cooperative action.[15]

Promotion

Promotions in municipal police work are for the most part effected in two ways: (1) as a result of a written examination on police procedures, supplemented by physical tests, and perhaps weighted for length of police service or for what is known as "veterans' preference"; (2) as a result of political or other pressures. Sometimes one or the other of these methods is used and often they occur together. Political pressures are most common in those cities which have never experienced professional police service, but they also may prove highly effective in communities that have operated under civil service controls for decades. Their effect upon police work is often

---

[14] Schools are regularly conducted by the Police Department of the City of New York as follows: (1) Recruits' Training School; (2) Officers' Training School; (3) School of Detectives; (4) Traffic and Street Safety School; (5) School of Horsemanship; (6) Motor Transport School; (7) Motorcycle School; (8) Specialized Training School for Radio Recorders; (9) Pistol Instruction School (in three cycles). In addition, specialized courses are conducted for (1) plain-clothes patrolmen; (2) policewomen; (3) civilian employees; also in the following subjects: (1) regimental drill; (2) preparatory pistol instruction; (3) rifle instruction (44/40 rifles, 12-gauge shotguns, and .45-caliber submachine guns); (4) ditto (30/06 automatic rifle); (5) physical and moral welfare of children.

[15] Cf. Chap. 9.

bad. Written promotional examinations, on the other hand, do not test those qualities of leadership or administrative capacity which are presumably a major consideration in promotions to higher rank. Such qualities are therefore largely ignored because the more familiar techniques of personnel management do not attempt any such evaluation of human personality. Rarely does an American city conduct a promotional examination with the aid of an oral interview, although its use in the selection of police chiefs shows some sign of gaining ground.

The reluctance of a large majority of civil service commissions to employ the oral examination or interview method is likely to be based on two considerations. Some personnel administrators cling to the belief that a formal written test can be developed that will meet all the requirements of the interview, and at the same time lend itself to a simple and easily demonstrable system of grading; but the most common objection to the oral examination is that it may arouse popular distrust concerning the fairness of the examination process. Since the systems used in grading are those of the examiners and the results are not susceptible of check and review, there is always some danger that the oral interview will be attacked as a device for avoiding the restrictions placed upon individual judgment by civil service controls.

In the limited number of instances in which the interview method has been employed as a part of police promotional examinations, this danger has been avoided through the designation of special oral examination boards consisting of persons obviously above such criticisms. Whether these specially constituted boards of lay members can ever be considered a full substitute for the free play of executive judgment is another question. As matters now stand, it may at least be said that the oral examination is an important supplement to the written test, and that it can be so administered as to avoid any reasonable suspicion of personal bias or partisanship on the part of the examiners.

A possible substitute for the oral examination is a review of all subordinates by their superiors, at regular intervals, and use of one of the personnel rating systems in this connection. While there is some evidence that such methods have proved valuable in certain types of private and public employments, they have not yet generally commended themselves to police administrators. The reasons are various. In some cases the police have not troubled to master the technique of rating, or have not given the rating system a fair trial. In other instances, and partcularly in the larger police establishments, different sets of superior officers have graded their subordinates according to differing standards which proved difficult to reconcile.

The specific reasons for the partial failure of rating systems no doubt vary between departments. There are, however, common weaknesses which can be corrected by administration. That a personnel rating must always be subjective rather than objective is too seldom recognized. In consequence virtually all rating forms call for an evaluation of fifteen or twenty personal characteristics: appearance, loyalty, vigor, and so forth. Actually these forms can be greatly simplified, and provide a more honest evaluation if they are confined to rating the man "as a whole," without attempting to fragment his personality and achievements. While many ratings call for a determination of degrees of goodness (or badness) ranging from three to as high as ten degrees, it must be apparent that an excessive number of rating choices is impractical. To simplify rating procedures, and to make them understandable to the rater, a few departments have, commendably, limited the number of rating degrees to three: below average, average, and far above average.

The problem of the proper command level to perform personnel ratings has received too little attention. It is apparent that the commissioner in New York City cannot know 24,000 men personally. Perhaps not so apparent is the observable fact that a street sergeant who works closely with his men is, by the nature of his relationship, "too close to the forest." Raters must be close enough to their subordinates' day-to-day activities to know them well, but sufficiently distant organizationally to express their evaluations freely. This, too, is being done in a few departments.

Most departments which attempt personnel rating systems employ some system of averaging; either by an equalization board, or by accepting ratings by ranking officers who may not be in the direct chain of command to the rated subordinate. Neither of these expedients works well, perhaps because they violate the principle of unity of command. Better practice has been the rating by one, or at the most two, direct-line supervisors who are in a position to evaluate personality and performance.

Thus the methods employed in effecting promotions in municipal police forces are for the time being in an uncertain stage of development. The cut-and-dried written examination still prevails in most cities, and will probably continue for many years to provide the chief measure of qualification for promotion in police service.[16]

Discipline

The control exercised by any administrative head rests upon his power to discipline the members of the rank and file. In most organizations such powers are rarely used. Their mere existence provides sufficient support for the executive authority.

It is otherwise in police service. The very nature of the work—the large powers entrusted to police, the fact that they often operate alone and far from supervision of any kind, and the corrosive influence of almost continuous association with criminals and delinquents—tends to make infractions of disciplinary rules a matter of more frequent occurrence and of more serious moment. Hence the disciplinary powers of the police administrator need to be kept in good working order because there is likely to be frequent need for their exercise.

Yet this is rarely the case in our municipal police force. The vast majority of them, as we have seen, are subject to civil service regulations that restrict the free play of executive judgment and discretion. Either by law or by regulation, the police administrator is told in no uncertain terms that he cannot take major disciplinary action with decision and vigor. For, once "covered in" by the termination of the probationary period, the policeman acquires a kind of estate of freehold under our prevailing patterns. The law and the rules, which appear to be so pliable in matters concerning selection and promotion, suddenly acquire a new and sterner quality when disciplinary action is involved. The police administrator soon finds himself confronted by obstacles—sometimes a whole series of statutory and regulatory hurdles—that must be surmounted before even the most salutary discipline can be applied.

No matter how flagrant the offense, the policeman must be subjected to formal trial. In some systems, such trials are conducted

---

[16] The promotional techniques employed by federal and state police are sometimes developed quite outside the sphere of civil service control. These are treated in the following chapter.

by the head of the police force, or by a person or persons specially designated by him for the purpose. In either event, appeal lies to the civil service commission and sometimes, in addition, to the entire hierarchy of state courts. Thus the administrator faces the possibility —indeed, the probability—of interminable delays in the course of which the effect of vigorous disciplinary action upon the rank and file is largely dissipated.

Often the setup is even less favorable in that the case must be tried in the first instance before the civil service commission and subject to the usual judicial review on appeal. Under such circumstances the police administrator temporarily loses his position as the responsible superior of the delinquent policeman and becomes a mere complaining party. If the decision goes against him, his official prestige with the rank and file is bound to suffer.

Police administrators naturally shrink from such unpleasant contingencies. They seek to avoid, if they can, bringing the general run of police offenders to trial. Is the policeman tardy or lazy? Inefficient? Corrupt? Active in fomenting discontent in the force? Quarrelsome, overbearing, or violent? Intemperate, or given to public intoxication? Then let him be transferred to a post where such lapses will do the least harm or where they will at all events be less conspicuous! Thus are the disciplinary requirements of a quasi-military body reduced to the level of almost complete ineffectiveness. In the course of time the police force becomes burdened with an undue proportion of drunkards, contumacious characters, guardhouse lawyers, and grafters.

Even when an occasional police offender is separated from the force, after repeated "disciplinary" transfers, or administrative trials followed by reversals, it does not follow that this action is final. The personnel records of our city police are replete with examples of the reinstatement and even repeated reinstatement of police offenders who have spent a considerable portion of their official lives under suspension and awaiting trial on charges. Here the fault lies solely and simply at the door of what is loosely known as "politics"—or more accurately, perhaps, of the influence that professional politicians exercise upon public officials in behalf of people who have no influence of their own. It follows that this rather common fault in municipal police administration is not confined to cities operating under civil service rules, but appears in most of our urban communities without discrimination. It constitutes one of the most impressive indices of the great influence once universally exercised by political pressure in police affairs, and of the continuing strength of that influence in many cities both large and small. Even though the actual number of reinstated policemen may not be large in a given city, it is difficult to overestimate the damage to police morale and discipline which accompanies the practice.[17]

Thus most city forces have a long way to go before their disciplinary methods can meet the test to which they are subjected by the special requirements of police work. If the influences engendered by ward politics and the greed and corruption which accompany vice and crime could be removed or made ineffective, then prevailing disciplinary practices might be continued. But until there is some evidence that this millennium is at hand, many improvements in municipal police administration will continue to be retarded by the use of inappropriate disciplinary methods. A sound discipline will probably contribute more to the solution of our municipal police problems than any other single recourse now available.[18]

Welfare Provisions

When the police recruit reports for active duty he is usually under the necessity of providing himself with a uniform and with various pieces of required equipment.

The initial cost of uniforms and equipment may run between $200 and $250, an item of considerable magnitude to the young recruit and one which should cause police administrators some concern; this for the reason that ward heelers, loan sharks, gamblers, and others who tilt at the criminal law show themselves ready and willing to advance police recruits the necessary funds. In order to avoid the implications of such practices, a few police forces now undertake to finance the cost of uniforms and equipment and to

---

[17] For specific examples of the varying results secured under different disciplinary systems, see the following firsthand studies: Missouri Association for Criminal Justice, *The Missouri Crime Survey* (1926), pp. 35-39; Citizens' Police Committee, *Chicago Police Problems* (1931), pp. 70-79; L. V. Harrison, *Police Administration in Boston* (1934), pp. 78-83; Institute of Public Administration, *A Survey of the Bureau of Police*, Pittsburgh, Pennsylvania, New York (1937), pp. 28-32; "San Francisco Police Department Survey Report" (published by the San Francisco Bureau of Governmental Research in *The City*, Vol. XVII, No. 3, July, 1937, p. 60).

[18] The disciplinary systems of federal and state police are described in Chap. 6.

make installment deductions from the police recruits' pay checks.

There is a strong argument favoring department-furnished uniforms for all personnel: they can be maintained at a standard of quality and appearance, the individual officer will be less hesitant to damage his uniform in line of duty, and the uniform can be reclaimed upon the police officer's separation from the service. However, an increasing number of departments have provided cash allowances, usually about one hundred dollars a year, to reimburse policemen for uniforms. Primarily this has been recognized as a subterfuge to increase police pay without proportional increases for other municipal employees. In practice it has not benefited the appearance of uniforms, and is therefore a less desirable administrative step than is the outright provision of uniforms and equipment.

Also bearing upon the attractiveness of police service are such matters as hours of duty, rest days, vacations, sick leave, and pensions for disability or superannuation. In the matter of hours of duty, American police forces have benefited from a general reduction in industrial working hours during the past several decades. The eight-hour day is almost universal in police service.

Thus far there are few indications that the hours of duty for police may be reduced below the eight-hour level, because of the administrative convenience of the three-platoon system and the great cost which any further reduction in working hours for police would involve.

Allied to the foregoing question is the matter of days-off-with-pay. Nearly all American cities allow two-days-off-in-seven to members of the police force. A few allow none whatever, with the balance ranging between one-in-seven and one-in-thirty.

An annual vacation of approximately two weeks is allowed in four-fifths of the municipal forces. Practically all the rest have longer annual holidays.

The administration of sick-leave arrangements for police raises a number of difficult questions. About 12 per cent of the cities make no regular provision for paying the ill or disabled policeman; all the others have some degree of established policy. A small proportion (7 per cent) allow half pay during sick leave, but the majority allow full pay, with limitations ranging from a few days each year up through various gradations until a level carrying no restrictions is reached. About a quarter of the cities have no established policy concerning the allowance of sick leave with pay, so that each case as it arises is handled without reference to any general rule. Experience with such loose systems indicates that they are distinctly liberal in their application, so it seems safe to count this rather large group as in general following a full-pay policy.

The foregoing summaries conceal many refinements of procedure that are chiefly directed at discouraging malingering by police who are being carried on the sick and disability rolls. To this end some cities place the sick policeman on half pay for a few days and thereafter extend full pay. Others reverse the process and reduce the rate of pay during extended illnesses. Such diverse methods merely serve to emphasize the patent fact that no hard-and-fast rule can be expected to be fair both to the police force and to the policeman in all cases. Forces served by competent and active police surgeons who are able and willing to use their professional talents in the furtherance of a sound discipline come closest to a solution of this vexing problem, because only in this way can each case be determined according to its individual merits.

In all but the largest cities police surgeons are either private practitioners who are engaged on a part-time basis or they perform other duties as public health officers. These, together with the occasional full-time police surgeon, raise delicate questions of a professional nature. The layman can scarcely be expected to pass judgment upon such abstruse matters as physical fitness. Hence the police administrator concerned with maintaining the force at the highest possible level of effective strength is sometimes confronted with a situation over which he can exercise no direct and positive control. On the other hand, the part-time police surgeon cannot be expected to have thorough knowledge of the exigencies of police work or a realization of the need for a full complement of manpower at any given time. Furthermore, it is not in the professional nature of the private practitioner of medicine to order a man back to work as soon as he is fit, and without the unnecessary loss of a single day, although this is exactly what the police force should require and in any case is the prime reason for the employment of police surgeons. While there is real need for bridging the gap between police management and the medical profession, it does not appear to be a matter which can be handled satisfactorily by uniform standards or by generalized procedures. A solution will probably continue to depend upon a clearer understanding between the administrator and the physician, with the former taking the initiative in attempting to clarify and reconcile the differing viewpoints likely to prevail.

Occasional instances of lax enforcement of medical discipline by police surgeons spring from indifference to and neglect of official duties. Here the lot of the police administrator is partciularly unfortunate because he is not able to challenge the professional judgment of his subordinate effectively and can do little more than wait for some striking and deliberate act or omission to pave the way for dismissing the police surgeon from the service.

The introduction of retirement systems for police has spread so rapidly through American cities that nearly all now have such arrangements. In most cases such systems involve contributions by the prospective pensioners, which range from purely nominal sums up to 20 per cent of salary. Contributions of only 2 or 4 per cent of salary are, however, so common that the majority of pension systems rest primarily upon annual deficiency appropriations by the city governments. Thus in most instances police pension systems are wholly unsound in an actuarial sense and may ultimately throw such unexpected burdens upon the local governments concerned that complete or partial defaults will follow.[19]

It is probably because little attention has been given to the actual cost of pension systems that the arrangements are for the most part generous to police. Service pensions (that is, for superannuation retirement) are usually allowed at 50 per cent of base salary and often after only twenty or twenty-five years of service. Disability pensions generally rise to even higher levels, sometimes reaching as much as 75 per cent of base pay at the time of retirement. Such pension arrangements are available at the option of police who can qualify under their terms. Special arrangements, however, are required to introduce provisions under which the administrative head can force a police officer to accept retirement. It is an interesting fact that only about one-third of our municipal forces make any provision for compulsory retirement upon administrative

[19] Cf., for example, Albert H. Hall, *A Summary of Actuarial Surveys of Seventy Local Police and Fire Pension Funds in New York State*, Publication No. 34, Bureau of Training and Research, New York State Conference of Mayors, 1935.

order. Where such provisions exist, the age range for compulsory retirement ranges from 60 to 70 years, with the largest single group favoring age 65. In all other cities compulsory retirement can be effected only under the pension law, which usually means that some degree of incapacitating disability must be shown. There are as yet no accepted standards for measuring such incapacity in police work. Accordingly many policemen continue to draw full pay long after they might have retired on pension because they find it easy to secure light-duty assignments so that no pressure of work induces them to go on the pension roll. There is only one answer to such abuses. It consists in providing a fixed age limit beyond which the administrative head may retire a policeman at will. Fixed limits are the rule in military establishments since they tend to lower the average age, which in itself is a desirable thing in any service involving great physical activity.

Health insurance, death benefits, and the like are occasionally available to police forces. Most of these are operated by police benevolent societies and do not derive their support from public taxes. Public support, whether direct or indirect, does not seem to be justified since the management of the funds is not under governmental control and their purpose is not within the ordinary scope of public assistance to police welfare

Viewing the composite picture of police compensation and welfare, one cannot fail to be impressed by the substantial gains scored by police in securing liberal treatment. In some instances these ends have been achieved through the pressure exerted by thinly disguised police unions and in other instances the pressure has been of a political character, but for the most part police have asked the American public for generous consideration and have received it without much question. Thus the American policeman stands today as the best paid and best housed of his kind in the world.

Future Role of Municipal Police

While it is true that brilliant police management and execution are becoming familiar in some of our cities, other urban forces have had to fight their way up from the depths of degradation. If the scars of that contest still remain, and if most police units even yet have not fully met the challenge thrown down to them, let it be remembered that this is no sham battle, nor is it one in which the highest ethical standards always prevail. On the contrary, the record of police advancement has been marked by many regrettable incidents—of policemen who were "framed" and sent to prison or forced into an ignominious retirement; of civic leaders who assumed police command with high purposes, only to relinquish their posts after a few months with the settled conviction that police problems defy solution; of promising police officers who were shunted aside into obscure assignments because their vigorous activity was found objectionable.

In city after city these things have happened and will continue to happen to a uniformed service which necessarily stands between the underworld and the upper world and so suffers from a damaging crossfire. At one and the same time it is the target of every vicious, selfish, and criminal influence of the city which it serves and also of the inexperienced and impatient reformers who want to effect a police "shake-up" whenever anything goes wrong. The police veteran of even a few such skirmishes comes to understand that these are all in the nature of preliminaries to decisive engagements which may never occur. Though one side or the other may get the upper hand for a time, the struggle has no end. So the experienced police officer leads no crusades, strikes no attitudes, and makes as few enemies on either side as is possible under his oath of office. He bears the burden of an inglorious police past with resignation, but keeps abreast of advancing police techniques.

These at least are the marks of the new professional policeman as he is found in the modern American city. Upon him rests the hope for much of our future development because the city police-man is the typical policeman. One may entertain serious doubt concerning the future role of the sheriff, the constable, the village marshal, and a host of other local, state and federal police agencies, but there can be little uncertainty concerning the future importance of the police of great urban centers. As nearly as we may judge, ours will continue to be an urban civilization for a long time to come, and the place of the city police force in that setting seems assured. With all their political crosscurrents and other unfavor-able features, municipal police seem destined to make the same deep impression upon the police developments of the future that has been theirs in the recent past. If they do not accomplish this by skill and effort, they will do it by sheer weight of numbers.

CHAPTER 6

STATE AND FEDERAL POLICE

Most of our state and federal police forces are of recent origin. They have been created and expanded in response to a variety of influences, chief of which have been the widespread popular discontent with the functioning of certain portions of the local police systems and a realization that decentralized police authority could not effectively deal with crimes having wide ramifications. Other influences have sprung from less worthy motives. Some of these central agencies were created in response to incessant demands for political patronage, and have enlarged their numbers and their powers by methods characteristic of entrenched bureaucracies.

While any general treatment of state and federal police forces must recognize the operation of such unfavorable influences in various services, the fact remains that the general average of their administration and performance has been at a level substantially higher than that attained by the constable, the sheriff, and the vast majority of urban police forces. From the standpoint of partisan influences, the new agencies have been removed from the contaminating atmosphere of ward politics, and while some of them have merely exchanged the political control of the city hall or county courthouse for that of the state or national capitol, they have thereby escaped from at least a part of the ancient police tradition and have had an opportunity to develop along new lines and with wider horizons.

So much, at least, must be said for the state and federal systems as a whole. Above and beyond such cautious appraisals of the mass stands the almost palpable fact that some of these agencies are among the best that have been developed in this country—forces which do not suffer by comparison with the world's best. Their achievements are a novel feature of the American police scene. In some quarters they have produced the conviction that centralized police administration alone is capable of dealing with present-day crime and criminals. Nonetheless it is significant that a mere handful of local police agencies has been abandoned since the new facilities were created, and that the authority of the latter continues to be restricted in many respects.

All of the federal forces are controlled by the constitutional limits of federal jurisdiction over crimes,[1] and for the most part are concerned with the enforcement of special groups of federal statutes directly relating to the governmental department within which each force operates. Thus through constitutional limitations and a series of historical accidents, the federal police system is rather closely limited and except for the broad powers of the Federal Bureau of Investigation, the system has been split into a number of minor fragments and narrowly specialized agencies.

Likewise in the sphere of state police there has been no real centralizing process. On the contrary, general police authority has been denied to many of the state forces, and when granted by statute in some jurisdictions it is exercised only within carefully defined limits. Even in those states which have conferred full police powers, severe restrictions upon the numerical strength of the state force sometimes have prevented application of a really vigorous law enforcement policy, while the evident antipathy of a considerable number of county, township, village, and city police units operates to impose geographical limitations upon state police work which were not contemplated by law. Thus the state police experiment acquires diverse characteristics that become more and more confusing as the years pass.

1. THE STATE POLICE

The earliest state police forces did not come into existence in response to the challenge of inadequate rural police protection.

---

[1] Cf. *U.S.* v. *Hudson*, 7 Cranch 32 (1812), holding that the courts of the United States have no common-law jurisdiction over criminal cases because not within the powers delegated to the federal government by the Constitution.

They were the result of what now appear to have been rather bungling attempts to provide a few commonwealths with a police arm which could enforce various unpopular state-wide regulations without depending upon unreliable or reluctant local police agencies for cooperation and support.

Upon occasion the governors of some of our states have openly expressed dissatisfaction with their positions as general executives. Their responsibilities, while broad, either were not buttressed by the necessary authority or they lacked the compelling power of a suitable enforcement body. Since there were no means to compel sheriffs and constables to perform their duties, the governor of Indiana found it necessary to order out the state militia to enforce a statute prohibiting race track gambling.[2] The governor of Colorado experienced a somewhat similar difficulty, declaring that he was "required by the [state] constitution to enforce the laws. But," he observed, "there is not a sheriff or other county officer that is dependent upon me; he can defy me; he can say 'I will not enforce those laws.' What is the efficiency of my office under those circumstances? The only power I have is to call out the militia to suppress something."[3]

Still another state executive, in Pennsylvania, described his situation in supervising the enforcement of the state's laws with a touch of humorous exaggeration. He said:

In the year 1903, when I assumed the office of chief executive of the state, I found myself thereby invested with supreme executive authority. I found that no power existed to interfere with me in my duty to enforce the laws of the state, and that by the same token, no conditions could release me from my duty so to do. I then looked about me to see what instruments I possessed wherewith to accomplish this bounden obligation—what instruments on whose loyalty and obedience I could truly rely. I perceived three such instruments—my private secretary, a very small man; my woman stenographer; and the janitor, a Negro. So I made the state police.[4]

[2] Cited in *Annals of American Academy of Political and Social Science*, May, 1913, p. 252; and see also *ibid.*, p. 61, for the situation in Missouri.

[3] *Proceedings of the Governors' Conference*, Washington, 1910, p. 216.

[4] Governor Pennypacker, of Pennsylvania; quoted in Mayo, *Justice to All*, pp. 5-6.

Origin and Extension

These and related considerations provided the basis for the first state police agencies. The earliest form of state police force to make its appearance was that represented by the Texas Rangers, established back in the days of the Texas republic. Three Ranger companies, authorized in 1835 by the provisional government of Texas, were made subject to the direction of the military authorities and were intended for, and actually employed in, military service on the Mexican border. This function of border patrol persisted for many years although general police work, including criminal investigation, ultimately became their primary function.[5]

In 1865 a few "state constables" were appointed in Massachusetts. While their chief function was the suppression of commercialized vice, they were also granted general police powers to be exercised throughout the length and breadth of the state. Massachusetts may therefore be said to have been the first to establish a general state police force. The new body was rudimentary in its conception and organization, and became the subject of recurrent legislative revision. In 1879 this process culminated in the establishment of the Massachusetts District Police, a state detective unit, which in turn was absorbed by the division of state police set up in the new Department of Public Safety in 1920.

Following the inception of the Massachusetts system in 1865, there was a long period which witnessed no extension of the state police idea. In 1903 a small state force was established in Connecticut. Succeeding to the powers and duties formerly exercised by the Law and Order League, a quasi-public instrumentality, it was to a considerable degree modeled after the Massachusetts District Police of that day. Like the latter, the Connecticut force was chiefly intended for the more effective suppression of commercialized vice, with particular reference to enforcement of the liquor and gambling laws, but it was also charged with certain inspectional duties and with the investigation of suspicious fires. The force was so small as to make any system of regular patrols impossible. Its organization

[5] In this treatment of the origin and development of state police, some of the data have been drawn from the writer's earlier study. *The State Police; Organization and Administration* (1925). See, also, Vollmer and Parker, *Crime and the State Police* (1935); Weldon Cooper, "The State Police Movement in the South," *The Journal of Politics*, Vol. I, No. 4, 1939, pp. 414-433.

was loose and responsibility for administration was ill-defined. After experiencing many vicissitudes, it gradually acquired the characteristics of a state detective force operating under the control of an ex officio administrative board, and continued in this status until the extensive reorganization of 1920.

The Arizona Rangers were established in 1901 and the New Mexico Mounted Police in 1905. Both were virtually border patrol forces on the order of the Texas Rangers, and both were abandoned within a few years, having apparently become involved in state politics.

The Pennsylvania "State Constabulary," as it came to be known, was the next to appear; an event which has since had far-reaching results both in Pennsylvania and in other states. It will already have been observed that the years between 1835 and 1905 had witnessed a highly tentative and uncertain approach to the state police question. The forces which came into existence during this period originated either from the need for frontier patrols in the newer commonwealths or in an effort to enforce unpopular liquor and gambling laws which often became a dead letter when their execution was entrusted solely to local police authorities.

Such motives do not seem to have played any part in the creation of the Pennsylvania State Police. Its origin was inspired by three apparent needs: The first was that of a general executive arm for the state. The second was closely related to the disturbed industrial conditions in the coal and iron regions, and the demonstrated incapacity of sheriffs, constables, and the organized police forces of small communities generally, to contend with them successfully. The third arose from a realization that the sheriff-constable system had broken down, thereby exposing the rural districts to the danger of inadequate police protection.

Recognition of all three conditions in Pennsylvania was to have an important bearing upon later police developments elsewhere, but the rural protection aspect challenged attention from the very outset and has exercised a compelling influence upon state police management in many parts of the country from that day to this. Other agencies and devices for maintenance of the peace and the protection of life and property had been painfully evolved—for centuries in the case of sheriffs, constables, and city police, and for several scores of years in the case of the earlier state police forces.

But the Pennsylvania force was not evolved in any strict sense of the term. In the terse expression of Governor Pennypacker, it was "made," and in the making, whether from accident or from design, there was a sharp break from established tradition. Schemes of organization and control which had become embedded in accepted police practice were ignored in the formation of this new body. Its establishment in 1905 marked the beginning of a new era in rural police administration.

The distinguishing characteristic of this force consisted in the extensive administrative powers granted to the superintendent of state police, who was made responsible to the governor of the commonwealth alone. From the very beginning it operated as a mounted and uniformed body which, using a widely distributed system of troop headquarters and substations as a base of operations, patrolled the rural and semirural portions of the entire state, even to the little-frequented byways and lanes. In its highly centralized administrative powers, its decentralized scheme of structural organization, and its policy of continuous patrol throughout the rural areas, the Pennsylvania State Police constituted a distinct departure from earlier state practice

In 1917 the agitation which had been going on in New York for a decade or more took definite form. The state police force created in that year closely followed the pattern first laid down in Pennsylvania. Following the World War and partly as a result of the states' difficulties in perfecting local defense arrangements, the state police idea was greatly accelerated. The Michigan State Police, hastily organized in 1917 as a war measure, acquired permanent status in 1919. The Colorado Rangers also owed their creation to the war emergency but were disbanded in 1923 after a political campaign in which they were a leading issue.

Other state forces now made their appearance in rapid succession. In 1919 the West Virginia Department of Public Safety was set up. Despite the broad administrative implications of its name, this body was devised solely for general police work. The scheme of organization provided a wide departure by introducing a bipartisan board of commissioners who divide with the superintendent responsibility for the control of personnel. New Jersey, in 1921, and Rhode Island, in 1925, established departments of state police with statutory bases similar to those of Pennsylvania and New York.

Meanwhile some of the older state police forces were undergoing extensive revision. Massachusetts effected in 1920 a complete consolidation of all state agencies in any way related to the administration of the public safety function. Coincident with this was the establishment of a state-wide, uniformed, patrol force patterned closely after the Pennsylvania model. Connecticut likewise abandoned its loose scheme of overhead organization, involving general direction and control by a police board composed of ex officiis members, and in 1927 completed a series of major changes bringing the Connecticut State Police more nearly into line with Pennsylvania and the other states which had followed its lead. Even in Pennsylvania, the bellwether of the state police was consolidated with the state highway patrol in 1937, under the style of "The Pennsylvania Motor Police." Following a brief period marked by some ill-conceived experimentation and political interference, the new and greatly enlarged force has returned to its original patterns.

In 1929 the state force which had been developed in Maine for the primary and specific purpose of enforcing the motor vehicle laws on state highways extended its powers and functions to include the maintenance of general police patrols and the conduct of criminal investigations throughout the state. This departure was of special significance because it became one of a whole series of similar examples.

Rudimentary State Police Forces

The development of state highway patrols has made rapid strides since the advent of the motorcar and the vast network of hard-surfaced state highways brought new problems of traffic regulation and accident prevention to the rural districts. For in addition to the states which adhere more or less closely to the Pennsylvania plan and hence enforce all laws, including traffic regulations, there have sprung up more than a score of state highway patrols which are usually organized as subordinate units under the commissioner of highways, the commissioner of motor vehicles, various fiscal officers, or other state functionaries. In some of these states the highway forces have been clothed with general police powers which are exercised in some degree but not extensively enough to make them directly comparable with those adhering to the Pennsylvania system. There are other differences. Thus, by the very nature of their constitution, these forces are not directly responsible to the governor of the state alone. More significant than all else, they do not partake of the state police tradition. Political considerations still play an important role in their recruiting policies, their training programs are defective, their discipline is uncertain, and the volume of general criminal work they perform is relatively so small as clearly to distingush them from the older state police bodies.

At best, therefore, the forces which have cautiously advanced from specialized traffic control units are but an intermediate stage between the state police proper and the more recent highway police organizations. The latter exercise powers strictly confined to the enforcement of the highway laws and traffic regulations. They need not specially concern us here except to note in passing that almost every one of them shows some indication of seeking extension of its police powers, with every reasonable prospect that they will eventually acquire full police status.

Duplication of State Police Forces

In addition to the basic state police agencies which include uniformed patrols as an essential feature, a number of states have set up rival, or at the very least independent, police forces. Some of these are concerned with criminal investigation exclusively, others with special aspects of motor vehicle law enforcement, while twenty widely distributed states maintain liquor law enforcement bodies with field agents who are clothed with police powers.

The central investigation forces hold special interest because they represent a recognition by the state governments of existing weaknesses in justice administration, but an unwillingness to commit the state to an integrated police system. Thus Iowa, Nebraska, South Dakota, and California operate state detective bureaus which are separate from and independent of the highway patrol forces. Bodies such as these illustrate the extreme caution with which certain commonwealths approach the question of delegating full police authority. On the other hand, some states have set up plural forces from what appears to be sheer prodigality in such delegation. For example, there are a number of state clearinghouses of identification which are wholly separate from state police or highway patrol forces, as in California, Illinois, Nebraska, New York, and Ohio. Again, state bodies concerned with the enforcement of the highway and motor vehicle laws operate side by side with the regular establishments of state police, as in Massachusetts, New Jersey, Arizona, and Nevada. Sometimes these independent state police and highway patrols are rivals in actual fact, though this condition is more often disguised by an agreement to divide the field of enforcement. New York and Pennsylvania entered upon similar duplicate enforcement programs, but each abandoned the experiment after several years of trial. Especially to be noted is the extraordinary degree of overlapping in Oklahoma's protective arrangements. These include: (1) a Department of Public Safety, consisting of a state highway patrol and a division of investigation, both operating primarily in the field of traffic law enforcement, though each possesses emergency powers of a general police character; (2) a Bureau of Criminal Identification and Investigation, which conducts criminal inquiries under the supervision of the governor and the attorney general; (3) a body of "special" investigators attached directly to the governor's office, with broad powers which are exercised under the governor's direction. In the multiplication of minor police units, no state has as yet challenged Oklahoma.

For such vagaries of administrative organization there seems to be no cure. They represent confused thinking about the realities of police duty, and are likely to occur whenever collision of political interests renders the establishment of a single unified state police force impracticable. Yet the creation of a series of fragmentary police services differentiated along functional lines does not produce the protective effect which one simple, complete police organism would have, nor does the adding of one inadequate police force to another yield satisfactory results. The number of men involved may be sufficient and the total cost may be immoderately high, but the results in terms of service to the public are always disappointing.

Diverse Patterns in State Police

Still it is apparent that a number of influences now at work may materially alter the original character of the state police movement. Ignoring for present purposes the random developments in the nineteenth century, the sixty years since elapsed fall naturally into three major periods. The first modern state police forces appeared between 1905 and 1919. They were six in number and all but one was on the general order of the Pennsylvania establishment. The next decade, following the World War, saw extension of the state police idea to nineteen other states, only nine of which have conferred anything approaching general powers upon their state forces. Between 1930 and 1940 all of the remaining states acquired some form of police force, with this period featured by a further decline in the proportion of full-fledged agencies. Some of them are so rudimentary in design as scarcely to justify the appellation of police, while others employ various euphemistic descriptions calculated to indicate that the state body is no very powerful or compelling factor in law enforcement. State patrols, highway patrols, safety patrols, traffic patrols, and maintenance patrols abound, with Colorado reaching a hitherto unattained degree of inoffensiveness with a "State Highway Courtesy Patrol."

It is difficult to find in such cautious juggling of titles any evidence of a nationwide determination by the state to take over the police function heretofore devolved upon local governments, or to set up central law enforcement agencies as ultimate substitutes for the police of cities, counties, towns, and villages. This impression is fortified by the fact that thus far only thirty-six states have conferred anything approaching full authority on their police agencies, and that less than half this number make any real effort toward general law enforcement. In some instances broad authority has been granted with no intention that it should be exercised; in others the wide dispersion of a hopelessly inadequate force throughout an entire commonwealth renders it inadvisable to attempt more than a mild regulation of the use of the state highways. Pennsylvania, California, New York, and Michigan have forces in excess of a thousand men. Several states have less than fifty men, with the grand total for all state units running at less than fourteen thousand men, 30 per cent of whom are departmental employees without police authority. The active strength is distributed among the various commonwealths in accordance with no discernible rule. Unlike urban police, the numerical strength of the several state forces seems to bear no common relationship to the population, area, mileage of state roads, or other easily determinable factors. A part of this variation is due to the differing police duties with which they are charged—and part also to underlying levels of county, village, and township police agencies, some of which are still active arms of the law, while others have abdicated their public responsibilities.

The Standard Type

Clearly, then, if state police constitute a significant departure, it is in those jurisdictions in which persistently high standards of police administration are fortified by a numerical strength that is reasonably adequate to the task of general law enforcement. Within this restricted definition not more than a dozen state forces can be included, while a few others are worthy of note because of special features of their administration. Even within this small group it is not difficult to single out Pennsylvania, New York, New Jersey, Massachusetts, and Michigan, as being in a class by themselves. Although all have been subject to occasional executive or legislative attack, they have for the most part avoided political involvement with a consistency that stands in striking contrast with the past and present alliances of the sheriff-constable system, and with those of most city and county police forces. In their successful avoidance of political influences, the state police have doubtless profited because their administrative headquarters are necessarily rather remote from nearly all the smaller fry of urban and rural politicians who have privileges to secure and favors to bestow. Of equal importance is the fact that most of these forces have come into existence within recent years, and accordingly have not been profoundly influenced by the police tradition that handicaps so many of our older police establishments. Finally it should be noted that in many instances the administrative heads of the state police have been men of unusual personal force; men who were marked by a determination to protect the rank and file against political interference, whether exercised from high places or from low.[6]

Owing to one or several of these factors, or perhaps to a combination of all of them, the general standard of state police administration, in large questions of public policy as in lesser matters of daily routine, is far in advance of that prevailing in the local police systems. As to those singled out for special mention above, they are quite the best of all such police agencies in the United

[6] J. H. Harwood, "State Police Forces," in *Traffic Quarterly*, Vol. III, No. 1 (1949), pp. 5-13.

States. They will stand comparison with the most famous police systems of western Europe.

State Police Jurisdiction

Speaking generally, the standard types of state police owe their existence to recognition that in the preservation of the peace the state government has a duty to perform, a right to defend, and that there are interests to protect which require its intervention. The relative emphasis placed upon such duties, rights, and interests varies somewhat from state to state.

In the commonwealths here under review the state police are vested with all the general police powers possessed by sheriffs, constable, municipal police, or other peace officers and are territorially limited in their exercise only by the state's boundaries. In Pennsylvania, New York, West Virginia, and New Jersey the state police are also designated as fire, fish, and game wardens; they may accordingly command the aid of all persons in extinguishing forest fires, and may search game bags without judicial warrant. In view of the continuous rural patrol which these forces perform and their direct and continuous responsibility to higher authority, there would appear to be no sound reason why equal powers should not be extended to the forces of the other states. The practice holds no concealed dangers.

Thus far no state police organization has been vested with the unrestricted right to command the *posse comitatus,* or "power of the county," such as is commonly conferred on sheriffs. In West Virginia, however, the state police are authorized to take command of all peace officers and the *posse comitatus* upon the request of the sheriff or the order of the governor. In Michigan the commissioner of state police may with the governor's approval demand the help of the local police, and in Connecticut any member of the force may request any sheriff, municipal policeman, or constable to assist him, whereupon such officers become temporarily vested with state-wide criminal jurisdiction and are paid by the state as such. Members of the Connecticut force cannot, however, require any local officer to serve outside his appropriate district without first receiving the consent of the governmental authority to which the local officer is subject. The commissioner of public safety in Massachusetts, with the approval of the governor, may require the assistance of the

Metropolitan District Police, the administration of which is controlled by the state. The Texas Rangers are merely authorized to "accept the services of such citizens as shall volunteer to aid them."

The right to call upon the *posse comitatus* has always been carefully safeguarded and limited, and properly so. It was granted to the sheriff at a time when he was the direct representative of the Crown and a high and responsible dignitary. The centuries have brought many changes in the office, which now has descended a great way from its former high estate. Nevertheless, the sheriff still exercises this important power. In view of the responsibility placed upon the state executive for the preservation of the public peace, it would appear altogether reasonable that the governor should be authorized in grave emergencies to delegate the power of the county to the state police, as in West Virginia.

Special Duties

In addition to the foregoing powers, state police have certain special duties and obligations placed upon them. In Michigan they may be required to execute civil process in actions to which the state is a party; in New York they are required to act as court officers for justices of the peace on Indian reservations; and in Connecticut and Pennsylvania they conduct road tests for motor vehicle operator licenses.

Still other activities are delegated to, or assumed by, the state police as a natural consequence of the fact that they are part and parcel of a state government which exercises a broad territorial jurisdiction. Being widely distributed throughout the entire state, with their patrols in intimate daily contact with local conditions, it is perhaps inevitable that other administrative departments should turn to them for assistance. Here, ready to the hand, is a highly organized and relatively numerous body to which may be delegated certain duties which the other state departments are not equipped to perform. It is apparent that this practice may hold serious difficulties in store for the police, particularly where the other departments retain administrative supervision over the delegated function. But keeping always in mind that nonpolice functions cannot safely be added to the duties of police without jeopardizing their utility as police officers, the experiments of a number of states in this field deserve consideration.

Thus far the state police have been eager to aid and to cooperate with other state departments in performing duties not directly concerned with the enforcement of criminal statutes. This is particularly true of the forces which have been under heavy attack from organized labor, and in one or two cases there is reason to believe that they may have welcomed additional functions as a means of strengthening their positions in the state government, and thereby becoming so far as possible indispensable to its administration.

Yet no matter how closely allied such additional activities may be, or how important their effective enforcement from the standpoint of state administration, the fact remains that they cannot be performed to any considerable extent without reducing regular and systematic patrols to the disappearing point. Since some distinction must be drawn between the various types of regulatory and inspectional tasks, it seems reasonable that only those duties should be delegated to the state police as can reasonably be performed as a routine matter in the ordinary course of patrol. Whenever a special squad becomes necessary or men are regularly diverted from patrol duty in order to serve other state departments, the dispersion of police effectives has commenced.

Back of all such devices lies the pronounced disposition of legislative bodies, both state and municipal, to widen the scope of governmental regulation without providing the funds necessary for effective supervision and enforcement. The police sphere is already so wide as to make it but a short step to add functions that are wholly foreign to police duty. Hence it is the cumulative effect that threatens seriously to diminish the number of active patrolmen and to divert the attention of the remainder from what must always be the fundamentals of police work.

Limitations on Police Powers

Although the jurisdiction of the state police is of the broadest nature, being in some instances extended to include activities beyond the ordinary scope of police administration, the legislatures of several states have imposed certain limitations upon the exercise of the powers which they have granted. Some of these are without special significance and constitute merely assurances that the force shall be employed in a proper and a legal manner, or declarations of a policy to that effect. Thus in West Virginia the state police are enjoined not to "interfere with the rights or property of any person except for the prevention of crime" and are prohibited from acting as election officials or detailing or ordering any member to duty near any voting precinct. Such formal provisions reflect not only legislative distrust of a compact, highly organized and armed body, but also a past record of failure in the democratic control of public agencies other than the newly created state police.

Far more important are those statutory provisions restricting the exercise of state-wide power with respect to riots and disorder. Quite without exception these have been introduced to meet the demands of organized labor and as a formal disavowal of any intention arbitrarily to interfere with the lawful rights of participants in industrial conflicts. There is also the challenging fact that American communities are inclined to resent the use of outside forces for the suppression of local disturbances. If all these were able regularly to maintain order without other aid, the matter might easily be settled. Experience has shown, however, that actual and flagrant disorder has frequently required the interposition of the military power of the state or nation. Where adequate state police forces have been established the state government has naturally employed them whenever local conditions seemed to require intervention. The question has thus been squarely raised as to what restrictions, if any, should be placed upon their use.

The beginning of such limitations may be traced to a practice that originated in Pennsylvania. This force was placed in the field in 1906, and almost from the outset found itself engaged in recurrent strike duty. It also found that the sheriffs in certain sections were rather too prompt in demanding aid from the state police when the gravity of the situation did not warrant it. Some local officers, at least, were glad enough thus to avoid a duty which is always unpleasant, and upon occasion may be both politically and personally hazardous. It therefore early became the invariable custom of the superintendent to require a statement from the local authorities declaring that the situation was beyond their control and asking for the assistance of the state force. If such statement was supported by the findings and reports of the local state police detachment, and the governor gave his approval, the necessary detachments were mobilized at the point of disorder and took charge. This policy has been continued without modification up to the present time.

Provisions based upon the Pennsylvania practice have been incorporated in the statutes constituting several other forces. When the New York State Police was established in 1917, a concession was made to organized labor by a statutory restriction on the use of the state police in the suppression of public disorder. The act creating the New York force provides that it shall not act to suppress riot or disorder within the limits of any city except by direction of the governor or upon the request of the mayor when approved by the governor. Somewhat similar limitations, established either by law or by regulation, have been adopted in New Hampshire, Rhode Island, Maryland, Indiana, and Louisiana. On the other hand, full control over the use of state police for riot duty is denied to the governor of New Jersey, where the force may not be employed "as a *posse*" in any municipality having a regularly organized police force except by order of the governor acting upon request from the local governing body.

It will be noted that the self-imposed practice of Pennsylvania differs from the statutory requirements of the other states in that it applies not alone to cities, as in New York, or to municipalities generally, as in New Jersey, but extends to all portions of the state. The New Jersey statute would seem to be open to the criticism that it permits the governing body of the municipality to decide whether or not the state police shall be called upon. Although the issue has not as yet been raised there, it is easy to imagine the obstructive tactics which might be resorted to in a city or borough council whenever the question of state intervention was raised. Maintenance of the public peace and good order would immediately become the subject of debate. Indeed, the exacting requirements of the New Jersey statute go so far in their effort to destroy both local and state executive responsibility that they may partially defeat the real purpose. For if in any given situation the mayor or the governor becomes convinced that state intervention is required, there is nothing to prevent the mayor requesting, or the governor commanding, the National Guard to mobilize for that purpose. In all serious emergencies, the best that the New Jersey provision can hope to accomplish is delay, and it may fairly be questioned whether this does not operate squarely against the public interest.

Occasionally the restrictions upon riot duty are so shrill and incisive that even the stilted phraseology of statutes cannot conceal the underlying distrust of an armed and disciplined police body. Thus a Mississippi act declares that ". . . the state highway patrol shall never, by anyone, or under any circumstances be ordered, instructed, required, or obligated to perform the duties or functions properly devolving under the law to the organized militia of this state, nor shall said patrol ever be used in any strike, lockout or other labor controversy . . ." Though the police problems arising in connection with industrial disputes are far from being solved, it may fairly be questioned whether such broad and undiscriminating prohibitions upon a civil police organization offer solutions more promising than the use of armed force by the National Guard, or the declaration of martial law.

In Connecticut the activities of the state police in suppressing riots or civil commotion are limited to cases which have received the approval of the governor, and then only after preliminary warning has been given to the rioters. Massachusetts has introduced a novel and highly significant element into the situation by requiring that the force "shall not be used or called upon for service in any industrial dispute, unless actual violence has occurred therein, and then only by order of the governor." This provision goes to the root of the entire matter by placing the emphasis upon suppression of violence. With the practice and experience of Pennsylvania, New York, and Connecticut as a background, it may well serve as a basis for a more harmonious adjustment of the labor difficulty.

Management of Personnel

Unlike most urban forces, four out of five state police establishments operate outside the ordinary restrictions of civil service control. Although some of the organizations so administered have grossly abused the opportunity for the free development of personnel policies thereby offered, the best state forces are all still to be found in this independent category. So while there are confusing cross-currents at work which through a process of erosion may ultimately wear away the distinctive state police procedures, they have not as yet made any material impression upon forces of the standard type. In Pennsylvania, New York, New Jersey, Massachusetts, Rhode Island, and Michigan the sole authority in the selection, promotion, discipline, and control of the rank file is the administrative head.[7]

[7] The Pennsylvania State Police, however, do utilize the state Civil Service Commission to conduct recruit examinations which are advisory (only) to the superintendent.

In some instances, as in Massachusetts, these essential powers may be delegated in part to a board of officers who recommend action to the administrative head, while in other states the chief administrator acts alone. In either event, the limitations provided by law permit the exercise of a wide administrative discretion. Although tenure-of-office acts are now in effect in one-third of the state forces, they are for the most part moderate in tone. Hence they have not, as yet, materially interfered with rigorous disciplinary standards.

So it has come about that the state police of a number of jurisdictions have made long strides toward fitting their personnel policies to practical police needs, while at the same time adhering to the highest standards of nonpolitical administration Their standards of selection are materially higher than those usually imposed by civil service commissions, character investigations are rigorously conducted, procedures for determining the relative efficiency of aspirants for promotion have been developed, elaborate training programs are regularly offered, and a strict discipline is at all times enforced.

It is a safe generalization that no group of police agencies employs the modern arts of recruit training more assiduously than do the state police. With few exceptions they have adopted the policy of giving the new state trooper a thorough and practical foundation in the principles, the laws, and the established practices which govern his calling. The training period varies from a month or six weeks in some forces up to six months, as in Pennsylvania. The influence of intensive technical instruction during some three to six months, to say nothing of the disciplinary effect of constant supervision and group coordination acquired through close-order drill, works an impressive change in the state police recruit. This is reflected in his bearing, his manner of address, his familiarity with the fundamentals of police practice and procedure, and many other desirable features of the modern policeman. When he finally dons the uniform of his corps and is assigned to duty in company with an experienced trooper, he constitutes a highly promising, though as yet untested, instrument of organized society. For while the selective process continues throughout the period of instruction, and unsuitable candidates are eliminated during this stage, experience has shown that only a vigorous disciplinary system can ultimately perfect the work of selection. Although most of the state police forces

emphasize military discipline during the training period, it is relaxed somewhat after assignment to active duty is made. From that
point onward the task of protecting life and property is conducted
in the customary police fashion, with military bearing and precision generally continuing to mark the state trooper's work throughout his police career.

Supplementary instruction for those eligible for promotion, as
well as for troop officers generally, is a common feature with the
state police. Such advanced training has been especially well developed in Massachusetts, while in Indiana a four-year course and
in Michigan a five-year cadet course are operated in conjunction
with state colleges and universities. By such devices all ranks are
impressed with the fact that they are concerned with a living and
growing body of technical knowledge, and that their professional
horizons must widen as their practical experience increases.

Compensation and Welfare

The methods employed in compensating, clothing, and housing
the state police remain to be considered. Owing to the large areas
to be protected and the modest numerical strength of the police
establishments, it is only under the most pressing conditions that
efforts have thus far been made to provide circulating patrols
throughout the twenty-four hours of the day. It follows that the state
trooper is subject to the demands of his calling at all hours of the
day and night. Hence it is important that he should be housed in
such a fashion that he may be immediately available, when "off
duty," both to the general public and to his official superiors. Special
housing arrangements carry with them the necessity for feeding the
rank and file, not only at the various divisions and troop barracks,
but throughout a widely distributed system of substations also. It
is to this incidental feature of modern rural protection that the
so-called military characteristics may largely be attributed. The fact
that the standard type of state police are commonly fed, quartered,
clothed, and equipped by the state, are trained in the formalities
of military bearing, address, and courtesies, lends them a super-
ficially military appearance.

Until recent years a high fraction of state policemen were unmar-
ried, and therefore accepted barracks quarters as a part of their
compensation. In response to the demonstrated use several of the

older state police forces constructed rather elaborate barrack buildings as a part of troop and substation installations. Since the end of World War II the state police members are characteristically married, and these men prefer a settled home life over a shifting barracks life. State police barracks costing several hundreds of thousands of dollars, providing sleeping and recreation space for fifty or more men, now may house but three or four men. It is likely that this trend away from the barracks will continue, and that in many respects it is healthy.

Closely associated with the sharp increase in married state troopers is an equal increase in personnel problems involving assignments and transfers about the state. Administration is no longer free, as a practical matter, to assign any member to that point in the organization where he is needed or best suited. Instead, from the standpoint of assignment and promotion, the troops and substations become in effect separate police forces. It is in fact not uncommon for troopers to prefer to remain at a fixed station, if necessary relinquishing a promotion, rather than to transfer within the force but to another section of the state.

The compensation scales of state police do not lend themselves to direct comparison, largely because of the varying policies of the several forces with respect to providing subsistence and quarters, or commutation thereof. They range almost as widely as do municipal police salaries, though generally at a lower dollar level. Even this spread is further amplified in some instances by the state providing various commodities and services which are not included under most state or local police systems. Thus the military parallel is emphasized. Yet in all essential matters they are civil officers like other police, but subjected to a more exacting discipline than local police authorities are commonly able to apply.

Although the states have been slow to provide disability and death benefits, or adequate arrangements for superannuation retirement, this feature of state police management is coming to be emphasized more and more as the years pass. Owing to the fact that many of the state forces have been established during the past forty years and that their personnel turnover has been more rapid than in most municipal forces, the problem as it affects the rank and file has seldom assumed serious proportions. The isolated instances which have appeared from time to time have been taken care of by special means and without the aid of an established policy. The time has now arrived, however, when such questions must be squarely faced by state executives, legislators, and police administrators alike. With seventeen forces having neither death nor disability benefits for the rank and file, and with only a mere handful of the older organizations enjoying any provision whatever for superannuation retirement, most states are confronted with the need for immediate action in these neglected fields. However inadequate certain of the existing retirement systems may be, there is ample evidence that they will be extended and improved as the need for such changes becomes clearly apparent. Meanwhile, future obligations are being assumed without current provision for their ultimate discharge.

Law Enforcement

The great majority of state police forces employ uniformed patrols as their chief medium of law enforcement. Loosely articulated forces like the highway patrols often set up district headquarters for the purpose of administering field activities, but permit each patrolman to function largely as an independent unit, operating from his own home as a base. The better organized forces avoid this dispersion of strength by maintaining not merely district (or troop) headquarters but also substations which are directly and continuously responsible to the district command. District stations are usually large, completely equipped, and well-manned centers. The substations, on the other hand, may either be small state-owned buildings housing a limited personnel in charge of a noncommissioned officer, or they may be of a temporary character and subject to occasional change, thus providing all parts of the patrol area with the quieting influence which the presence of a police station is assumed to afford. The district headquarters are intended to serve not alone as administrative bases and as transport and communication centers, but also as fixed points on which to establish such reserves and mobile emergency units as the size of the force permits. The twenty state police establishments which make some effort at administrative decentralization along the lines described above maintain, all told, over four hundred district stations or substations, about one-fourth of which are located in Pennsylvania.

Under the pressure of political expediency the Pennsylvania State

Police have placed at least one district station or substation in every county but one; and one county has four substations. From the financial standpoint these stations are costly, being rented at a price as high as $400 a month. A 1955 survey report[8] recommended the discontinuance of nine substations outright, and the combination of twelve more into four locations. In practice unneeded substations in Pennsylvania draw needed manpower from patrol, as each substation requires a trooper on telephone-radio watch to receive and pass on citizen calls for police assistance. The trooper on telephone-radio watch is not available to perform a police service outside of the substation himself, and thus adds no security to the neighborhood.

Because of the large areas involved, transportation is an especially important factor in state police work. The earliest forces either antedated the automobile or they came into existence before motorcars had acquired the universality which they enjoy today. Hence the first state police were mounted forces and so acquired a romantic quality which still adheres. Although the mounted trooper served to bring law and order to many remote districts, the ever-extending network of fine highways has diminished the need for him, and he has now virtually disappeared. The few horses still found in state police stables are employed in the training of recruits, for the control of certain types of highway traffic, and for occasional riot duty or the regulation of large assemblages. New means of transport consist of automobiles primarily. It may fairly be doubted whether any extensive police system anywhere has such a wealth of transport facilities as that enjoyed by the state police.

Communications are in general those used by other types of police systems, with the public telephone, teletype, radiophone, and radiotelegraph most commonly employed. Despite the great areas to be covered by broadcasts and the technical difficulties encountered in securing anything like full coverage, nearly all state forces have set up radio networks through which they not only maintain contact with a far-flung system of patrols but bring these police facilities within the reach of many small local forces which could not otherwise be apprized of major crime occurrence. Teletype systems also are operated by state police, though to a lesser extent, and here too

[8] A Report of Survey of the Pennsylvania State Police, page 56 et seq., by Bruce Smith, Jr.

local forces are encouraged to participate in their use.[9]

Two-way radiophone communication between stations and patrol cars is now the merest commonplace in state police work, while the radiotype has been introduced on a limited experimental scale. These new devices render the areas of the several states far more compact, in a police sense, than they were when the first state police were placed on the road. Hence our severely localized police systems may eventually be consolidated because of the improved administrative controls provided by the new transport and communication systems. In any case it appears certain that the state trooper of the future, while enjoying better intelligence services than his early counterparts had at hand, will have less initiative and be less self-reliant than they were. The age of the motorcar and the radio has marked the passing of many fine and noble human institutions. The mounted trooper who brought law and order in his saddlebags to remote settlements and to the open country is surely not the least of the casualties due to mechanization.

Relatively few of the state forces include detective bureaus in their setups. The familiar argument against dispersion through specialized personnel comes pretty close to being conclusive when applied to state police. Their numbers are too small to permit much subdivision of their work. They also experience somewhat the same difficulties in selecting suitable raw material for their detective bureaus as do the city forces, because adequate and reliable tests simply do not exist. The state police, for the most part, have been bound by no statutory mandates in this matter and have recognized no administrative distinction between crime suppression and criminal investigation.[10] Where special capacity is required in conducting an investigation, a trooper who possesses the necessary qualifications may be taken from patrol and assigned to the case. He does not thereby come under the immediate control of any other authority. He is still responsible to his troop captain, and he returns to patrol

[9] A further description of state police communication systems appears in Chap. 9.

[10] Except in Massachusetts, where a state detective body under civil service control is maintained side by side with the noncivil service state patrol force. Even so, many members of the latter body operate regularly as detectives. Cf. Commonwealth of Massachusetts, *Report of the Special Commission on Taxation and Public Expenditures*, Part VII, pp. 16-17, 19-22. Other states maintaining detective forces, such as New York and Pennsylvania, select their investigating personnel by relatively informal methods.

duty when the case is closed. There are no complex administrative processes to be observed, there is no temporary shifting of responsibilities. The system is direct, simple, and comprehensive. The only question of which it does not completely dispose is the matter of special training for special tasks.

It is in deference to the latter feature that some of the larger forces exercising general police authority have established specialized investigative agencies for the assistance of the uniformed state patrols, and of any local forces which care to avail themselves of such central services. The results have not always equaled the expectations. The difficulties usually encountered in selecting competent detectives, and the rivalry of local forces which often resent state police participation in criminal cases, operate to discount the hopes once held out for this method.[11] Such limitations upon their full effectiveness will continue to apply until the state police either are able to increase their numbers to a point where greater decentralization of investigative activities is possible or until consolidation of local forces removes some of the overlapping layers of police service and thereby simplifies the problems arising from duplicate investigations.

One of the more difficult features of law enforcement in rural areas has been the overwhelming burden of highway traffic imposed upon the local constables. Abuses of their power in the form of speed traps or alliances with rural justices have been one of the influences favoring establishment of the state police. Another factor has been the obvious need for some general authority capable of applying uniform standards in traffic regulation. As already noted, many of the state police forces are in effect traffic law enforcement agencies and nothing else. Yet even the forces exercising general police authority have been confronted by the need for giving the

[11] A formal statement made by the governor of Massachusetts over seventy years ago is still so apt in its current application as to bear repetition. In his inaugural address, delivered on January 4, 1867, Governor Alexander H. Bullock declared: "It [the state constabulary created two years before] has demonstrated that the representative of the power of the Commonwealth commands a respect and attains results which the municipal officer, embarrassed by local influences and associations, has failed to secure.

"I regret that the local police have not in all cases cordially cooperated with the constabulary of the state; and that in some instances they have manifested a disposition to impede rather than to assist this department of the executive power."

rural traffic problem a considerable part of their attention. In a few instances, and notably in Pennsylvania, New York, and New Jersey, there has been specialization of function for the rank and file, with general police work and traffic work allocated to separate administrative units, while Massachusetts, Michigan, and Indiana have been impelled to set up special headquarters units for intensive study of traffic hazards in order that the rank and file may be more effectively employed in reducing highway accidents.

The advent of specialized accident investigation techniques now promises to throw new burdens upon uniformed state patrols, which may result in further dispersion of effective strength because of the apparent need for specialization. The situation differs so widely in the several states that no broad conclusions can easily be drawn, though it may be confidently predicted that, unless present tendencies toward specialization are curbed, the uniformed state trooper, like the city patrolman, will become a vanishing institution.

Politics in State Police

With the extension of the various state police patterns to cover the entire country, certain features characteristic of the forces constituted along the lines of the Pennsylvania model have been lost. Indeed, it is difficult to avoid the conclusion that as state police have increased in quantity, they have declined in quality. A very few state forces have plumbed the depths of political degradation. Such cases, though readily distinguishable from the general average as well as from the superior forces, are nonetheless a burden to the state police movement and to the large changes in our local, state, and federal systems which must precede its further development.

Although the environment in which the state police experiment has been conducted is certainly more favorable than that surrounding the police department of a large city, with political influences somewhat more remote in their application, the heads of even the most successful state forces can attest the partisan pressure that has been brought to bear upon them from time to time. In some of the older forces such efforts to influence the administration of the state police have so consistently proved unavailing that the administrators' hands are now entirely free. In the light of American experience with the management and control of police, this freedom from partisan influence acquires special significance. For, while state

police are not alone in winning a position of professional independence within the public service, they have accomplished it in a
larger proportion of cases than have the local or federal forces. Thus
the states promise to continue as a proving ground for some of the
latest adaptations of the theory and practice of public management
to the severely practical task of police administration.

II. FEDERAL POLICE

In the police systems thus far considered, much of the fragmentation of the police function has been due to a desire to avoid the
creation of unduly strong and cohesive police forces, while overlapping police activity has arisen largely from the fact that state
and local governments themselves overlap in many respects, and
that few exceptions have been made in favor of police lest local
autonomy be invaded.

Such influences had no part in shaping the federal police system.
If that system is broken into many fragments and is featured by
many overlapping patterns, it is largely because the law enforcement activities of the federal government were of slow growth, and
only within recent years have emerged from obscurity. Most of them
were created in the first instance as minor investigative agencies
which after the lapse of several decades gradually acquired law enforcement aspects of significance. Hence they are so solidly built
into the bureaucratic structure that nothing short of a general
administrative upheaval can be relied upon to dislodge them.

This interlacing of law enforcement activities with others of a
varied nature also renders it difficult to distinguish between agencies
of a police character and those which, though they have their law
enforcement aspects, are primarily concerned with intradepartmental inspections and investigations. Accordingly, there is a certain
amount of debate, with resulting uncertainty, concerning the actual
scope of federal law enforcement work and the agencies charged
therewith. For example, the Coast Guard, a large seagoing unit
which patrols the sea and lake shores of the United States, is charged
with general powers of criminal law enforcement. Here, quite
clearly, is a police agency with a broad statutory jurisdiction, though
one that is exercised largely within the limits of coastal waters. Yet
the Coast Guard is not a civil police agency in the full sense of the

term. Its recruiting, training of officer personnel, and discipline are more closely related to military and naval precedents than are police forces proper. Symbolic of this traditional relationship is the fact that in the event of hostilities the Coast Guard is automatically transferred from the control of the Treasury to that of the Navy Department, and finds itself arrayed with the naval forces actively engaged in the national defense. Thus it acquires connotations similar to those of the Military Intelligence Division in the War Department and of the Intelligence Division in the Office of Chief of Naval Operations in the Navy.

Agencies with Auxiliary Police Authority

Other units possessing certain minor police characteristics include:

1. Public Health Service (Treasury) is concerned with preventing the introduction of epidemic diseases into the United States.

2. Division of Investigation (Interior) investigates offenses committed by officers and employees of the Department of the Interior, as a kind of intradepartmental disciplinary agency.

3. Various bureaus in the Department of Agriculture exercise limited police authority in connection with intradepartmental activities.

4. Several bureaus in the Department of Commerce are similarly authorized.

5. The Veterans' Administration, through a force of field examiners under the solicitor, seeks to protect the federal government from fraudulent claims made by veterans and others.

6. Two personnel units—the United States Civil Service Commission and the United States Employees' Compensation Commission—also investigate fraudulent representations as a part of their regular administrative functioning.

7. Certain more or less independent agencies are concerned either wholly or in part with unlawful trade practices; namely the Federal Trade Commission, Securities and Exchange Commission, Federal Alcohol Administration, Federal Communications Commission, Interstate Commerce Commission, and United States Maritime Commission.

8. Police operating within the National Park Service; Office of Indian Affairs (Interior); Bureau of Insular Affairs (Army); Division of Territories and Island Possessions (Interior); Office of Island Governments (Navy); together with the regularly constituted police in the Territories and the Canal Zone.

Among all of the foregoing agencies, those in the last category alone exercise general police authority within prescribed territorial limits. The others are auxiliary in their organization and functioning, and therefore do not properly belong within the police sphere.

Regular Civil Police Agencies

Our concern, therefore, is not with these.[12] Rather it is with the federal police agencies of a civil character that enforce penal statutes of general application throughout the domain of the national government. The units falling within this category may be broadly classified according to their purposes, as follows:

I. Protection of the National Revenue:
1. Intelligence Unit of the Bureau of Internal Revenue (Treasury), concerned primarily with major violations of internal revenue laws, including income tax laws.
2. Enforcement Division of the Alcohol Tax Unit, Bureau of Internal Revenue (Treasury), concerned primarily with violations of laws imposing taxes upon intoxicants.
3. Division of Investigations and Patrol, Bureau of Customs (Treasury), concerned primarily with smuggling and illegal exportation.

II. Protection of Life and Property and Enforcement of Penal Statutes Generally:
1. Federal Bureau of Investigation (Justice), exercises full police jurisdiction over all crimes which are not the immediate and special concern of other federal police agencies.
2. Secret Service Division (Treasury), concerned with counterfeiting and forgery, and the protection of the President, his family, and the President-elect; with a broad though ill-defined jurisdiction over crimes affecting a long list of federal agencies.
3. Bureau of Narcotics (Treasury), concerned generally with all violations of statutes directed at the control of narcotic drugs.
4. Post office inspectors, concerned with mail losses, mail depredations, and violations of the postal laws generally; also

[12] For a more detailed treatment of the investigative and law enforcement units here excluded from further consideration, cf. *Report on the Organization of Federal Law Enforcement Activities*, prepared by the Brookings Institution for the Select Committee (Senate) to Investigate the Executive Agencies of the Government, 75th Congress, 1st session, Washington, 1937, pp. 1-4, 6, 122-124.

with many noncriminal and administrative investigations which consume two-thirds of their time and effort.

5. Immigration Border Patrol (Justice), concerned primarily with the smuggling of aliens and allied crimes.

Numerical Strength

Despite the transcontinental scope of the investigative and patrol agencies, the statutory jurisdictions of most of them are so narrow that they do not maintain a large personnel. The Federal Bureau of Investigation has, all told, about 1,300 employees, of whom only 45 per cent are directly engaged in investigations. The enforcement division of the Alcohol Tax Unit and the two border patrols stand next in order of size, with a total of about 4,000 men, while the remaining federal agencies are substantially smaller. Even including the services that are auxiliary to patrol and investigation, the entire federal police establishment totals a little over 20,000 men.

On the other hand, there are many more criminal investigators in the seven federal agencies employing them than could be mustered by all other police units in the United States taken together. It follows that the federal police establishment is not nearly so unimportant, in a numerical sense, as superficial comparisons with large patrol forces might seem to indicate. The most rapid growth has been experienced by the Federal Bureau of Investigation, which has had its jurisdiction greatly increased by Congress during the past three decades through a more complete utilization of federal powers to regulate interstate and foreign commerce, and the exercise of various postal and taxing powers. Notable additions to its criminal jurisdiction during this period have included the National Stolen Property Act, the federal (Lindbergh) kidnaping statutes, and others relating to extortion, fugitives, racketeering, firearms, and bank robberies. During the same years the growth of various central services conducted by the FBI for the benefit of local forces— identification, crime reporting, police training, and crime laboratory —has increased by leaps and bounds, thus requiring larger and larger quotas of headquarters employees for their current operation.[13]

---

[13] In addition to the 6,000 agents engaged on investigative duties, the FBI employs about 7,000 fingerprint experts, technical men, and clerks. A description of these central services appears in Chap. 9.

Management of Personnel

There is notable lack of unity of design in the personnel systems of the various law enforcement services. Nearest approach to a prevailing pattern is in their civil service status. With the single exception of the special agents of the Federal Bureau of Investigation, the enforcement officers of the various agencies are all recruited, promoted, and disciplined under civil service regulations. Thus the FBI is singled out at the very start by its departure from accepted patterns. Here, as in the best of the state forces and a few municipal police establishments, one finds the highest standards of recruitment, training, and discipline under what is customarily viewed as the dubious auspices of a noncivil service regime.

The FBI demands of its recruits that they be young, of sound physique, and of good educational background. Appointments are made from graduates in law or accountancy, and for the special agent such professional training is an absolute prerequisite. The other federal police services accept many kinds of qualifications which are generally related to their specific work. Thus applicants for admission to the Secret Service must be "experienced in detective work"; the Narcotics Bureau declares a preference for men with formal training in medicine or pharmacy, but through various alternatives will accept as little as one year of practical experience in these fields, plus one year of service as a criminal investigator; while the Post Office Inspectors, who are selected under civil service rules from those having four years of prior experience in the postal service, are apportioned both by states and by party affiliation. That such partisan influences and artificial residence qualifications should have survived so many major improvements in personnel management merely serves to heighten the contrasts in federal police work.

All of these agencies provide some form of in-service training. The FBI requires that the recruit shall receive full-time practical and theoretical instruction for sixteen weeks at the outset, with qualifying examinations of frequent occurrence thereafter, and annually supplemented by two to four weeks of review courses. The Immigration Border Patrol subjects its recruits to three months of intensive instruction at the beginning of their official service, with retraining courses made available for those who are able to attend in special groups from time to time thereafter.

Police training in some of the other federal agencies appears casual and indifferent by comparison. The intelligence unit of the Bureau of Internal Revenue provides its recruits with preliminary training through the medium of syllabi and correspondence courses covering a period of six weeks or less; in the alcohol tax unit's enforcement division, personal instruction or correspondence courses are given for two or three weeks; the Bureau of Narcotics offers a correspondence course in "Constitution and law," which is supplemented by practical instruction in the handling of firearms; while recruits in the Secret Service are individually schooled at district headquarters for a week or two, and in addition receive practical instruction in the processes of manufacturing genuine and counterfeit money and securities, and in the examination of questioned documents. The training programs of the Customs Border Patrol and of the Post Office Inspectors are also informal and decentralized.

The only units giving any special recognition to the probationary period as part of the selective process are the Immigration Border Patrol (one year), and the Post Office Inspectors and Narcotics Bureau (six months each).

With such widely varying standards in the management of personnel, it is but natural that the salary differential of the several federal forces should be rather pronounced. In such a heterogeneous collection of unstandardized grades and positions, it is difficult to draw hard-and-fast comparisons between the several forces. Yet this much may be said and said positively: grade for grade the compensation scales of the Federal Bureau of Investigation are the highest in the federal police service, and in most instances they hold this position by such a wide-margin that there can be no doubt of their primacy. This is not to suggest that the scale is excessive. On the contrary, it may merely be one more manifestation of the willingness and desire of the American people to pay well for superior service.

Distribution of Personnel

Federal police personnel is located not alone at the seat of government but throughout the length and breadth of the United States, its territories and possessions. Such a scheme of distribution, necessarily wide, involves problems of organization and supervision that are of the first magnitude. The generally successful operation

of these federal agencies with their far-flung systems of local offices
and detachments indicates that the difficulties involved in the administrative control of police over a wide front are not insuperable.
But fragmentation of federal police jurisdiction does operate to produce duplicating activities and duplicate field offices, each with its
supervisory, clerical, and stenographic personnel. Said the Brookings
Institution in 1937: "No two of these agencies have adopted the
same system of districting; but in a number of cities it is possible to
find the district headquarters, or at least a suboffice, of each of the
agencies. . . . The districts coincide much less frequently than do
the locations of the field offices."[14]

With over 400 field offices located in 50 states, a situation was
thereby created seriously threatening to any integral character the
federal police system might have. So far as the various Treasury
units are concerned, the situation has been recognized to the extent
that they have been fitted into a scheme of fifteen law enforcement
districts, with a single headquarters city designated for each district.
By means of interbureau coordinating committees some problems
have been simplified, but without removing the duplications or improving relations with police in other federal departments.

The situation of the Customs and Immigration Border Patrols,
maintained by the Treasury and Justice departments respectively,
has proved to be especially difficult. These two patrol bodies are
distributed along the land and sea borders of the United States, on
which the Customs Patrol maintains 9 headquarters offices and 15
substations and the Immigration Patrol operates from 10 district
headquarters and 23 subdistricts. As already indicated above, these
two bodies exercise their respective jurisdictions in entirely separate and distinct spheres of law enforcement. At least they are distinct so far as the statutory definitions of subject matters are concerned. Yet in a geographic sense they overlap each other for almost
every mile of our international boundaries. While one force is
primarily concerned with the smuggling of goods and the other with
the smuggling of aliens, each is projected into a situation where it
is obliged to exercise the jurisdiction granted to the other. The
Customs Patrol seizes not only general merchandise illegally brought
into the United States, but also narcotics and intoxicating liquors.
It apprehends persons engaged in smuggling such goods, and also

14 *Op. cit.*, pp. 100 ff.

those who participate in the illegal entry of aliens. Conversely, the Immigration Patrol emphasizes the traffic in aliens, but also makes many arrests and seizures for customs violations. It is difficult indeed to see how these two rival services could act otherwise than as they do, although the claim of each that its separate existence is necessary to adequate enforcement of a special type of penal statute is not supported by their actual operations.

At some of the small stations along the national frontiers, only one of these patrol services will be represented, with the understanding that it will enforce both the customs and the immigration laws and regulations. Both sides admit that this makes for economy, but object that the performance of the rival force is unsatisfactory because of lack of interest in enforcing statutes lying beyond the narrow horizons of the patrol service concerned. This represents the most common, as well as the most objectionable, result of overspecialization.[15]

Problems of Jurisdiction

Thus problems of jurisdiction and of interforce administration crowd in on every hand. The points at which duplications occur are roughly indicated in Fig. V. With 28 possible duplicating relationships, 20 are actually involved in this restricted group of 8 police agencies. If a broader definition of federal police were employed so as to include the other investigative units listed above, the situation would defy graphic representation.

Conflicts among federal police agencies are of so varied a nature that they sometimes run almost the entire gamut of bureaucratic rivalry, distrust, and intrigue. This is not to say that interdepart-

[15] When the Department of Labor conducted an inquiry some years ago into the operation of joint services by the two patrols, the committee in charge declared that it was "impressed with the showing that at many small ports of entry . . . as many as four officers are simultaneously on duty at one small port, with insufficient work to keep one man busy. . . . There is no doubt that at these small ports of entry one officer, if clothed with the necessary authority, could take over the duties now being performed by the several officers." Yet the committee expressed concern about "unsatisfactory work of customs officers" when entrusted with immigration functions, and listed what it described as "glaring examples" of "lack of cooperation" and "uncoordinated activities" of the two patrol forces, and proposed that they be consolidated under the control of the immigration authorities. (Memorandum submitted by a "committee of immigration officers representing both the Canadian and Mexican Borders," on *The Possible Consolidation of Border Activities and Discontinuance of Unnecessary Government Officers*, typewritten manuscript dated October 23, 1933; cf., also, typewritten memorandum of November 15, 1933, re: *Practicability of a Consolidated Border Patrol Service*.)

mental cooperation among the various police forces is not attempted, or that it does not yield substantial results. Such cooperation is necessary as a *modus vivendi* for each of the agencies and much time, thought, and effort are expended in maintaining it. Yet as a discriminating student of the subject has observed, "one should not gain the impression . . . that the federal crime control agencies live and work together like members of a happy family, each zealously observing the Golden Rule. As a matter of fact, each is busy trying to dig out from under its own work; and naturally each thinks of itself first."[16]

Quite different considerations apply to the overlapping police jurisdictions of the state and federal governments, since these arise not only out of administrative relationships, but also from the fact that some of the national crime legislation has been frankly directed at enlarging the federal police sphere, at the ultimate expense of that of the state and local governments. For example, when Congress enacts laws punishing attacks upon banks brought within the orbit of federal control, such penal statutes are intended not merely to supplement state laws on the subject or to fill the interstices which may exist between the state and federal systems of criminal law and administration. On the contrary, it is the purpose of such laws to give the federal government the power to punish criminal acts which are already punishable under state laws, and to prosecute persons who violate the federal statutes if the national government can apprehend them before the police of state or local governments can do so. Some of the statutes have produced duplication where none existed before. In this fashion the problems of interforce cooperation between local police agencies have in effect been bypassed, with a single federal force conducting an integrated investigation over large areas and without regard to state or local boundaries. Such departures have had, for the most part, enthusiastic police support from all levels of government, and seem also to have enjoyed the unqualified approval of the American people, grown weary of the cycle of futility imposed by voluntary cooperation among thousands of local forces. Still there is no blinking the fact that a new type of police duplication has been created, and that it will require the most careful administrative guidance of federal, state, and local police if ruinous collisions of interest are to be avoided. This, and this alone, offers hope for practical solutions in

[16] A. C. Millspaugh, *Crime Control by the National Government*, p. 103.

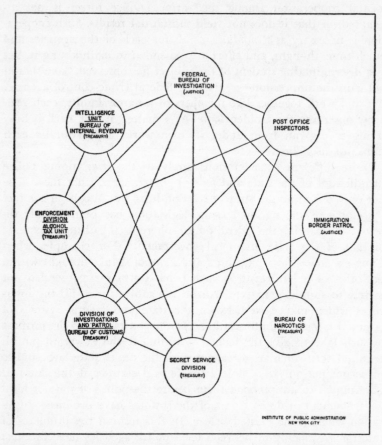

Figure V Interrelations in federal law enforcement. Generalized chart showing the points at which duplication in police jurisdiction occurs most frequently.

both present and future, since the duplications involved in federal and state penal laws cannot be eliminated without destroying the very element of untrammeled action by federal police that the new acts of Congress were intended to provide.

Coordination versus Consolidation

One notes a rising interest in the administrative problems created by our overlapping federal police agencies, and many and varied are the plans for correcting the defects that arise from them. Three general types of proposals are advanced: (1) those involving a re-allocation of police functions among the federal departments, bureaus, and divisions, without abandoning any of the existing police units; (2) those consolidating the various police units and set-ting up a single federal bureau of investigation and patrol in the Department of Justice; (3) those providing some form of coordina-tion of the existing machinery, such as interdepartmental commit-tee or a single law enforcement coordinator (attached to the Bureau of the Budget or elsewhere in the Executive Office of the President), with advisory powers only.

Standing alone, no one of these devices seems to promise a solu-tion of the federal police problem. Any mere redistribution of ad-ministrative responsibilities and authorities would at best be a kind of statutory cheeseparing, and might greatly complicate the practical business of law enforcement by building even higher the bureau-cratic fortifications now separating some of the agencies. At the other extreme, any thoroughgoing plan of consolidation would be vigorously opposed by federal officers with administrative axes to grind, as well as by those who are fearful of the political and social effects of any concentration of police authority. Efforts at outright consolidation in the past have been easily thwarted by such in-fluences. The third angle of approach is almost barren of promise of any ameliorative effort if it merely takes the form of an in-teragency committee which is charged with securing cooperative action. For this device is predicated upon the assumption that there are vested interests in the several units which must not be impaired by anything that seeks to regulate the functioning of independent police units or by anything resembling administrative authority or compulsion. Hence it is objectionable upon that ground alone. The proposal for a single coordinating officer who is independent of any of the law enforcement agencies may possess some merit, particu-larly if he were authorized to work out detailed programs for the transfer of functions among the several agencies; for the consolida-tion of functions in those specific instances where the facts strongly indicated the desirability of such action; and for the constant main-tenance of a coordinating influence among the twoscore other fed-eral agencies, which will in any case continue to exercise their respective fragments of the law enforcement function.

When all the available evidence is put together, one feature stands out. Some degree of consolidation is clearly necessary if the federal police machine is to possess any discernible coherence whatever. Most clearly falling within this category are the general law enforcement activities of the Secret Service division and the Post Office Inspectors, which could be absorbed by the Federal Bureau of Investigation without any extension of its present statutory powers or major change in its structural organization. At a single stroke a considerable part of existing administrative conflict and duplication of effort would thereby be eliminated.

There is less agreement as to some of the other independent agencies; for example, whether the Customs and Immigration Border Patrols should be consolidated, or whether they should merely be required to work out a more complete interchange of responsibility at various ports of entry.[17] Other questions on which there is no agreement revolve around the transfer of the enforcement division of the alcohol tax unit, and the Bureau of Narcotics, both now located in the Treasury, to the Federal Bureau of Investigation.

Perhaps time and the light which further study should provide will offer more clear-cut solutions. That mere lapse of time, which is not employed in clarifying these and related problems, will not alone operate to place the federal police system upon a more satisfactory basis, seems self-evident. To produce a smoothly functioning machine there must be not only a transfer of functions, but also consolidation of certain agencies and a close administrative coordination of others. Meanwhile there appears to be little foundation for the fear that centralizing tendencies in police work may operate to aggrandize unduly the position of the federal government in law enforcement. The whole constitutional basis of our federal system and the position of the states within that system operate to limit the scope of federal law enforcement. Added to this is the patent fact that a national government that is unable to piece together the few

[17] On May 23, 1940, President Roosevelt transmitted to Congress *Reorganization Plan No. V,* prepared in accordance with the provisions of Section 4 of the Reorganization Act of 1939 (Public, No. 19, 76th Congress, 1st session), approved April 3, 1939. The Immigration and Naturalization Service (including the Immigration Border Patrol) was thereby transferred from the Department of Labor to the Department of Justice. While this major shift in administrative control did not simplify the problem of synthesizing the work of the two border patrols, it is important in that it brought partial integration of federal police agencies one degree closer to fulfillment.

score fragments into which its police authority has been broken would be overwhelmed by the task of absorbing some tens of thousands of local police agencies. Though our police mechanism needs simplifying, that is a job both for the states and the federal government, each operating within its own constitutional sphere. For the present at least, the traditional system seems secure from any acquisitive designs by the federal government.

CHAPTER 7

POLICE CONTROL

The term "police control" is almost inherently ambiguous. It consists of two elements: popular control over general policies, and the control commonly exercised by administrative heads in directing the day-to-day operations of the rank and file. Theoretically there is no conflict between the two objectives. If popular controls are to be effective they must not only guide the major policies of the police force, but must also indirectly influence the manner in which such policies are applied by the several ranks and grades in conducting the routine of police work. It is for this reason that the term "police control" in its broader sense has proved to be a useful aid to generalized thinking on police problems and has served to focus attention upon both administrative programs and the manner of their execution.

Nevertheless, the constituent elements of the term involve widely differing factors. Police control in the sense of popular determination of basic policies involves many abstract ideas concerning the democratic process, as well as certain severely practical considerations that arise out of the defective functioning of that process. It invades a field of political theory enjoying few scientific features and is a blend of historical perspective, high aspiration, and a shrewd judgment of the possibilities and limitations of people in the mass.

By contrast with such vague concepts, police control in the sense of regulating the details of police operations is relatively concrete. It involves such matters as the technical means for so organizing the available personnel that competent police leadership, when secured, can operate effectively. It is concerned not so much with the extent to which popular controls can be trusted to guide and direct the course of police protection as with the administrative relationships which should exist between the component parts of the police organism.

In view of the widely differing angles of approach characterizing these two elements of police control, it is necessary and even desirable to treat them separately, though the point is worthy of the emphasis of repetition, that under our democratic patterns these elements are intimately related and sometimes exercise a direct influence upon each other.

The search for some means for keeping police operations within the bounds of constitutional rights and guaranties, and of preventing them from becoming unduly repressive, probably is inspired in part by the age-old popular fear and distrust of armed force. Professional military and police forces both came into existence in response to the need for defensive measures, to be executed by trained specialists who are armed with extraordinary powers to act with vigor and decision. Both have therefore been the subject of concern, lest they override not only private rights of long standing, but also the established processes of civil government. One device for controlling military power is to place its general regulation and control in the hands of a nonprofessional administrator who is displaced with sufficient frequency to prevent eventual domination by the technically skilled military caste. Something akin to this device has been used also in regulating the police function. Professional police administrators have been subordinated at times to the daily supervision of legislative committees, administrative boards, and lay directing heads, who, no matter what their general competence might be, could make no pretense at specialized skill in police management. The favorable and unfavorable effects of this policy upon police leadership are reserved for later consideration. It is necessary here, however, to trace its development as a major device of popular control.[1]

Early Forms of Police Control

Popular election was the earliest of the various expedients to make its appearance. During the early colonial period, the sheriff and

---

[1] Fosdick's *American Police Systems* contains (pp. 58-187) what is still the most comprehensive and best treatment of the development of police control in American cities.

constable were the only police officers, who soon came to be chosen for short elective terms. With the rise of the cities separately organized night and day watches were organized, and at this point the practice of appointment began to make substantial headway.

The power of appointment, together with the general duty of controlling and directing police affairs, was often lodged in a standing committee of the city council. The origin of this practice traces back to the lengthy struggle for mastery waged by kings and parliaments. When the latter finally gained the upper hand, they consolidated their gains by subordinating executive authority to the legislative branch of government. The method was well established in England when our colonial governments were set up and, although the whole conflict between executive and legislative control was duplicated here, it reached the same conclusion and was of shorter duration than that which had earlier taken place in England. Thus the early history of police in America was marked by the dissensions that are an inevitable feature of practically all representative popular assemblies. Such collisions of policy have their value in the legislative process, but are a burden to administration. Under their impact, standards of consistent performance were forgotten and the emphasis of police operations was changed with each shift in the political scene. Situations requiring prompt action were subjected to the dilatory effects of prolonged debate. Others requiring vigorous and decisive handling were disposed of in accordance with legislative compromise. Appointments to police office, whether high or low, were made in strict accord with partisan interest and were often for limited terms. Geographical representation in appointments was assured through a logrolling process which gave to each member of the legislative committee the right to designate a certain number of police incumbents. Through it all ran the usual characteristics of the legislative scene—representation of interests, responsiveness to temporary changes in popular opinion, rotation in office, protracted debate, and the compromise of issues. Their effect upon police administration was so unfavorable that, while direct legislative control of police administration was ascendant, little or no progress in police methods could be made. So long as the system of legislative direction prevailed, the policeman's art was unable to emerge from its original stage of rudimentary watchman duty, performed by unskilled casual laborers.

Control by Administrative Boards

The next major change in the form of popular control occurred during the middle decades of the nineteenth century. It involved an abandonment of the practice of lodging administrative supervision in legislative committees, and the substitution of administrative boards which were sometimes ex officio in their composition, sometimes specially appointed for the purpose. Such departures were hailed at the time as impressive reforms in police management and ushered in a period of experimentation in multiple control that still exercises a certain influence upon American police forces. The new boards were of great variety. Judges, mayors, and city councilmen were propelled into the technical direction of police affairs. Private citizens who were engrossed with their own personal concerns and had no experience in supervising public undertakings were given similar responsibilities. Almost invariably such service was of a part-time character. Often it was not only inexpert, but meddlesome.

Charges of partisanship brought further changes. Bipartisan boards were substituted for unipartisan boards, and these revived the familiar logrolling devices employed by legislative committees. In desperation, new boards were set up under the style and pretense that they were nonpartisan in character. However, it does not appear that any of them, whether denominated unipartisan, bipartisan, or nonpartisan, ever rose above party and partisanship. Their composition as lay, inexpert, and representative bodies went far to assure that result. Both police management and police protection continued to flounder in a morass of political uncertainty, intrigue, partisanship, and corruption.

As the nineteenth century wore on to its close, the urbanization of America was accelerated. The "Shame of the Cities" was in the making. Rural constituencies viewed such developments with alarm. They clung to the early American culture, but the great sprawling cities were producing a new culture—polyglot, alien, and a menace to the old order. Mounting urban populations threatened the legislative control which had been exercised by landed proprietors great and small. Police corruption was well publicized and rode high on this rising tide of urban domination. So state legislatures, which still reflected a predominant rural influence, struck, and struck swiftly. In practically every great city of America, and in many smaller places, local control of police was swept away by statute, and police administrators appointed by state authorities were substituted.

State Control of Local Police Forces

Quite aside from abuses arising under local control, there was a certain theoretical justification for such drastic action. After all, the states retained certain attributes of sovereignty. In contemplation of law they were the reservoirs of police authority. The laws which the local police enforced were state laws, and the state appeared to owe a duty to its citizens to assure an adequate and equal enforcement of them.

So ran the theory justifying state intervention, and even today, after more than half a century of unsuccessful experience, it is difficult to pick flaws in this underlying philosophy. Yet the scheme met with little success. The reasons for its failure are apparent on the surface. For one thing, the theory of state control of the police function was not uniformly applied. It was primarily directed at the larger cities, by legislatures seeking to assure a continuance of rural domination in public affairs. Hence it became necessary to continue to impose the burden of fiscal support of the police upon the locality affected, and in some cases to require local legislative bodies to appropriate whatever sums the state-appointed police authorities might require, under penalty of fine and imprisonment for failure to comply. Since the police authority thereby virtually becomes the fiscal appropriating authority, it is usually constituted as a deliberative body, and thereupon the whole system is affected by the familiar weaknesses of board control.

Moreover, the cities thus singled out as objects of attack were generally of a differing political party inclination from that prevailing in the rural districts. Naturally, and almost inevitably, the police officials designated by the state government were not in political harmony with a majority of the people whom they were charged with protecting; and although rural standards of private conduct differed materially from those prevailing in the large cities, an effort was made to impose them.

Thus the whole scheme was foredomed to failure. Collisions between municipal authorities and those managing the police force on behalf of the state were of common occurrence. Police costs rose because police boards were not even indirectly responsible to the local taxpaying public which they served, and with a few exceptions, the quality of police service was not improved. So in city after city the unsuccessful experiment was abandoned and the local forces were returned to local control.[2]

Effect of Commission Government Charters

The next major change in police control occurred in the first decade of this century, with the enactment of so-called commission government charters for many cities. Their outstanding feature is the combination of both executive and legislative powers in a small commission elected by popular vote. Usually the commission numbers only five members, among whom the various departments of the city government are parceled out for purposes of administrative supervision. Quite aside from any basic shortcomings of this scheme as a form of local government stands the fact that the member of the commission who is designated as commissioner of public safety is charged with the management not only of the police force, but of the fire-fighting force as well, with building regulation and occasionally also health and welfare thrown in for good measure. Thus amateur supervision by a popularly elected and transient police administrator is complicated by the demands of other important municipal services.

Police forces enjoying even a moderate success under such control devices are so few and far between it may confidently be asserted that the future of police development does not lie in this direction. Indeed, the entire commission government plan has gone into a decline during recent years, many of the cities which adopted it either turning to the council-manager form or reverting to the older mayor-and-council system under which they had previously operated.

Unity of Command

During the later stages of the municipal police developments which have just been traced, the police facilities of the state and

[2] The system still endures in Missouri (St. Louis, Kansas City, and St. Joseph); Maryland (Baltimore); Massachusetts (Boston and Fall River); Maine (Lewiston); New Hampshire (Berlin, Dover, Exeter, Laconia, Manchester, Nashua, Portsmouth, and Somersworth). In the foregoing cities police boards are appointed by state authority, except in Boston and Baltimore, each of which has a single administrative head of the police force who is designated by the governor.

federal governments were winning increasingly important places for themselves in the field of law enforcement. It is a highly significant fact that these more modern agencies have with few exceptions avoided multiple control—whether exercised by legislative committees or by administrative boards—but rather are placed under unified command, such as has characterized many local forces from the very beginning of modern police systems.

Even more significant is the manner in which unified direction of the older municipal forces has persisted down through the years, unaffected in its basic outlines by the rather wide variety of substitutes with which it has been obliged to compete. Recent decades have seen a steadily accelerating movement away from the device of popular control by popular election and also from the cumbersome mechanics of multiple control by administrative boards.

As matters now stand the situation may be summarized in broad and general terms as follows: the police of most of our cities and states, and all of the federal police agencies, are directed by appointed administrators rather than by elected heads or administrative boards. Appointment of town and village constables is becoming increasingly common and the sheriff remains the sole type of law enforcement officer who characteristically enjoys elective status. Thus although there is as yet no uniformity of practice, the trend is too clear to permit real doubt as to the ultimate result. American police administrators seem destined to be appointed by general executive officers and to exercise their proper powers free from the indecisions and confusions that go hand in hand with multiple control.

That the vivid lessons of experience have not been more quickly and generally learned is probably due to the fact that as a people we fear executive authority and almost instinctively turn to legislative assemblies for protection against executive abuses. Police service is so prominently associated with executive authority in the public mind that it is but natural it should find itself more narrowly restricted by control devices than most other functions of civil government. Possibly this popular attitude of suspicion will continue indefinitely to influence police patterns; but it does not follow from this that the old and outworn formulae will be repeatedly revived and applied in our later efforts toward police control.

Control through Lay Administrators

Remaining to be considered is another device to bring police activity into focus with popular attitudes. It consists in selecting the police commander from the mass of the people generally, rather than from the ranks of the police force, sometimes coupling this with provisions concerning official term which give some assurance that the tenure of the incumbent will not be unduly long. When limited terms are thus allied with technical inexperience the results, while not always downright bad, are seldom really good. The history of American police administration is replete with examples of the failure of lay direction. There have been, it is true, a few notable successes, though in each case the successful lay head seems to have possessed unusual personal or professional qualifications, and in addition was able to remain in office long enough to consolidate the hard-won administrative gains of his leadership.

The lessons of experience in this field seem to point more to the failure of short-term direction than to the failure of nonprofessional direction as such. Here the issue is particularly critical because upon it may hinge many future determinations of policy in the matter of police control. For it will be recalled that the device of nonprofessional police direction, with limited tenure, was apparently borrowed from a similar method employed to assure civil control of military affairs. That method seems to have given a fair degree of satisfaction under varying political conditions throughout the world. Its possible applicability to police administration is therefore worth considering seriously. Yet it should be noted at the outset that the military and police aspects of the question are not strictly comparable. Civil direction of military affairs has been guided and supported by expert and well-trained general staffs selected from the similarly trained and professional body of the military establishments. In other words, civil direction has been materially aided by the professional qualifications of the permanent personnel. No such favorable conditions prevail in the vast majority of American police forces. With certain notable exceptions, our American police have not, in the past, been recruited with an eye to the future leadership of the force. Admission standards have been low, training programs were either superficial or nonexistent, and the standards for promotion to higher command were of uncertain value. Although such defects are now in process of being corrected in many police jurisdictions, the occasional striking improvements in personnel management do not yet reach into the thousands of small and obscure police forces nor into some of the larger units. In any case, the highly commendable changes now being inaugurated will require years of persistent application before their effects upon police leadership become apparent. It takes time for the carefully selected and trained police recruit to ripen under the test of practical experience until he is in the full sense prepared to assume the burdens of responsibilities of command.

Incidental to this question of qualified professional support for the nonprofessional administrator, but throwing some light on the whole question, is the experience of some of the leading state police forces.[3] As indicated in the preceding chapter, though of recent development they have established new standards of police administration in a number of important respects. In every case the original administrative heads of these forces were entirely without practical police experience when appointed. They were, in short, amateurs in police management. Yet almost from the outset the police units under their command moved forward into an advanced position in the police field.

The causative factors underlying such favorable developments are doubtless numerous. Some will emphasize the high personal standing and general competence of the police administrators concerned. In this there will be general agreement. Yet the mayors of American cities have repeatedly appointed estimable men without police experience to the command of local police forces and have generally found nothing but disappointment in the ultimate results.

Probably the best explanation of the successes of state police administrators consists in the fact that, from the very day the several state forces were organized, the recruiting, training, promotion, and disciplinary procedures were of an unusually high order. Being in every sense new forces, there was no deadwood occupying key positions. The directing head acquired experience in police administration, while the rank and file were becoming proficient in the policeman's art. Lay police leadership proved effective because the force was generally composed of competent, enthusiastic, and loyal

[3] The state police in Pennsylvania, New York, New Jersey, Massachusetts, Rhode Island, and Michigan are to be particularly noted in this connection.

subordinates who were subject to a vigorously applied discipline. Under these circumstances the lay police administrator may reasonably hope to achieve success, but there is nothing in our police history to indicate that he can do so with any great frequency when the police force reflects the neglect and mismanagement of generations.

Assuming that generally favorable conditions prevail, there are other factors making it desirable to appoint to police command men of high personal qualifications and competence who have no specific experience in police work. Thus the police administrator drawn directly from civil life is more closely in touch with public attitudes, more sensitive to popular needs, and therefore better adapted to the purposes and requirements of popular control. He is more likely to have enjoyed the advantages of broad interests and wide experience than is the man risen from the ranks, who has been subjected throughout his career to the deadening and narrowing effects of official routine. While corps loyalty and enthusiasm are aids to management that have real value under most circumstances, they are susceptible of diversion into channels which may be directed against the public interest and devoted solely to selfish and professional ends. The lay administrator is less likely to be subject to such unfavorable influences, and therefore is perhaps better adapted to the ends of popular control. Given the proper underlying conditions, there is real substance in the practice of appointing police administrators from the upper reaches of commerce, industry, the Army, and the learned professions.

Next to sheer police technique, which can be acquired only by experience, the greatest advantage enjoyed by the locally trained professional administrator is derived from the fact that he has a considerable fund of firsthand knowledge concerning the strong points, weaknesses, and special aptitudes of the force that is his to command. He has this information ready at hand from the moment of his appointment and therefore can move swiftly and certainly toward his objectives from the outset. The administrator who has not risen from the ranks is in a more difficult position. At best he can merely select a few trusted advisers within the force, and rely heavily upon them in forming his personal judgments. That is far from a perfect method, though it often seems to work satisfactorily. In any event, the relative disadvantage of the lay administrator is merely temporary, and he is compensated for it by the fact that he does not assume the responsibilities of general command with burdens such as long and friendly association in the ranks sometime imposes upon the newly elevated police official.

Control through Technically Trained Leaders

Finally, there is the widely recognized fact that true professional status involves the observance of certain ethical standards. The police service now emerging to something like a professional level is deliberately seeking to formulate such standards and to enforce them through group action. But even without the encouragement and support of such formal methods there is ample evidence that professional police administrators are developing their own codes which, however vague and uncertain in their present outlines, hold great promise for the future. Prominent among them is a determination on the part of certain police leaders to avoid participation in political activities, to leave the formulation of public policies to the elected representatives of the people, and to confine themselves to the meticulous execution of such policies once they are clearly defined and accepted.

For the present such trends are none too positive or general, but they do exist and if extended may go far toward removing the greatest single objection to placing our police forces wholly under the direction and control of men who have mastered the techniques of administration through firsthand experience with police service.

As some of the recruits of recent years rise from the ranks, the superior personal qualifications which they brought to police work may be expected to encourage a more and more frequent recourse to management by trained police officers. Also worthy of consideration is the fact that the designation of a lay police head is likely to have an unsettling effect upon the rank and file, who are uncertain of the attitude he may take toward police routines produced by lengthy experience. Such an administrator comes to his task with certain predilections concerning police duty which may not stand the test of practical application. The time spent in educating the lay administrator in the realities of police duty may be so extended that the day-to-day functioning of the force meanwhile is impaired. Another objectionable feature is that selection of the police administrator from sources lying outside the police force limits the possibilities of promotion to that extent, and hence may discourage the recruitment of especially able and ambitious aspirants who may be attracted to police service with an eye to eventual succession to the highest administrative post. Conversely, it may be argued that, if the lines of promotion to the very top are kept open, there is a larger and continuing incentive to the members of the rank and file to improve their educational backgrounds, to profit by their experience, and to enlarge their outlooks and horizons.

Practical Applications

It would be a fruitless task to weigh these various and conflicting factors in an effort to strike some balance between them and thus determine once and for all whether lay or professional heads are to be preferred. There are cogent arguments for and against both systems, and neither should be employed to the complete exclusion of the other. On the whole, it is fortunate that this is the case because certain severely practical considerations must be recognized. First and foremost of these is the demonstrated fact that capable police administrators do not grow on every bough. At the particular moment when an appointment must be made it may well be that the police force cannot muster a single aspirant who meets all reasonable requirements. After all, its numbers are limited, and narrow limitation in the field of choice should be avoided. On the other hand, the much larger field from which a lay head may be drawn is really much smaller than it appears to be. Success in business or a learned profession does not in itself indicate aptitude for police management, nor for the nice balancing of official and public interests it involves. Some of those qualified in other respects either lack "the common touch" the job of police direction demands or have a distaste for public employment, or are not attracted by the limited financial rewards it affords to the incorruptible administrator. Even more serious is the increasing realization that the cut-and-dried methods of civil service control do not offer a promising medium for successful police management.

Under such a complex of circumstances, it is better that the judgment of the appointing authority, whether national, state, or local, should be unfettered in its selection of an administrative head for police operations. Considering the difficulties that beset police management, the best qualified leader will prove difficult enough to find and attract without raising artificial barriers to a free selection. Even in a force that is able to breed its own future leaders there will be continuing need for occasional excursions into the wider field. Selection of the leader from the force itself—provided always that the selection squares with the judgment of the rank and file—can provide a stimulus to corps pride and morale. But if the practice is repeated again and again without variation, certain new dangers appear. For after a man has spent a considerable time as part of a well-organized and smoothly functioning machine he may come to accept it as a matter of course and cease to cudgel his brains in devising ways and means for improving it. He may even arrive at the comforting conclusion that the administrative organism with which he has been familiar for so long has at last attained perfection and that nothing remains for the directing head to do but to supervise its daily operations. Yet the job of the police administrator does not properly consist in directing his force in the conduct of a particular case or of any number of cases, no matter how numerous or how important. Rather his task is to provide the most effective methods and the most satisfactory instruments which can be fashioned to that end. Both the methods and the instruments must always be on trial before him. Is this method, or that man, or such-and-such device meeting all requirements? If not, is it satisfying all reasonable expectations? Can a change of method or routine be made advantageously? . . . What are the facts? What are the probabilities? . . . What then?

Paradoxical as it may appear, the more efficient the administrative machine the less likely it is to produce a leader of marked perception, with an alert sensibility to changing conditions, and of vigorous and constructive thought and action. Long attachment to familiar methods serves to dampen his ardor in the criticism and rearrangement of the existing mechanism so that it may anticipate impending crises, or at the very least satisfactorily meet them after they have arisen.

While great leaders have come from the ranks of efficient police machines and will continue to do so, they are men whose native ability and fresh viewpoint could not be impaired by the deteriorative effects of routine, nor by the continued subordination of their own judgments to the general plan. Such men will always be essential to the advance of police administration along a wide front. If possible they should provide the bulk, as well as the quality, of our police leadership. But the way must also be left open for new ideas and new influences arising directly from the great mass of the people who are protected and served—and who incidentally pay the bill. Human experience with police management, as well as with other callings, has conclusively shown that occasionally a layman can be found who is able to exercise leadership in developing the techniques of the trained specialist.

Lessons from American and Foreign Experience

Here in the United States are no fixed patterns determining with any degree of precision the policies to be followed in selecting the administrative heads of our police forces. As already stated, popular election is still employed, though this is now largely confined to such rudimentary police agencies as sheriffs, constables, town or village marshals, councilmanic committees on police, and to public safety directors under commission government charters. Many of the federal, state, and municipal police administrators are regularly appointed from the higher grades of the respective police forces, sometimes by formal civil service examination, sometimes by free executive selection; often, too, the selection is made from outside the force, and there are a few police jurisdictions in which no established practice prevails, the appointments going to police or to laymen according to no set plan or tradition.

Thus far only one or two fairly safe conclusions can be drawn from all this varying practice. The first and most clearly defined is that the method of popular election is wholly unsuited to the selection of police administrators, and that popular control, if thus secured, is bought at an unnecessarily high price—at the expense of competence, character, continuity of service, and professional standing. Second, the appointment of lay administrators is somewhat more likely to be tinged with partisan considerations than if technically trained heads are designated, and the official tenure of the layman tends to be somewhat shorter than that of the man risen from the ranks. The distinction here is none too pronounced, however, and may possibly revolve about wholly local factors more than any inherent characteristics of the two methods.

Of special interest are the methods employed in selecting chief constables in Great Britain. A majority of the chief constables in

the cities and boroughs are appointed from the regular police establishments, whereas the county chief constables, who command, in
many instances, large, well-trained, and modern police forces, are
more likely to be drawn from the ranks of the Army. In any case
the selection is made by the local authorities—by the watch committees of the cities and boroughs or by the standing joint committees of the counties.

Concerning the situation in England and Wales generally, a Royal
Commission has declared that

long experience and good service in the lower ranks of the Force
are not the only, nor even the most important, qualifications for the
higher posts, which ought to be filled in all cases by men who,
besides being themselves upright and fair-minded, are capable of
impressing their own standards on their subordinates. We should
therefore regard as inimical to the public interest any system which
limited appointments to the higher posts to those who had entered
the Police as constables and we are of the opinion that such posts
should be filled by the best men available, irrespective of the source
whence they are drawn.[4]

The foregoing generalizations on British practice may be supplemented from the experience of the Metropolitan Police. This body
of 20,000 men, which protects all the London metropolitan area
(except for the square mile City of London) is incomparably the
largest police unit in the island. The gravity and complexity of the
problems encountered there, the importance of the area in all affairs
of the kingdom, the predominating influence of the national government upon the Metropolitan Police force, and the prominent
place which it holds among the great police forces of the world,
all serve to lend special interest and significance to its procedures.
It is therefore more than an ordinary striking fact that during
the century and more that has elapsed since the inception of the
Metropolitan Police, the force itself "has never yet produced a
Commissioner, or (with one exception) a Deputy or Assistant Commissioner. It has also been found necessary to recruit all but a few
of the Chief Constables from outside the Force."[5]

[4] *Report of the Royal Commission on Police Powers and Procedure,* Dated
16th March, 1929, p. 20.

[5] The chief constables of the Metropolitan Police are generally assigned as district commanders. The chief constables of other British forces are police administrators in the full sense of the term.

Commenting upon this situation, an especially qualified English observer and police administrator says that "it should cause no surprise that the Commissioner's post has been filled otherwise than by promotion, or that it has been successfully so filled. Expert knowledge is the province of his subordinates: the Commissioner has to hold the scales between police and public and between different branches of the police, a task which . . . is of such magnitude and delicacy, and requires such a wide knowledge of men and affairs, that it can well be undertaken by one who has had the opportunity of acquiring the exceptional qualifications necessary in some wider sphere than that of the police service."[6]

Turning now to the methods employed for the selection of police leaders in the countries of western Europe, it may fairly be questioned whether their policies can throw much light upon the present or future of American developments. Their traditions of local government rest upon far different historical bases than do ours, and the extent to which their municipalities and other minor political units are subjected to national control and supervision finds no counterpart here. A scheme of rather extreme centralization is reflected in their police patterns, with a closely knit bureaucracy recruited from the universities, the Army, the bar, and the minor judiciary occupying to a great extent the higher police ranks and grades.

In so far as comparisons are both possible and illuminating, it may be said that the continental devices, while essentially foreign to those of English-speaking countries, are more closely akin to those of Great Britain than to those of the United States. Certainly we have not developed anything at all resembling an official class. Neither have we made notable progress in offering reasonable assurance of tenure to our police administrators, nor shown any marked disposition to recruit them from an extensive area. We do not provide the interlocking official hierarchies by which regular stages of promotion carry a prosecuting officer to a minor criminal bench and thence perhaps to command of a police force. The concept of an official class has not yet taken root here, and there is no reliable

[6] Sir John F. Moylan, Receiver for the Metropolitan Police District and Metropolitan Police Courts, in *Scotland Yard and the Metropolitan Police*, London, 1929, pp. 56-57. Home Office, *Memorandum on the Subject of Certain Changes in the Organization and Administration of the Metropolitan Police*, *Cmd. 4320*, London, 1933, pp. 4-5.

indication that it will do so in the near future. The matter of tenure, however, is a live current issue in American police administration, and the question of residence qualifications promises to be. Their backgrounds and future implications are therefore matters of some moment.

The Tenure of Police Leadership

It will be observed that throughout the many phases of American police control herein described one feature has often been present. Either by formal statute or by unwritten law, it has consisted in a short official term for the police administrator. The patterns thus established are by no means of exclusive police origin. They are to be found, in some degree of definition, throughout our public services, being most positive and clear-cut in the case of the police and, on the other hand, notably weak in their effect upon the public school systems.

Undoubtedly the device of short tenure has some influence in making democratic controls effective. When police administrators are subject to frequent replacement they tend to respond quickly and easily to changes in public sentiment. If that were the only objective and effect of the method, its utility would come close to being established. But it has other connotations. For example, the foregoing observations tacitly assume that changes in public attitudes are of a reasoned character and that they represent major changes of policy with respect to certain features of law enforcement and police administration. It is a notorious fact that this is seldom the case; on the contrary, public attitudes are in constant flux with respect to many aspects of criminal justice. The popular temper veers this way and that in unpredictable fashion, now being so urgent in its demands for rigid enforcement as to condone lynch law and the third degree, now insisting upon the fullest protection of private rights and personal liberties. It will enthusiastically endorse cleanup campaigns and then through apathy or diverted interest allow them to fail without even being aware that they have failed. It will urge rigorous investigations into police graft, but in jury boxes become the hot partisan of officers on trial for such offenses. Its course is so meandering and uncertain that only over fairly long periods of time can one discern any positive trend in its direction or conclusions. Short official terms are quite as likely to adjust police management to these capricious changes of public opinion as to the well-rounded, considered, and profound convictions of the popular will. Others have sought to adhere to the professional ideal, and to enforce the letter and the spirit of the law without regard to current opinions concerning the desirability of rigid or slack enforcement. If too doggedly pursued, this can produce a wholly unimaginative program untouched by the lives of the people at whom it is directed, and wholly uninfluenced by the popular will.

Leadership Turnover Here and Abroad

The real problems surrounding the tenure of police leadership therefore are concerned with retaining the essential popular controls without reducing the administrator's functions to those of a political weather vane. Probably a majority of police jurisdictions provide tenure at the will of the appointing executive authority. Some have short official terms or offer security of tenure for as much as five years. Others place the police administrator under the protection of civil service systems or of other hard-and-fast devices. which at their worst extend such complete independence to incumbents that they can thwart popular controls. The results under all of these are of an ambiguous nature, much depending upon local political backgrounds and local standards and traditions of the public service.

Taking them all together, and without regard to statutory terms or other formal provisions for tenure, it is apparent that the record of American cities is not an impressive one. A tabulation for 556 cities having between 10,000 and 300,000 population and covering a period of 21 years shows that the average tenure of the chief police official is slightly over four years. For the larger cities, where civil service status is less frequently extended to police administrators, the record is even less satisfactory, being less than two and one-half years in cities over 500,000 population.

Sometimes the changes are kaleidoscopic in their effect. During the six and one-half years of the Walker administration in New York City, there were five police commissioners, and in 1930 alone four commissioners moved in and out of the Detroit police headquarters. Similarly, St. Paul had eight chiefs of police between January, 1930, and May, 1936, only two of whom served more than one year, while El Paso had seven chiefs between 1915 and 1923.

Compare this record with that of any other country and the result is unfavorable. Under the highly centralized bureaucratic systems prevailing on the Continent, the rate of turnover is naturally low. Likewise in Great Britain, where insistence upon popular controls is certainly no less pronounced than it is here, the changes in city, borough, and county chief constables are few and far between. Even in London, where one might expect complex influences to operate to shorten official tenures at Scotland Yard, there have been only 16 commissioners in 130 years, three of whom served overlapping terms during the early days of the Metropolitan Police force. Thus the average tenure has been eight years, as contrasted with a little more than two years in our own large cities.

The greatest immediate need of police service in America is a reconciliation of secure tenure and popular control. For generations the two have been working at cross-purposes. Out of this conflict have come confused thinking and certain official practices which are nothing less than outrageous. From it we get ill-equipped and untrained political birds-of-passage for the command of our police forces, or selection by cut-and-dried methods from among the higher officers of the force, coupled with a tenure so secure that popular controls may be sacrificed· in the process. In the vast majority of cases we are offered a choice between nonprofessional, inexperienced, and temporary administrators, on the one hand, and a permanent professional head who only in rare instances arises above the general level of the force from which he is drawn. To persons impressed by the brilliant administrators who are occasionally secured by both methods, this comment will seem unduly severe. Still the facts justify the generalization, and there is little to indicate that the occasional successes realized under present procedures will in time become so frequent as to be commonplace.

Tenure During Good Behavior

During recent years the opinion of the "better element" in many communities has been crystallizing in behalf of civil service tenure for police administrators, despite the unimpressive record which that method has already produced and despite also the impairment of popular controls which it involves. Viewing all possibilities together, it seems clear that civil service status does not offer any real prospect of solving the more difficult part of our administrative leadership problem. Thus far no satisfactory formal tests for the selection of police administrators have been devised, so that mere security of tenure may be purchased at too great a price. In any event, it will not be necessary to set up civil police dictators who are beyond the reach of popular control, nor to protect official incompetence against vigorous and responsible executive discipline. It will be enough if we profit by our own experience to the end that police administrators are shielded to some extent from the caprices of popular attitudes and emotions, and are accorded some substantial protection against the coarser forms of partisan control.

If the police administrator is appointed without fixed term, and provision is made for his removal by the appointing authority only after due notice of the charge and the right to a public hearing, then adequate safeguards both for the public and for the administrator will have been provided. The grounds for removal should not be closely prescribed or otherwise restricted. It will be enough if the charge and specifications are clearly stated. Whatever the reasons for removal and whether they relate to official acts or to those committed in a private capacity, it is important that the removal shall be effected only after the entire matter has been sufficiently dramatized to capture and hold public attention. More complex devices serve only to confuse popular understanding; but a simple drama consisting of complaint, answer, hearing, and final judgment, will meet with no difficulty in holding public attention for the brief period required to accomplish an orderly removal.

The foregoing proposal will be attacked by political spoilsmen, because it goes too far in protecting the police administrator, and by the civil service reformer, because it does not go far enough. Yet it is in no sense a compromise of these two extreme positions. Essentially it represents the procedure followed by successful police forces in other lands than ours, and in addition constitutes the only major device for reconciling popular control with reasonable assurance of tenure which we have not already tried and found wanting. Its ultimate success will depend upon the traditions that surround it. That is the whole lesson of foreign experience. But traditions cannot be imported nor can they be introduced by statutory or administrative formulae. They must evolve through the years.

Under our existing tenure arrangements the chances are distinctly against any such process of evolution. One does not establish a tradition of tenure during good behavior by swapping police administrators with each change of political administration. Nor does one secure it by the civil service method. The latter merely "freezes-in" the incumbent without regard to merit, behavior, or continuing competence. The illusion of tenure-by-merit is bright, but the substance is not there.

What we need is a real test of the merit system and popular controls. We have no such test now. If the new system fails, it will be because popular control has failed to function and the applied art of self-government has disappeared in America. But there is nothing now to show that this gloomy prospect is before us. On the contrary, powerful civic forces, arising almost spontaneously in communities throughout the land, are now at work for better governmental personnel. If these forces are guided by police experience abroad, and make their influence felt on behalf of a revision of our provisions for police leadership, the foundations of a favorable tradition will have been securely laid. If they fail in this, there is little for us to look forward to but a continuance of the series of drab failures with which we are already familiar, even though there occasionally appears a brilliantly successful police administrator who advances the art and science of police protection to new levels of excellence. But such favorable interludes do not occur often enough to offset the constant drag of the long-established trend.

As matters now stand we use the short official term and uncertainty of tenure as means for assuring popular control, thus placing in the hands of the professional politician—the ward heeler and the fixer—a most effective instrument for assuring political control. In theory our partisan political machinery is a medium for registering the popular will, but in practice the ends and aims of the two are often divergent and the partisan objectives are most commonly realized. So the future of American police administration largely depends upon the prospect for reconciling our established democratic processes with the modern demands upon competent police management.

Residence Qualifications for Police Administrators

Reference has already been made to the fact that the qualifications for police leadership are so broad and so involved with elements of personality—tact, judgment, ability in handling men, resourcefulness, and the like—as to defy clear definition. There is one feature, however, which can be reduced to absolute precision. It consists in requiring that the police administrator, at the time of his selection, shall be a resident of so-many-years' standing within the jurisdiction which he is to serve. This requirement is not by any means universal in our statutes, but either by law or by established practice it comes close to being universal in its application.

Several other influences are constantly at work tending to confine the selection of the police administrator to the area in which he is to function. Most prominent of these is the perfectly natural disposition to deal with known rather than with unknown personalities. The search for qualified leaders in the local community, whether it be a city, a county, or a state, is a simpler, more concentrated task than if extended to a wider area. The local aspirant is more easily checked and appraised than one from a distance. Quite aside from such considerations, the element of local pride will probably always be a factor in limiting the field of choice.

The interest of the dominant political party likewise exercises a major influence. Its success as a partisan organization depends, in part, upon rewarding those who have fought in its ranks, thus excluding nonresident aspirants from any degree of consideration whatever. While such political patterns are by no means uniform throughout police jurisdictions in the United States, they still have a decisive effect in the vast majority of instances.

There is also the well-defined popular feeling, which is especially pronounced during times of economic depression and widespread unemployment, that local jobs, whether public or private, belong to local residents. The effect of this influence upon the selection of police administrators is too uncertain to permit even rough appraisal, but it probably does in some measure control the course of many appointments.

Finally, there is the purely theoretical argument which reasons that a police administrator drawn from among the residents of the community to be served will be more alive to its needs, attitudes, and complex forces than one who is in a sense foreign to them. While this has only a limited direct influence in shaping the conditions upon which a final selection rests, it serves to rationalize and justify the conclusions reached by the dictates of partisan or other interests. It is therefore a matter of some moment to determine to what extent this argument is valid, and whether it should exercise any influence in determining the choice of a police administrator.

It must be conceded at the outset that the argument has some force. If public opinion is to be accurately interpreted by the police administrator, and is to be employed by him in determining the extent and direction of popular control, it seems almost obvious that he will be aided by a thorough familiarity with the community and the standing of its spokesmen. The proposition is so nearly self-evident, however, that it is likely to be accepted and applied without weighing certain qualifying factors. For example, the question of making popular controls effective is not a pressing one in all jurisdictions, nor even in a majority of them at any given time. Thus there are many circumstances in which a nonresident police administrator of superior qualifications may be introduced to a local problem in full confidence that within a reasonable time he will acquire everything necessary to familiarize him with the special attitudes of the community which he serves. There are even situations in which nonresidence may constitute a primary qualification, as when the conflict of opposed interests becomes so irreconcilable that no local figure can be accepted by all parties as a detached and disinterested functionary. Under such circumstances the nonresident appointee actually enjoys a marked advantage in shifting the management of the police force to a new foundation upon which it can stand with greater expectation of popular support.

Diminishing Influence of Local Residence Rule

Owing to the operation of the influences listed above, only a small proportion of American police forces have at any time reached beyond their local boundaries in the search for their administrative heads, but the practice is becoming more and more common as the years pass, with professional policemen moving from one force to another and taking over the general direction of the new command. There have even been instances of the appointment of nonresident administrators, without police experience, to the highest administrative post, though it is unlikely that such cases will ever bulk large in numbers or importance.

Two lines of future development are clearly discernible. One of them is controlled by the fact that the prestige of some of the older state police organizations has encouraged a number of communities, both large and small, to seek their police administrators in these state forces without regard to local residence and with attention directed solely to technical qualifications, probity, and capacity in handling men. Coincident with this there has been some interchange of police administrators among local communities, and here also the tendency is increasingly marked. Much of the interchange has been confined to well-defined regions, but when a police chief moves from Rochester to Miami, and thence to Wilmington; or from Buffalo to Sacramento, one is encouraged in the hope that the tradition of local residence is weakening throughout the nation.

Nevertheless, that tradition, supported by statutory requirement in many jurisdictions, is still the controlling influence in most cases, and while both the law and the custom are probably destined to disappear as major factors in the choice of police administrators, they promise to disintegrate slowly; all this despite the fact that the conditions here described find no real counterpart in other parts of the world.

Residence Requirements Abroad

The high degree of centralization characterizing police service on the Continent avoids at the outset any likelihood of a local residence rule developing. But even in Great Britain, with a police system which, in theory at least, is just as decentralized and just as localized as our own, residence qualifications receive little attention from appointing authorities. In the county forces, as already noted, chief constables without professional police backgrounds may appear, and these have often been nonresidents of the counties for which they were appointed; and even in the cities and boroughs, where a larger proportion of police rise from the ranks to general administrative leadership, there is an impressive proportion of nonresident chief constables. In some instances chief constables have moved from one force to another as many as three or four times, each change being in the nature of a promotion, and each predicated on demonstrated capacity for police administration.

Thus the practice of wide selection is well established in Great Britain, for all its decentralized system. Conditions there clearly have been more favorable to such a development than those with which we in this country are familiar. British party organizations are of a rudimentary character when compared with those of the United States, and expect and receive far less political patronage than do ours. This relieves appointing authorities of the constant pressures exerted here on behalf of the local residence rule. Furthermore, statutes, ordinances, and other provisions formally incorporating the rule simply do not exist. There remains only the power of local opinion to support it, and such opinion, in so far as it is vocal, seems to be more concerned with the competence and character of the prospective chief constable than with the place of his abode during the years immediately preceding.

New American Patterns of Police Control

Viewing the general and more distant background of police leadership in America—the opportunities it has enjoyed, the obstacles with which it has been confronted, and the traditions it has passed along—there is little one can find to commend. For several generations American police administrators came to their tasks without adequate preparation of either a general or a technical nature; assumed their official duties under conditions that implied a heavy partisan obligation; were the willing or unwilling tools of political manipulators; and, when the political climate changed, failed to survive it and were succeeded by others who repeated the same unprofitable routine.[7] So much, at least, is true of the long-range view. If attention is focused directly on the record of the past forty years, a somewhat different and, on the whole, more agreeable prospect is unfolded. For in city after city, and state after state, one finds competent police administrators who through a fortunate combination of circumstances have exercised control over their respective forces for a period sufficiently long to make their influence felt. Some of these have risen from the ranks, some were recruited from other activities than police; but only a mere handful have been immediately succeeded by others of equal or greater competence. Against the general pattern of a thousand organized police forces sprawling across this continent, such occasional and isolated examples of highly successful police leadership may appear to have only slight

---

[7] The record of most other governmental functions is similar, except perhaps in the fields of public education, public health, and public works, which regularly draw their chief administrators from recognized and established professional groups.

significance. Still the trend seems on the whole to be favorable, even though too recently established to permit a sure appraisal of its ultimate extent and effect. So our police future promises to be far more attractive than our past, and if popular attitudes toward police control continue to improve, we may yet see whole regions covered by police forces which are competently and even expertly directed, and which can survive a change of political administration without experiencing a whole series of unsettling, ill-advised, and largely meaningless revisions in the administrative setup.

We may in time even develop a true career service in public administration from which police leadership, among other types, may be recruited. Whether such continental and British patterns can be successfully impressed upon the fabric of American political and social institutions remains to be seen. Clearly the time for their outright adoption has not yet arrived. Current efforts in this direction tend to accept the form of career service without its substance; to offer statutory or other guaranteed forms of tenure under civil service auspices as an incentive; and to destroy the ends of popular control by the very means directed toward its attainment. The realization of a career service for police administrators, as for other fields, must wait upon the orderly processes of gradual professionalization. It cannot be extemporized, nor its fulfillment hastened, without sacrificing the art of self-government to administrative science.

CHAPTER 8

ORGANIZATION

Although police leadership has been subjected to much random experimentation, the problems of administrative structure are often neglected or ignored.

The broad principles of organization that have won such wide acceptance in military and industrial circles[1] find ready application to the structure of police forces. In general, it is their purpose to simplify as much as possible the complex interrelations of any large-scale human venture; to reduce them to some clear and systematic basis; and thereby do contribute toward making the official leadership effective.

When police forces have failed to apply the techniques of organization, it is usually due to one of two causes. In the first place, nearly all police agencies, even the largest of them, have sprung from small beginnings and have only gradually acquired complex structural features. From mere lapse of time, various stopgap and temporary devices come to be accepted parts of the police organism, and procedures grow up around them which resist all but the most vigorous efforts at uprooting.

A second underlying cause of defective police organization may consist in the fact that only in the rarest instances have American police forces been led by men with prior experience in large-scale operations, or by men who have enjoyed a sufficient background of general knowledge and administrative performance to make them aware even of the existence of a problem of organization. The po-

---

[1] Cf. Gulick and Urwick, *Papers on the Science of Administration*, pp. 49-88. An ingenious and illuminating application of the principles of combat to police organization and administration is contained in Colonel George F. Chandler's *The Policeman's Art*, pp. 15-17.

litical influences controlling the destinies of the vast majority of American police forces have not often elevated to the highest command those members either of the police establishment itself or of the community at large who possessed personal or professional qualifications in any marked degree. So it has come about that our police have generally been directed by men who were not prepared to deal with the problems of organization with which they were confronted. To expect solutions under such circumstances is to invite disappointment.

Fortunately, local conditions are not always so unfavorable to the development of a sound structure of police organization, and examples of a more satisfactory treatment of organization problems are increasing in number and significance. Some of this improvement is due to a higher order of police administrator; some of it, to the fact that the new facilities for police communication produce so many new interrelationships that outdated organization structures prove incapable of further piecemeal adaptation, and are completely revised.

Despite such occasional departures, the vast majority of American police agencies continue to function according to patterns laid down several generations ago. If a given police force has grown but little during the intervening years and is still serving a small population in a compact area, the chances are that its structure is still adequate; but if there has been a considerable growth in the numerical strength of the force or in its territorial jurisdiction, there is every prospect that its organization is now so complex as to baffle all but the most resourceful administrative leadership. For in the process of growth there is inevitable specialization, and unless specialized units are carefully fitted into the general scheme of things, they tend to operate independently and without regard to the police program as a whole. Thus minor and casual activities may acquire a disproportionate importance in the plan of organization. Sometimes these unrelated units entirely escape from administrative control and become to all intents and purposes independent, and perhaps rival, agencies. This represents the very antithesis of organization, the ultimate purpose of which is unity of action.[2]

[2] Organization has been defined as the subdivision and arrangement of activities to secure economy of effort through specialization and coordination of work, thereby leading to unity of action. Cf. Urwick, *Executive Decentralization with Functional Coordination* (1935), p. 1.

Stages of Organization Growth

Perhaps the best approach to the problems of police organization can be made by tracing the processes of growth in a police force.[3] The simplest and most common type of American police agency is the one-man police force, such as is found in many rural towns and townships, and in the smaller villages, boroughs, and other incor-

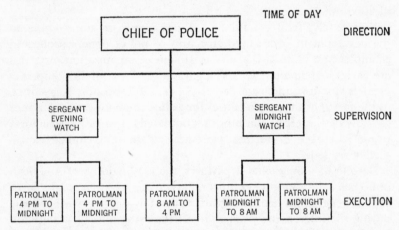

Figure VI   Typical organization of a small force, with subdivision by time of day.

porated places. This lone functionary may be appointed by the mayor or by the village or town board, or may even be elected by popular vote, but in any event he is the sole local representative of law and order. He combines in himself both direction and execution; and may personally cover the entire range of police work from uniformed patrol and traffic regulation, at one end of the scale, to criminal investigation, identification, and crime recording, at the other. The nature of his job may be such that it is not necessary to subdivide, arrange, specialize, and coordinate its several parts; but even though it were necessary, it would not be possible to do so.

[3] The eminent authority on industrial organization, Henri Fayol, declares that "the general form of an organization depends almost entirely on the number of employees." *Industrial and General Administration*, p. 42. While the character of work to be performed also has an important bearing, it remains true that mere size alone produces many problems of organization.

Assume now that the community in question enjoys a rapid growth in population, as has so often been the case in America. In time it reaches the status of a small city in which, as has already appeared, the average strength of the police force is about eight men. At this stage, as shown in Figure VI, some subordination of authority becomes necessary. The work performed by each patrolman may still run the entire gamut of the policeman's art, and the distinction between patrolman and sergeant may rest more upon insignia of rank, length of service, and pay scale than upon any differentiation of work. But if there is any such differentiation it consists in the fact that the higher ranks direct and supervise the tour of duty; that is, there is *subdivision by time of day*.

With further growth in the size of the force some degree of specialization of function is almost certain to develop. Figure VII illustrates how this process of *subdivision by kinds of activity* may take place in an organization which is still extremely simple in its conception.

The arguments for and against specializations have been so widely debated as to require no extensive treatment here. In effect they may be reduced to this: that specialization is desirable in that it permits training in highly developed skills and development of a degree of expertness which could not otherwise be realized. On the other hand, some administrative heads are reluctant to introduce much specialization into their establishments, for fear that it may weaken the sense of responsibility of the individual member for seeing to it that the entire task is performed. This objection to specialization is particularly applicable to police work, which because of its emergency character cannot always be reduced to carefully planned procedures.[4] Yet even the most cautious must concede that there are certain types of police activity which can be reduced to a more or less fixed routine involving such special skills as to invite subdivision along specialized lines. For example, Figure VII shows that three men are assigned to headquarters desk duty, dividing among them the twenty-four hours of the day in three eight-hour shifts. The desk man on duty at any one time is no highly trained specialist, but he does perform certain tasks at the headquarters station which bear at least some relationship to each other and are easily

[4] In any case, mere specialization of function falls far short of the goal, unless there is also specialized training of the rank and file.

distinguishable from the work of the patrol force.[5] As the size of the police force increases, subdivision by kind of activity, with attendant specialization, becomes increasingly common.

A point is finally reached when further attention to the facilities for supervision becomes a pressing matter. In the small force represented by Figure VII, subdivision by levels of activity has not been carried too far. This is a workable scheme until the quantity of work involved in the various specialized operations and the problem of supervision of the number of personnel assigned to those operations require further subdivision. Figure VIII shows a typical organization for a department of perhaps one hundred to two hundred men. Communications and records have assumed a more important organizational pattern, the uniformed force has emerged as a separate entity, and traffic control and detectives are usually subdivided into more specialized squads. It should be clearly understood that local conditions, personalities, and chance all introduce variations in organization; these schematic tables of organization presented herein are not an ideal, nor are they the best in any town or city.

If the territorial jurisdiction of a force becomes so widely extended that it cannot be effectively served from one central point, some degree of *subdivision by areas of activity* may also be necessary. The structural weakness introduced into the organization when this type of decentralization is effected constitutes a persuasive argument against its use except under compelling circumstances; but since such circumstances prevail in all the federal and state forces, and in the larger local police agencies as well, it is necessary to recognize this device. It is applied most frequently to the patrol force, which operates primarily on a basis of area; hence Figure IX is designed to illustrate the specialized organization of a patrol force in a rather large police department. Here the area to be protected is shown as being divided into four police districts, each commanded by a police captain and in each of which the patrol strength is divided into three shifts or platoons. Coordination of the work of the four districts is effected by placing the captains under a supervisory

[5] Such a headquarters detail in a small police force would probably be responsible for the following activities: (1) communications (operating the telephone switchboard and the local radio transmitter); (2) records (maintaining records of crime, criminals, and miscellaneous police services); (3) custody of persons temporarily confined in the police headquarters cell block.

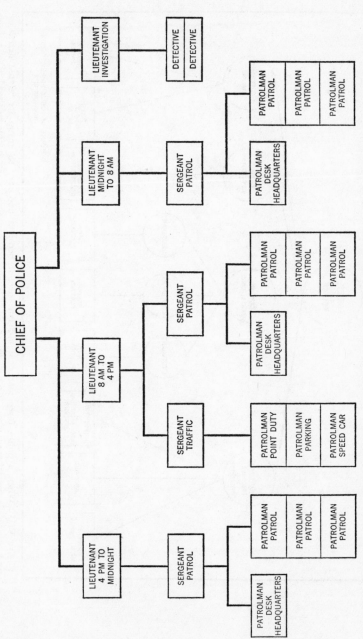

Figure VII Further development of the organization of a small police force, with subdivision by time of day.

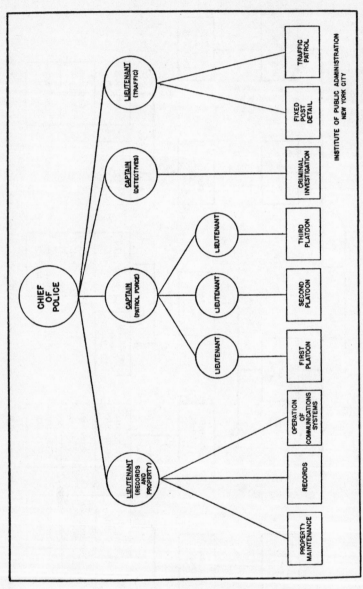

Figure VIII When a police force reaches a sufficient size, it becomes necessary to group its related activities and to provide special supervisors for each group. Such supervisors are directly responsible to the chief of police.

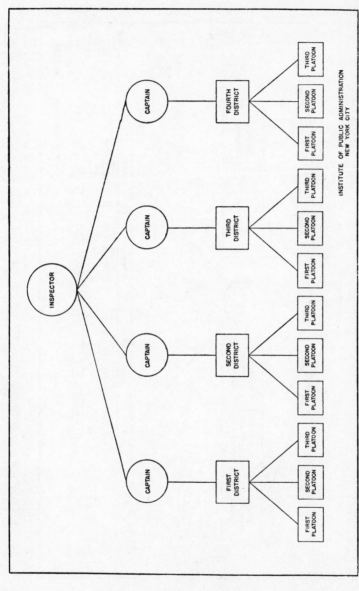

Figure IX Further development in the organization of a patrol force. When the area protected reaches a sufficient size, it may be necessary to subdivide it by areas of activity—that is, by police districts.

INSTITUTE OF PUBLIC ADMINISTRATION
NEW YORK CITY

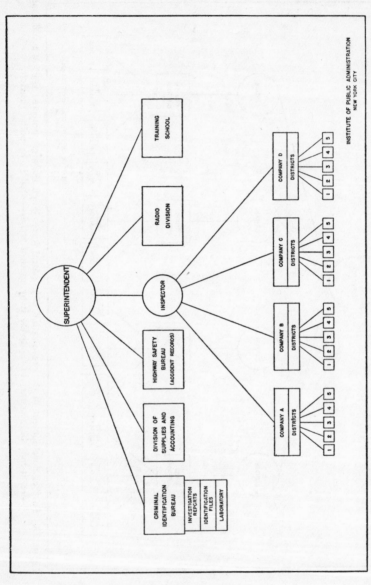

Figure X Organization of the West Virginia State Police. Unusually simple in design and structure because the commander of each company is directly responsible not only for patrol services in his area, but also for criminal investigation, crime prevention, and traffic control. This type of decentralization is especially desirable when large areas are involved.

Within the figure:

SUPERINTENDENT

CRIMINAL IDENTIFICATION BUREAU
- INVESTIGATION REPORTS
- IDENTIFICATION FILES
- LABORATORY

DIVISION OF SUPPLIES AND ACCOUNTING

HIGHWAY SAFETY BUREAU (ACCIDENT RECORDS)

RADIO DIVISION

TRAINING SCHOOL

INSPECTOR

COMPANY A — DISTRICTS — 1 2 3 4 5
COMPANY B — DISTRICTS — 1 2 3 4 5
COMPANY C — DISTRICTS — 1 2 3 4 5
COMPANY D — DISTRICTS — 1 2 3 4 5

INSTITUTE OF PUBLIC ADMINISTRATION
NEW YORK CITY

patrol officer, who is denominated an inspector in Figure IX. In such a scheme the inspector would be an immediate subordinate of the chief of police.

Subdivision by areas of activity may be carried to a point where the number of police districts is too great for one inspector to co-ordinate them all. In that event, additional levels of supervision must be provided. For example the 81 precincts (police districts) into which the City of New York is divided for patrol purposes (1) are each commanded by a police captain; (2) groups of precincts are allocated to some 20 divisional inspectors, (3) who are supervised by 7 deputy chief inspectors, (4) who in turn are directly responsible to the chief inspector, (5) who is an immediate subordinate of the police commissioner. Thus five separate and distinct levels of authority are involved, without counting the subordinate layers existing within the precinct organizations.

These arrangements, necessarily complex for the patrol force in New York City, are followed in almost identical fashion by the detective division, and to an only slightly lesser extent by the traffic division. Even crime prevention is parceled out among local geographical areas of the great metropolis. In no other American city is decentralized organization applied to so many activities, chiefly because New York is unique in the numerical strength of its police force. It is also distributed over an extensive area which in turn is subdivided by large bodies of water. These factors always operate either to encourage or to compel decentralization.

The Span of Control

The term "span of control" is applied to a principle—the concept that one supervisor can control only a limited number of sub-ordinates directly. It is a term used and abused to justify a variety of organizational patterns. Urwick, Graicunas, and others have contended that "no human brain should attempt to supervise directly five, or at the most six individuals whose work is interrelated."[6] The fact is, however, that a span of control of five or six is exceeded frequently with good results in operations wherein the problems of control are minimized by the personality of the supervisors, the quality and training of subordinates, the concentration of sub-ordinates in a single location, the concentration of subordinates by

[6] Gulick and Urwick, *Papers on the Science of Administration*, pp. 52-57.

time of day, and by the similarity of assigned functions. Too narrow a span of control, conditions considered, is as destructive to organizational effectiveness as is a too broad span.

A determination of the proper span of control must rest upon informed opinion in each specific situation, though no doubt a span of five or six is proper in many instances. Many municipal departments of approximately a hundred men have a specialized traffic division, subdivided into squads for enforcement and accident investigation, supervised by a sergeant or an officer of higher rank.

At any moment in time a traffic sergeant may have three or four subordinates actually working, these being spread over the entire city. Experience demonstrates that under these conditions the span of control for the sergeant is too wide due to dispersion, and that better results in supervision must be achieved through supervisors responsible for perhaps more men but concentrated in a smaller area.

As this is written, New York is successfully merging much of the traffic division manpower with the general patrol, thus sharply reducing the manpower assigned to the specialized traffic division.

The other extreme of the problem of span of control is exemplified by the Pennsylvania State Police. That force of 1,900 men is organized into the usual headquarters functions plus sixteen troops located about the state. The troops themselves are grouped into squadrons: five troops in Squadron One, four in Squadron Two, three in Squadron Three, and four in Squadron Four. On the face of it the state police conformed with textbook span of control. In practice, however, the squadron level was no more able to exercise control over its far-flung troops than was state police headquarters; the consequence being that in practice the squadron level was bypassed by headquarters in dealing with the troop commanders. A survey report by Bruce Smith, Jr., recommended a reorganization which would recognize and strengthen the degree of headquarters control.

For the vast majority of American police forces—whether they be supported by cities, villages, towns, counties, special districts, or states—the broad classification of police activities appearing in Table III should prove of some assistance in effecting a preliminary grouping of activities for the purpose of structural reorganization. In small forces, which do not require or permit such complete breakdowns by type, certain of these classes may easily be combined. For example, the records, property, and personnel activities may be grouped together in one unit, and under the immediate supervision of one head; or the patrol and traffic forces may be closely associated for administrative purposes; or criminal investigation, crime prevention, and morals regulation may be similarly combined. Hence the list of major groups of police activities, as presented in the left-hand column of Table III, may be viewed as being subject to consolidation, or to extension.[7]

TABLE III

CLASSIFICATION OF MAJOR POLICE ACTIVITIES[8]

Major Grouping	Related Activities within Each Group
1. Patrol Force	All protective patrols—foot, mounted, or motorized Recording and checking patrol-box calls Patrol wagon service Booking prisoners at district stations Custody of prisoners at district station lockups Operation of patrol and district station records
2. Traffic Regulation	All traffic regulation posts and patrols—fixed post, mounted, or motorized Traffic engineering and planning Accident prevention squads and records Accident records and reports Junior traffic patrols
3. Criminal Investigation	All organized crime detection activities conducted by agencies other than the patrol force: street and general duty details, specialized squads, pawnshop squad Criminal correspondence Crime laboratory Photography of crimes and criminals

[7] The dictum that the span of control must not exceed five or, at the most, six subordinates (cited *supra*) is predicated on the assumption that their work is so closely related that there is constant interplay between them requiring administrative control. If the dictum is valid, the interrelations upon which it rests must be of a more complex character than is encountered in police organization problems. At all events, no difficulty has been experienced by police administrators in extending the span of control to seven or more subordinates.

[8] In some jurisdictions prisoners serving sentences in the city prison or on the prison farm, as well as those awaiting trial, are placed in custody of the local police force. In that event, an additional major activity is created, which proves difficult to adjust to regular police work. The custody of such prisoners involves questions of institutional management and of penology, which are foreign to police administration.

4. Communication and Records Control	Files of crime and investigation reports Arrest records Identification files[9] Central Complaint Room (communication and crime reports center)[10]
5. Property Management	Accounting and payrolls Purchasing Maintenance of police buildings and equipment (including electrical signal systems; telephone, telegraph, teletype, radio, traffic and recall lights, patrol boxes, police vehicles, etc.)
6. Personnel Management	Examination and investigation of recruits Qualification and efficiency records Promotion standards Training Disciplinary trials Police surgeons
7. Crime Prevention	Protective work with women and juveniles Supervision of delinquent boys' activities Juvenile aid programs
8. Morals Regulation	Headquarters squads for controlling prostitution, narcotics, intoxicants, and gambling

Even in a state department of public safety, which is often burdened with duties considered to be extraneous to police work, it is possible so to correlate the various activities that the administrator's span of control is not unduly extended.[11] Nevertheless, despite the recent origin of the state police forces and highway patrols, many of them show defects of organization differing only in degree from those which characterize the older municipal forces. In contrast with such loose construction, some of the state police have organization plans which are models of their kind. The organization depicted in Figure X provides a good illustration of the simple structure possible in a force of moderate size which is required to render police service throughout an entire state. There is ample reason for this simplicity of construction. It will be noted in Figure XI that the number of specialized services is limited. There is no

[9] May be operated as a criminal investigation adjunct if necessary or more convenient.

[10] A general description of central complaint room organization and procedures appears *infra*.

[11] *Report of the Massachusetts Special Commission on Taxation and Public Expenditures, Part VII*, Department of Public Safety (1938), pp. 10-14; Bruce Smith, *The State Police*, pp. 65-72, 111-119.

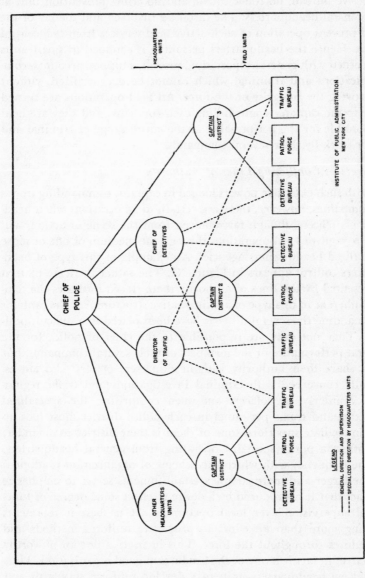

LEGEND

——— GENERAL DIRECTION AND SUPERVISION

- - - - SPECIALIZED DIRECTION BY HEADQUARTERS UNITS

INSTITUTE OF PUBLIC ADMINISTRATION
NEW YORK CITY

Figure XI Generalized chart illustrating a common and inherently dangerous type of headquarters control over decentralized field activities.

detective bureau, no traffic squad, and no crime prevention unit at the general headquarters. The distances involved and the lay of the land prevent operation of such active field services from one central point. Hence the headquarters personnel is confined to small units concerned with general supervision, records, supplies, accounts, communications and training, which cannot be decentralized without destroying the integrity of the force. All field operations are turned over to the captains commanding each company, and they are held responsible for the performance of the entire range of criminal and traffic work by their several commands.

Dangers in Conflicting Lines of Authority

With such extensive powers lodged in captains commanding troops or companies, however, there are certain to be occasions when headquarters officers, though far removed from the scene of action, will seek to control local operations through the medium of one or more specialized headquarters agencies. An example of this type of headquarters control appears in Figure XI. The rather intricate pattern represented by the lines of authority there traced indicates the dangers inherent in this type of administrative structure. For the captains commanding the several districts have been placed in a difficult position. They not only are responsible to the chief of police for the general performance of the members of their several commands, but must share their authority with headquarters officers who are especially concerned with criminal investigations and traffic regulation. Similarly the officers and men comprising the specialized detective and traffic personnel in each police district must look to two immediate superiors—one of them is their district commander; the other, a police specialist operating from general headquarters.

The frequency with which this scheme of organization is adopted by the larger and more complex establishments serves to emphasize the fact that it is produced by a desire to effect some degree of functional supervision over local operations. At its best it represents nothing more than an effort to propagate uniform methods and procedures throughout the force. This in itself is not an unworthy objective; in fact it is one of the products of good organization. Thus specialized headquarters units may develop uniform standards and methods for traffic law enforcement, and for stores control, crime reporting, and a host of other matters. When these have been promulgated by the chief they become the obligation of the district commanders to apply and enforce, subject to an audit or review of results by specialized headquarters agencies. No confusion of the lines of responsibility occurs under such circumstances. That such functional supervision can be effective even with reference to major field activities like criminal investigation has been repeatedly demonstrated, and notably so by the Federal Bureau of Investigation.

But when specialized headquarters officers exercise actual power to direct local operations under any given set of conditions, the chain of command is weakened, administrative responsibility is destroyed, and the morale of the force is soon impaired by the effect of conflicting orders and directions. Much of the fear of specialization springs from this type of situation; from a profound distrust of some of the uses to which specialized techniques may be put, rather than from any failure of specialization as an essential feature of the organization process.

Aides of the Administrative Head

Relatively few police forces provide for immediate aides to the administrative head. In fact, few forces are of a size to warrant such supplementary officers. Even when deputies or assistants are provided, it is rarely indeed that they function as such. Sometimes the deputy performs the duties of chief of police during the night hours; sometimes he heads up a group of auxiliary services at headquarters, or commands the patrol force or detective division. Although such supervisory activities are either necessary or desirable features of a closely knit police organization, they are special in character, and do not involve general responsibilities for planning and execution.

Confusions arise concerning the relation of the deputy or assistant to the chief administrative officer. In some forces the second-in-command is especially designated by the chief and holds this status at the pleasure of the latter. In other cases the rank of deputy or assistant chief is a distinct grade in the permanent civil service, or is conferred by the general executive head of the government concerned. Such differences may not appear to be of basic importance, but under some circumstances they can exercise a far-reaching influence upon the functioning of a police force.

When the deputy is an official creature of the administrative head, the latter is provided with an alter ego who can be employed at will in any and all stages of the administrative process. The aide thereby becomes just so much additional capacity for planning or to be used whenever and wherever circumstances may dictate, and to free the chief from time-consuming details. He may work side by side with his chief and exercise a considerable degree of general command or responsibility or he may work on special assignments, as the exigencies of police management require. In either case, and in any event, he enjoys the full confidence of his superior. When the administrative head is absent from his duties for any reason, the deputy temporarily moves into his place and carries out the general program strictly within the framework already established.

On the other hand, when the deputy holds a permanent civil service rank or is an appointee of the executive head of the government, this relation of full trust and confidence does not always prevail. Even though the deputy accords to his official superior the most complete measure of formal loyalty, the temperaments of the two men may be so different and their customary manner of approaching administrative questions so widely divergent that they cannot work together in that close harmony which their official relationship implies. Under these circumstances the deputy is likely to be assigned to the supervision of an auxiliary or field service, or to a group of such services, and thereby takes a subordinate place in the regular chain of command. In effect he exercises the functions of a deputy only when his superior is absent from duty.

Sometimes, however, the deputy who enjoys civil service status in that rank is so profoundly out of sympathy with the official policies of his chief, or is so actively disloyal to him, that he cannot be entrusted even with a circumscribed responsibility for a given activity or group of activities of the kind normally assigned to superior officers in the chain of command. Under such untoward circumstances the position of the administrative head is most difficult. One recourse for him is to relieve his chief subordinate of all official responsibility of a regularly recurring nature and thereby leave him with nothing more than minor clerical functions. This is sometimes done. But no rule, regulation, or order can deprive the deputy who enjoys full civil service status of his position as first alternate to the chief of police. Let the latter but suffer some temporary disability, or leave the jurisdiction on a holiday or on duties connected with his official position, and the deputy (who may be his rival in every respect) steps into his shoes and at once acquires plenary authority. As acting chief, the deputy may cancel general orders, suspend certain activities, change the structural organization, make appointments and promotions, and apply discipline, to the detriment of the regular regime. The sole method by which the chief can protect himself from such a complex of administrative misfortunes is through virtually continuous presence within the police jurisdiction. Thus he becomes the prisoner of a faulty structural organization.

It is only when the administrative head has power to designate his deputy or assistant, and to remove him, that the essential administrative relationships are maintained with any consistency. In that event the deputy is bound to his chief not only by the usual bonds of undivided personal loyalty, but by what in a practical sense is of even more importance, the ties of self-interest. Owing his place directly to his immediate superior, and subject from moment to moment to the latter's disciplinary powers, the deputy is far less likely to curry favor with higher executive authority in the hope that he may thereby displace his chief. So he is more easily trained to fulfill the latter's requirements and may be entrusted the more readily with the execution of his policies.

It is at this point that a second reason for the complete subordination of the deputy becomes apparent. If the scheme for a routine though temporary succession to the position of command has any rational basis at all, its purpose is to provide continuity of administrative policy during the absences of the commander. Though ill, or disabled, or traveling at a great distance, he is still the responsible leader. For the moment his is the largest stake in the game, and the control which he exercises over his temporary substitute should be unqualified.

So much for the situations arising out of brief absences. In the event of a more prolonged interregnum there may be justification for the executive head of the government, or other appropriate general authority, to intervene in the interests of popular control. Thus in the event that the chief is unable to resume his official duties within thirty, sixty, or ninety days, but is to continue in office, the governor or mayor may be authorized by law to designate an administrative head of the police force ad interim. Executive responsibility and popular control are thereby conserved without upsetting the necessary and normal relationship of chief and deputy as it should exist from day to day.

There are few set patterns or titles determining this relationship. Sometimes the aide bears the title of deputy, sometimes that of assistant. While it would be easy and natural to distinguish between these two in such a way that the status of deputy would imply temporary succession in the absence of the commander, whereas that of assistant would not, no such distinctions exist in fact. Some assistant chiefs are alternates to their superiors, and some deputies enjoy no right of temporary succession. In any case, such vagaries in titular forms are unimportant except as they indicate the lack of precision characterizing both law and procedure in this field.

Several well-organized police departments have no single deputy chief, but rather three or more deputies to command functions: such as a uniformed force, detective division, and administration; or the deputies may be assigned for line or staff supervision under a time of day or area basis. Whatever the scheme of organization, there may be convincing arguments that if a department is large enough to warrant one deputy chief, it may be large enough to warrant more than one deputy chief. Those departments which are organized with more than one deputy, designate one deputy to act as department head when the chief of police is absent. This arrangement offers the department head a choice and latitude in the selection of a representative to effect his policies during an absence.[12]

Application of Organization Principles

The foregoing pages have been concerned primarily with general principles of organization and with their application to certain kinds of police forces. Each such application is necessarily a unique problem, because no two forces are identical in their powers, territorial jurisdiction, or numerical strength. Yet despite such diverse factors, one feature is common to them all; for in the last analysis the question resolves itself into one of complexity versus simplicity. Simplicity in the scheme of organization reduces the number of responsible officers with whom the administrative head must deal, and whom he must at all events control if his policies are to be

---

[12] One of the best discussions of organization was written by Chief William H. Parker of Los Angeles for the *Annals of the American Academy of Political and Social Science,* January, 1954, page 5 *et seq.*

effective. It also reduces to a minimum the conferences, the petty misunderstandings, the personal rivalries, and the open conflicts that serve to retard the efficient functioning of the police mechanism. By means of a simple and direct form of organization, the attention of the responsible head is freed from preoccupation with minor details and from the frequent necessity of reconciling opposed groups within the organization, each standing on its own little set of rights and privileges, each defending its sphere of action from intrusion by a coordinate unit. Such conflicts arise out of ill-defined powers and vague responsibilities. When spheres of action are clearly and boldly outlined in the scheme of organization, the occasion for intradepartmental warfare is removed, and the whole energies of the police force are marshaled, ready for systematic application to the varied forms of police work.[13] When this condition is realized, the administrative head may find it necessary to devote but a small part of his attention to daily operations, and to reserve his energies for the examination of problems which are as yet unsolved, for testing the value of various expedients to which recourse has been had, and for formulating plans for the consistent and orderly development and expansion of the force.

If a police chief's freedom from the preoccupations of petty routine be a test of sound organization, then few American police forces, large or small, can qualify on this ground. It is almost a matter of common knowledge that our police administrators are inundated with a flood of problems which, if not strictly concerned with matters of partisan politics, are of so minor a nature as not to warrant their attention.[14] Whether responsibility for this condition in any particular force rests with the police chief or with the community, it is certain that any effort expended in perfecting the structural organization will reduce the number of minor problems now exhausting the energies of so many police administrators. Large-scale advances in police administration wait upon the event.

[13] The importance of one simple direct plan is emphasized by Colonel George F. Chandler in his monograph, *The Policeman's Art* (p. 16). He illustrates the point by recounting a story attributed to General Sedgwick, of Civil War fame. It appears, according to this yarn, that the general had a fool, a complete simpleton, on his staff, to whom he submitted every order before it was issued. In this way he is supposed to have gained assurance that each order was so clear and so simple that even a fool could understand it!

[14] For a description of a police commissioner's daily routine, see *Chicago Police Problems*, pp. 29-35.

Grouping Related Activities

Meanwhile various other and more immediate practical benefits may be realized by a police force through careful reorganization of its structure and of its organic relationships. So long as police are operated under catch-as-catch-can rules, there should be little expectation that trained administrative leaders will be produced among the rank and file; but the systematic grouping of activities, imposed by observance of the span of control, makes it possible to develop capable successors for the incumbents of the higher administrative posts. Thus if a distinct personnel bureau is set up its supervision will require personal and technical qualifications which are equally well defined. The same is true of property management, which in any given setting is likely to be the most poorly administered of police activities. With the custody of property scattered broadcast throughout the force, and its management entrusted indiscriminately to the officers of auxiliary and field units alike, there is certain to be much preventable waste. Purchases are made at random, specifications are loosely drawn, careless storekeeping results in the destruction of supplies, inventories are allowed to lapse, thefts of gasoline, tires, and police equipment multiply for lack of stores control, buildings deteriorate too rapidly because timely repairs are not made, and contracts for gasoline, printing, and other commodities are entered into without regard for the rates paid by other large-scale enterprises. These faults are mere commonplaces in police administration because property management is so frequently entrusted to police officers who are without experience in the details of business procedures. If, on the other hand, the business activities of the police force are consolidated, the sum total of all such activities may be sufficient to justify the employment of an experienced property manager. Similarly, records administration will come to be entrusted to persons with some degree of clerical aptitude, and of capacity for analysis, while reserving the command of field units concerned with patrol, traffic control, criminal investigation and crime prevention to police officers with appropriate experience.

It is necessary to identify and clarify the problems of administrative supervision if such leadership is to be of a high order. Systematic grouping of related activities in the scheme of police organization is prerequisite to this process of clarification. Economies of manpower and other operating costs frequently result. If related activities are brought under unified supervision, part-time employments are more readily consolidated, and modern administrative processes and the use of labor-saving machinery is expedited.

Anything serving to define the tasks which a police force must perform tends to encourage the recruitment of persons having special qualifications for such tasks. An immediate result is an increase in the number of stenographers, clerks, mechanics, and laborers employed as such, and not as policemen. In most instances the "going wage" for such callings is substantially below that for police, with the result that special talents are secured for less money than was formerly required. Certainly there is no real justification for the practice, now so frequently followed, of using police for all manner of specialized tasks within the police force, as stenographers, clerks, janitors, sign painters, highway lane painters, motor mechanics, auto washers, gasoline pump attendants, dog pound employees, and the like. Employment of an occasional disabled policeman on such work may be a justifiable expedient, but not the regular assignment of highly paid policemen who have been selected, trained, and disciplined along entirely different lines.

Reorganization in Units Large and Small

Other manpower economies may be effected through the flexibility introduced into the scheme of organization when related activities are brought under unified command. So long as each activity operates independently and performs its own auxiliary services, there are certain to be numerous cases of malfunctioning, duplicating effort, lost motion, and just plain loafing resulting from lack of supervision. When related activities are brought together, however, there is an immediate pooling of effective strength and a coordination of effort that is likely to reduce somewhat the demands upon personnel. Added to this is the effect of supervision in stimulating the rank and file to greater activity. As to such economies, it must be stated that they are likely to be relatively more substantial and important when the process of reorganization affects rather small independent units than when the activities thus correlated are of considerable size. This is due to three factors:

1. The small units may engage only the partial services of various individuals whose spare time on the job cannot be employed in

other "independent" undertakings. When these are brought together into a unified bureau, the spare time can be more effectively employed. Losses resulting from such fractional employments are ordinarily less common in larger units, so that correlations of work produce relatively less impressive results.

2. When several small related units are brought together under single supervision, the reduction in lost motion and the advantages derived from the specialization now for the first time introduced are naturally more pronounced than if the reorganization affected larger units which presumably have enjoyed some measure of systematic treatment prior to their consolidation.

3. The stimulating effect of supervision upon small units is more apparent, since such influences have rarely been felt in the past. In the case of the larger activities, supervision has been a necessity from sheer weight of numbers, and hence it is not an added feature when these related activities are brought into administrative focus.

Yet while the issue of economy is likely to promise relatively larger returns in the case of the small forces, in the matter of improved service and smoother functioning, it is sometimes the large and ponderous organizations that profit most. Their very size may prove to be a burden, so that, unless the administrative mechanism which operates them is well adapted to the purpose in hand, there is real danger that they will collapse from their own weight.

Keeping the span of control within reasonable limits may also involve a reappraisal of the need for district stations. These decentralized means for patrol supervision are a necessary evil in large cities—an evil in the sense that they lengthen, and thereby weaken, the chain of command, but nevertheless necessary if the much greater hazards from over-centralization are to be avoided. Such considerations have led in a few instances to a re-examination of the need for numerous district stations, which generally produces the following conclusions: (1) district stations are convenient instrumentalities for decentralizing the distribution and supervision of the patrol force; (2) many districts and district stations were established several decades ago; (3) the new means of transportation and communication make it possible for a station to serve a much larger area than in the days when such districts were first established; (4) the manpower required for indoor assignments at district stations renders such structures surprisingly expensive to operate; (5) the cost of heat, light, and supplies often exceeds $6,000 per annum for each station. The interplay of these factors in recent years has led to a reduction in the number of police districts (with a corresponding reduction in the number of stations) in Cincinnati, Chicago, Richmond, Pittsburgh, Syracuse, Utica, Cleveland, Rochester, New Orleans, St. Louis, Providence, and elsewhere,[15] thus avoiding or minimizing unfavorable features in the structural organization of the police force, and effecting manpower economies as well as other substantial savings in building operation and maintenance.

Control Over Crime Reports and Investigations

Certain to arise in any review of police organization is the question of control over the record of investigations and of auditing the crime reports. While the performance of these two activities holds large potentialities for the administrator, there are still police forces which have not even attempted to introduce or exercise the necessary control procedures.[16] In so far as these revolve around questions of organization they require the establishment of a "central complaint room" which brings together under single supervision the operation of all police communication services and facilities, and the maintenance of systematic reports of crimes prepared at the moment each offense or complaint becomes known to the police. Thereafter the controls are exercised by a coordinate unit concerned with maintaining a complete record both of the complaint and of its investigation. The several major stages in this process of administrative control are as follows:

I. Action by the Central Complaint Room:
    1. Receipt of the original complaint requiring police action.
    2. Immediate transmission of the complaint.

[15] Cincinnati Bureau of Municipal Research and New York Bureau of Municipal Research, *Police Department: Administration, Records and Personnel,* Report No. 5, pp. 2-9 (three districts consolidated); Citizens' Police Committee, *Chicago Police Problems,* pp. 95-101; Bruce Smith, *Chicago Police Problems, An Approach to Their Solution,* p. 28 (two districts consolidated); *A Survey of the Bureau of Police, Department of Public Safety, Pittsburgh, Pennsylvania, 1937,* pp. 37-45 (three precincts consolidated). The police departments of Syracuse, Utica, and Lockport (New York) have abandoned all precinct stations and each now directs its field operations from one headquarters exclusively.

[16] For a detailed description of such procedures, cf. *F.B.I. Law Enforcement Bulletin,* Vol. 9, No. 1 (January, 1940), pp. 3-9; also the serial treatment of *Police Records Systems,* beginning with the February 1948 issue of the *Bulletin.*

(a) To the appropriate field unit, e.g., to patrol cars, district stations, detective bureau, etc.

(b) By means of radio, teletype, telephone, or otherwise, as the nature of the case may require.

3. Preparation of an original memorandum or "central complaint room report" (on a serially numbered and controlled report form) of the facts of the complaint so far as known at this early stage.

4. Routine transmission of the central complaint room report to the crime records unit.

II. *Action by the Crime Records Unit:*

5. Receipt of all reports of investigations conducted by field units (original investigations by patrol car crews, subsequent investigations by detectives, etc.).

6. Follow-up procedures to make certain that *every* report received from the central complaint room is adequately investigated.

7. Classification of all complaints of offenses committed, *in accordance with the facts as determined by investigating officers.*

8. Receipt of the formal official declaration by patrol or detective supervisory officers that the investigation is closed.

9. Preparation of summary statements of operations for the administrative head—an audit of crime reporting and criminal investigations.

Since the foregoing procedures are all aimed at control by general administrative officers, they cannot be entrusted to field agencies such as the patrol force or the detective bureau. Hence all necessary precautions should be taken to assure that one who reports a crime (whether by telephone or in person) is referred to the central complaint room, which has the full communication facilities of the police force at its disposal, yet is not responsible for the success or failure of individual policemen or field units in dealing with crimes and criminals.

The foregoing steps have been described in outline in order to clarify the nature of the organization problems involved. In very small police jurisdictions the entire scale of these services can be performed by the police officer assigned to headquarters desk duty. In large units the scheme of organization will become rather more detailed, as is indicated by Figure XII. The structural arrangement there depicted can be greatly simplified by consolidating closely re-

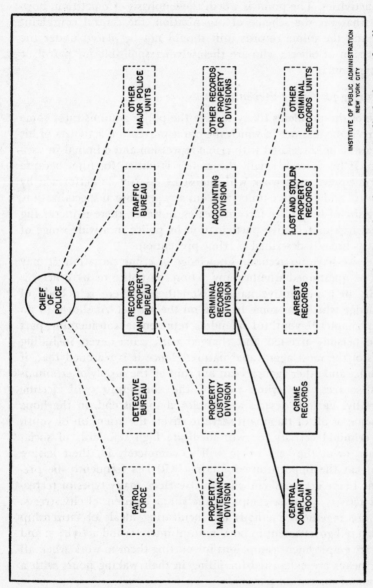

Figure XII Relation of the Central Complaint Room and crime records units to a generalized scheme of police organization. The units shown in solid line have a direct bearing upon control over reports of crimes and criminal investigations, and are independent of field units such as the patrol force or detective bureau. In small forces these arrangements may be greatly simplified.

INSTITUTE OF PUBLIC ADMINISTRATION
NEW YORK CITY

CHIEF OF POLICE

PATROL FORCE

DETECTIVE BUREAU

RECORDS AND PROPERTY BUREAU

TRAFFIC BUREAU

OTHER MAJOR POLICE UNITS

PROPERTY MAINTENANCE DIVISION

PROPERTY CUSTODY DIVISION

CRIMINAL RECORDS DIVISION

ACCOUNTING DIVISION

OTHER RECORDS OR PROPERTY DIVISIONS

CENTRAL COMPLAINT ROOM

CRIME RECORDS

ARREST RECORDS

LOST AND STOLEN PROPERTY RECORDS

OTHER CRIMINAL RECORDS UNITS

lated activities. The point is worth the emphasis of repetition, however: whatever the scheme of organization, the central complaint
room and the crime records unit should not be placed under the
supervision of officers who are themselves responsible for patrol or
investigation.

Organizing for Crime Prevention

One of the problems likely to give the police administrator some
concern is the manner in which the crime-prevention activities of his
force are to be correlated with crime repression and criminal investigation. If his force is small, the matter is settled for him, because
the crime-prevention work will almost necessarily be performed by
the patrol and detective units, without any pretense at specialization.
As the size of the police force increases, however, there is increasing
interest in a more active participation by police in a wide range of
activities broadly described as crime prevention.

Since we have no accurate knowledge of crime causation, it may
fairly be questioned whether any action, by police or by others, is
actually of a preventive nature. Nonetheless, there is a body of
knowledge which has some bearing on the subject. As shown in an
earlier chapter,[17] youthful offenders represent a considerable part
of the persons arrested and charged with crime, even including
crimes of the most aggravated nature. Hence it is reasoned that, if
the police and other agencies can but shut off the supply of criminals
at its sources, the crime rate of the community will decline
materially. Various devices are employed to this end, in the hope
that some or all of them will serve to divert the attention of youth
from criminal activity, or will inculcate high standards of social
conduct, or at the very worst, will so completely fill their leisure
hours that the opportunity for crime will less frequently be presented. There are boys' clubs in great variety, many types of recreational activity, summer camps for the young denizens of city streets;
there are ingenious methods for inculcating ideals of citizenship
through self-government in boys' natural interests and activities; and
there are employment campaigns for putting them to work when all
other means are exhausted for filling in their waking hours with a
program of supervised play.

As to all such efforts, one feature stands out: they are concerned

[17] Chap. 2.

with youths in the mass and not with youthful offenders as such. This basic fact would seem to dispose of the question of active police participation in such community programs, since it is estimated that only 2.5 per cent of the rising generation constitutes any serious problem for the police.[18] It is with this one child in forty that police should be concerned rather than with the generality of young persons, the overwhelming majority of whom are living normal lives as self-respecting members of a law-abiding society.

Yet even when these delinquents and predelinquents are duly identified and tagged, the opportunities for preventive work by police are none too clear or numerous. There is probation, it is true, but this is usually administered by the criminal courts; rarely or never by police. There is family case work and there are the procedures for dealing with defectives, but these are techniques lying within the proper sphere of the public agencies concerned with welfare and mental hygiene. Truancy, which is sometimes a forerunner of delinquency, is primarily a school problem and is dealt with as such. Where, then, is that portion of the crime-prevention field that is particularly suited to cultivation by police? While opinions on this point are certain to differ widely, there are two items upon which all should be able to agree. Places of commercialized recreation, such as amusement parks, dance halls, and the like, are likely to involve contaminating influences with which police, as general enforcers of the criminal law, are bound to be concerned. Experience has shown that women armed with the general authority of police can often patrol and regulate such establishments more effectively than most men. Hence some of the larger forces include women police on their regular rosters, not only for work of this specific type, but also for the entire range of police activities involving women or children in any respect—everything, indeed, from women criminals, prostitutes, and wayward minors to child vagrants, runaways, and peddlers.[19]

Another accepted field of police participation consists in maintaining contact with the school, welfare, health, probation, and parole agencies and with civic bodies, which taken together represent the totality of the public concern with the delinquent and predelinquent. Three hundred or more such composite groups, known

[18] Vollmer, *The Police and Modern Society*, p. 200.
[19] Hutzel, *The Policewoman's Handbook;* Owings, *Women Police.*

collectively as coordinating councils, exist in cities and villages throughout the land—in communities varying in size from the great City of New York to places of only five hundred inhabitants.[20] These constitute a necessary part of the police program because they deal either with actual delinquents or with probable delinquents, or with related agencies in juvenile work, with the activities of which the police should at all times be familiar.

If the program here briefly described appears much too modest to cover the possible approaches to crime prevention, it should be remembered that duplication of the proper work of other public and private agencies should be carefully avoided. Many of the crime-prevention and juvenile-aid activities now being conducted by police forces throughout the country overlap when they do not actually compete or conflict with the work of others. Police may conduct athletic contests, amateur theatricals, playgrounds, employment services, and many other parts of a broad public welfare program, without often coming to grips with problems directly and necessarily related to the police function or dealing with matters which clearly fall within the scope of their own experience and competence.[21] The one thing that comes closest to their proper sphere—the supervision of convicted offenders who have been released on probation and parole—is denied to them.

So it may be that the problem of organizing police work for juvenile aid and crime prevention is no problem at all, and that the greater part of it can be handled through the regular personnel on active duty in the field, supplemented in some cases by a police-women's unit or by other special auxiliary services.[22] General instruction of all ranks in the length, breadth, and character of the juvenile delinquency problem seems a far more promising angle of approach than a program of extreme specialization which may end by escaping from administrative control altogether. Such evasions of control

[20] For a description of the work of these community coordinating councils, cf. National Probation Association, *Community Cooperation for Social Welfare* (pp. 47-76) and *The Community Approach to Delinquency Prevention* (together with a selected bibliography at p. 153).

[21] Cf. *The Police Yearbook* (1938-1939) for the *Report of the Big Brother League Committee*, pp. 203-208; *A Boy Scout Program as an Aid in the Police Juvenile Problem*, pp. 209-212.

[22] One of the more complex and widely ranging of juvenile aid services is described by O. W. Wilson in *The American Journal of Medical Jurisprudence* (January 1939), Vol. II, pp. 1-8.

have occurred often enough to give the police administrator pause,
whereas general treatment by the entire force, when specially
instructed in the subject, holds no such concealed dangers.

Control of Commercialized Vice

Among difficult problems with which police forces have to deal is
the regulation or suppression of the various forms of commercialized
vice—prostitution, gambling, and the sale of narcotics and intoxicating beverages. The time is probably still far distant when public
opinion on all four of these activities will have crystallized sufficiently
to permit an orderly treatment of them by police and other agencies
of justice. Meanwhile the confusion of popular attitudes greatly
complicates the task of enforcement, with the so-called "standards of
public morality" in a constant state of flux. Not only do these
standards undergo numberless changes, but there is often a vigorous
demand for strict enforcement as to narcotics and prostitution at
the very time when public opinion is demanding a relaxed enforcement of the restrictions imposed by law upon gambling and intoxicants.[23]

This ever-changing problem of enforcement sometimes has a bearing upon the organization of a police force, because it requires a
considerable flexibility of administrative treatment to meet the
rapid shifts of popular temper. Such flexibility is difficult to secure
in a police force that has been instructed to look to the penal laws
for the true expression of public policy. So police administrators
have set up specialized vice divisions, either from considerations of
this character or because they desire to keep the corrupting influences
of commercialized vice confined to a particular segment of the force.
In large cities and in forces operating throughout extensive areas,
a point is sometimes reached where no headquarters unit can
possibly function effectively with reference to the whole gamut of
vice control. There then follows a whole series of decentralizing
and recentralizing stratagems. The vice squad is abolished and uniformed patrol units are made responsible for enforcement. Inevitably
this introduces a period of uncertainty, because the degree of enforcement and the emphasis on this or that regulatory statute will

[23] Shifting popular attitudes are well reflected in Woolston, *Prostitution in
the United States;* Fosdick and Scott, *Toward Liquor Control;* Harrison and
Laine, *After Repeal.*

differ in each patrol area. If charges are made against police, the administrator is likely to investigate them through the medium of a new headquarters unit, perhaps specially created for the purpose. Thus undercover squads and "shooflies" are introduced into the scheme of organization, to the detriment of police discipline.

After the process of centralization and decentralization has gone on for some time, a compromise may be struck which seeks to combine both methods. Responsibility for enforcement is laid upon the patrol force, but a headquarters squad is also maintained either for the purpose of checking up on such decentralized enforcement or as a means of conducting raids with a minimum of danger that their character and direction will be made known in advance to the parties operating the premises to be raided. Often, too, an element of specialized technique is involved, since a headquarters raiding squad can maintain special resources of information and also become experienced in meeting special judicial requirements as to evidence.

While new combinations of procedure and administrative structure are constantly being invented for vice control, these represent their major phases. At no point is there success in sufficient degree to warrant persistent application of any one method, because the underlying conditions for effective enforcement are not favorable. Vice is often the natural ally of local political machines, which in turn interpret the popular will and operate the police force in accord with that interpretation. Meanwhile popular attitudes become confused, and juries reflect the unwillingness of large parts of our cosmopolitan populations to observe the rigid requirements of some of our penal statutes. Rural standards are foisted upon urban communities, which retaliate with such flagrant lapses in enforcement that they are reminiscent of the wide-open towns of the advancing frontier. Thus each police administrator works out the problem as he finds it in his own jurisdiction and adjusts the structural organization of the force to meet current demands made upon it for vice control. If his force is able to function satisfactorily without the aid of a special squad for this purpose, so much the better. The ultimate responsibility for law enforcement is not then confused by setting up a new administrative agency to meet each new feature of the crime problem.

The Prospect of Overspecialization

Since all organization depends in some measure upon the subdivision of tasks, and therefore upon a degree of specialization in executing them, there is a continuing danger that this phase of the process may be overemphasized. Some administrators become so obsessed by the need for developing ever-higher skills through breaking down existing jobs into more highly specialized techniques that they eventually produce an organism dependent upon expert operation in all its details. Others arrive at an equally unfavorable result through the uncontrolled establishment of new administrative units for the performance of each new activity. In either event a dangerous situation is created, and particularly so when an emergency service like police is concerned. In many situations, whether the staff expert is on hand or not, police must act and act quickly. If the functioning of the force, or any major part of it, is to be made dependent upon closely articulated action by a number of specialized units or bureaus, the failure of one may destroy the effectiveness of all. While such difficult situations cannot be wholly avoided, since there is bound to be some degree of interdependence, all experience indicates that the police administrator will do well to subdivide police activities only when necessity clearly points the way. If selection, training, and discipline have in fact produced a rank and file of superior quality, simplification of police tasks through minute subdivision will become less and less necessary.

Particular care is required when units directly and actively concerned with law enforcement are involved. The basic and familiar subdivision of a police force into patrol and investigation units is a case in point. Nothing could be more obvious than this kind of separation, with its attendant differentiation between the uniformed and the detective personnel. Yet many a police administrator has viewed the collisions arising between his patrol commanders and his chief of detectives, together with the bitter rivalries these produce among the rank and file, and has wondered whether his force was in fact a unified body or was divided into two hostile camps.

It is a widely held belief that special aptitudes are required for the conduct of investigations, and that the average patrolman lacks the qualities deemed essential to the work. Therefore, the uniformed patrolman is expected merely to suppress or discourage crime; but once a crime is committed, particularly if it be a felony, the detective bureau is to be called upon to take charge of the case. The patrolman returns to his beat and resumes his routine duties. He is in the first line of defense, but when that line is broken the matter passes beyond his jurisdiction and sphere of responsibility for further action. It is for the trained investigator then to follow through to the end. So runs the line of reasoning, which rests upon the familiar proposition that there should be special aptitudes and special training for the performance of special tasks.

In its application this theory is beset with certain difficulties. At the very outset, for example, the administrator is confronted with the fact that there is no swift and certain method for testing aptitude for criminal investigation. Patrolmen are either transferred in and out of detective work in an effort to determine their relative capacity, or they take a civil service examination for detectives and thereafter become the one thing or the other. Meanwhile detectives go their own ways, operating in a sphere where the ordinary administrative checks and disciplinary methods do not apply, enjoying an almost unregulated discretion in the use and application of their efforts, and sometimes thrown largely upon their own resources. The patrol force observes this freedom, and resents it. Thus are engendered official rivalries which are inimical to good teamwork and hold grave danger for successful administration.

The problem has been variously dealt with. In some instances effort is made to bridge the artificial gap between patrolman and detective by assigning the patrolman who engages in the close pursuit of an offender to any later investigation conducted by the detective force. Others seek to break down the barriers of overspecialization by a more or less constant interchange of personnel between the patrol and investigating branches. Some of the state police have in large measure escaped from the dilemma entirely by turning all investigations over to the patrol force in the first instance, and supplementing their efforts with specialists and technicians of established qualification.[24]

Thus the never-ending shift between generalization and specialization of function goes on—in patrol, criminal investigation, traffic

---

[24] Cf. Smith, *The State Police*, pp. 204-214.

regulation, and other phases of police work.[25] While the increasing complexity of that work strongly favors the specialist, experienced administrators are alert to the dangers in this tendency and strive to maintain flexible arrangements whenever specialized techniques threaten unity of action.

Experienced police administrators also recognize that with few exceptions specialization in assignments invites political interference: appointments are almost universally treated as a form of patronage. As vacancies appear for specialized assignments the politicians within and without the department each offer a deserving candidate to the appointing authority. Unfortunately, the net result of specialization is too often a proliferation in specialist assignments for policemen whose friends constituted their only qualifications for the assignment. Due to the all but universal treatment of special assignments for patronage, those police departments which have attempted to work with a minimum of specialization (such as the Vermont State Police) are less troubled by intra-departmental rivalry than are such overspecialized departments as San Francisco.

Organization and Leadership

The theoretical and practical advantages to be derived from rigorous application of organization principles cover a wide range— so wide, in fact, as to invite the observation that good police management depends upon a sound structural plan. Still it must be admitted that much impressive evidence runs counter to such a sweeping conclusion. Some police forces standing high in the scale of administrative quality would make but a sorry showing if ranked according to their application of organization principles. These appear to succeed because of the joint operation of two factors or influences: (1) the centripetal forces set in motion by almost every human undertaking, even though the leadership may be weak, and the plan of operation uncertain; (2) the strenuous efforts put forth by many vigorous police leaders to keep the several parts of their administrative machines functioning in accord with a common purpose.

Thus even unsound plans of organization can be applied toward

[25] Inspector L. A. Hince of the FBI has superbly presented both the problem and its solution in *Police Responsibilities in Traffic Law Enforcement*, Eno Foundation Highway Traffic Conference Proceedings, 1944, pp. 17-20.

a successful result, particularly if the police force enjoys inspired leadership. If this could be secured with any high degree of consistency, problems of organization might with more complacency be left to solve themselves. But all police experience shows that the selection and retention of capable leaders is as yet one of the weakest features of American police control, and so long as this is true the structural outlines of our police forces will continue to be important to the success of large-scale programs for police improvement.

CHAPTER 9

MUNICIPAL POLICE PATROL
SUPERVISION

During the past twenty years there has been a growing problem in American policing: street supervision. At a time when police recruits were "given a badge and a gun, and put to work" the experienced street sergeant or lieutenant was the sole source of professional knowledge. The recruit, perhaps awed by an initial contact with a semimilitary organization, was receptive to training and discipline. In addition, the work of the street supervisor was comparatively simple insofar as locating the patrolman on post was concerned. The primary reliance upon foot patrol for watchman service limited the patrolman's post to well-defined limits, and it was a serious breach of department regulations to leave the post for any but the most pressing reasons.

Traditional Methods

The active street supervisor relied upon two basic supervisory techniques to train and control foot patrolmen: overt observation, and covert observation. On occasion the supervisor might walk a beat with his subordinate to observe conditions requiring police action, to observe the manner in which these conditions were handled by the subordinate, to instruct the subordinate in police technique, and to encourage the often lonely and discouraged officer to persist in his efforts to preserve the public safety. At other times street supervisors resorted to less obvious methods of control: observation of the patrol from comcealment, the use of simple traps to assure thorough patrol, and a frequent contact with citizens who themselves observe and evaluate police performance.

Older police officers still recall the friendly competition between the street sergeant and his subordinates to assure (and evade) adequate supervision. Each patrolman had a "hole" to which he retired for rest and comfort, although an alert eye was always necessary to detect the street supervisor in good time so that the appearance of active patrol could be maintained. If street supervision did not succeed in all of its objectives, at least a sincere attempt was often made, and the level of performance reflected the success of the attempt.

Supervision Is Essential

Virtually every police chief in the country today bewails the lack of effective street supervision. Almost universally the blame is laid at the door of the street sergeants, though a moment's thought will suggest that each level of command up to the highest in the municipal structure of government must be responsible. Wherever the fault, all recognize the need and the failure.

Street supervision establishes the chain of control between the police chief and his numerous and widespread subordinates. It is essential to effect the will of the chief, as the best thought-out administrative efforts can be frustrated by inferior performance, dishonesty, and laziness at the operating level. It requires no belabored argument to present the sorry fact that at different times and places policemen have been thieves, drunks, bullies, grafters, and worse. Less spectacular, but nonetheless serious, is the patrolman who loafs on duty, ignores requests for police assistance, or who fails to find and report on continuing violations which can be found and corrected by diligent police work. None of these faults are approved by the police themselves; they develop and persist for want of adequate supervision.

Street supervision is training, and properly applied can be a complete substitute for much formal training. Also, in matters relating to patrol technique it is the best type of training, as the street supervisor can know the specific hazards of an area and the means to cope with them far better than can a department-wide school in a large city, or an academy conducted by some distant department or unit of government. In fact, department-wide training of patrolmen can seriously undermine the authority of street supervisors by substituting a foreign doctrine for that which they may develop through local experience. An effective program for training by immediate supervisors is an assurance of satisfactory patrol performance; while a training program which bypasses street supervisors can be justified only on the grounds that street supervision has failed so abysmally that only shock methods can avert an imminent collapse of police service.

Street supervision is essential to morale. Men want to be observed by superiors when an assignment has been properly performed, as they expect action to be taken against fellow officers who fail in an assignment. Excellent patrolmen and investigators express discontent when their best efforts go unnoticed through the laziness or inept performance of supervisors. Recurrent violations of department rules of good procedure (if they remain uncorrected by supervisory action) also have a demoralizing effect upon men who have persisted in proper conduct at inconvenience to themselves. Much of the policeman's work is concerned with the seamy side of society. Arrests made at some personal effort and perhaps danger may be negated by improper administrative or judicial action. Victims of adversity, not too unlike the police officer himself, may be driven along an unhappy road by the stupidity of official or social agencies. There is boredom and discomfort to police work, occasionally punctuated by extreme demands for stamina, courage, and intelligent action. All of these problems which exist to some degree in every police department in the nation create the need for active and understanding street supervisors who can explain, and place them in perspective for operating personnel.

Causes of Slack Supervision

Apparently there are complex causes for the failure of street supervision during the past twenty years: an unwillingness by supervisors to perform a supervisory function, an inability of supervisors to adapt their techniques to the demands of motorized patrol and restrictions upon effective administration. These causes are all but universal, and have been met and corrected in but a few individual cases.

The unwillingness to supervise is rooted in a fear of censure from subordinates and from elected superiors. The urge to be popular, to avoid unpleasantness, to be a friend to all men has become a ruling passion with many. The fact that frequently promotions and special privilege have come to men who have pursued this popular policy has convinced its numerous devotees that they have discovered the secret to professional advancement. The New York City police commissioner has decried the prevalent attitude of supervisors toward their responsibilities as being the cause of a series of scandals in that department. Norfolk, Virginia, and San Francisco, California, have also experienced scandals attributable to slack supervision.

At least a portion of the blame for slack supervision stems from World War II. During the war thirteen million Americans experienced military leadership and discipline and were exposed to the workings of big organizations. Perhaps not surprisingly these men grew accustomed to crude, gruff methods of leadership and became correspondingly cynical. The dislike of such treatment leads men who have experienced it to disavow hollow and pretentious methods of leadership in their postwar callings, either as applied to themselves or applied by themselves. These were the men who were recruited to police forces in great numbers following the war, and today they are the men who are and will continue for some time to be in supervisory positions in police departments.

Yet a third important cause for the breakdown in leadership has been the increase in restrictions placed upon police administrators by state and local civil service laws. Intended as a protection to the police service against persecution for individual political convictions, civil service commissions and trial boards have tended to protect the policeman from the consequence of his misdeeds. Continued on a force with a reprimand or nominal suspension for drunkenness, brutality, or even murder, a policeman is a negation of all that supervision should stand for. It is little wonder that police administrators and supervisors have become discouraged about establishing discipline when their most aggravated offenders are returned to duty with back pay by civil service trial boards. That spiteful persecutions by politicians are undesirable to the police service is clear; but it is also clear that supervisors without the authority to discipline have been thus shorn of an essential power.

It is probable that the voting public is neither informed nor interested in the powers accorded to police administrators. Reliance has been placed upon reform movements and slogans whose vocal advocates are more familiar with textbook solutions than with the requirements of a semimilitary organization whose members are so frequently exposed to temptations. Few police administrators have had sufficient conviction to make a full effort to recover the authority essential to leadership.

The influence of police associations and unions has been by no means consistent, but has varied from time to time and from place to place. Many chapters of police associations still oppose any police administrative authority except their own: they have purposefully aimed to destroy the authority of leadership through laws and through pressure tactics. This is the traditional attitude of the past several decades.

There appears to be a new trend among police associations to back a stronger authority for the police leaders. At least a few union and association leaders now recognize the need for discipline and leadership, if only to prevent scandals which adversely affect the aspirations of the profession for higher pay. This trend back to strong leadership can and should be encouraged by police administrators by a fair and impartial exercise of disciplinary authority.

The demands and difficulties of supervising motorized patrols have with but few exceptions been insuperable. Given a willingness to supervise, traditionally foot patrols and stationary posts have been adequately supervised. Supervision of motorized patrols has been inadequate in all but a few jurisdictions. In the vast majority of cities, foot patrol has dropped in the number of men assigned to near the vanishing point. The extremes of weather characteristic of the eastern and midwestern portions of the nation have caused patrolmen themselves to prefer a motorized assignment to a foot patrol assignment. In addition, the far higher productivity of the motorized patrol in all types of police activity has favored the motor patrol. In the more moderate climate of the West Coast and South, patrolmen often prefer a foot assignment, but the demands for police service within a reasonable cost still dictates primary reliance upon motorized patrols.

Thus the primary method of police patrol today receives the least supervision, even from street supervisors who desire to perform the responsibilities of leadership. Actually the problems and objectives of motorized patrol supervision are the same as those for foot patrol, but they have assumed a different form. Patrol cars are normally assigned to a sector of the municipality for patrol and watchman service, but may be dispatched to any part of the city to answer a citizen's call for assistance. Specialized units such as accident investigation or traffic control may disperse a few motorized patrols over a large area for their specific function. Due to the large area in which they operate, motorized patrols do not lend themselves to as convenient supervision as do foot patrols.

However, the need for supervision of motorized patrols is of paramount importance as they bear the load of police activity and must cope with a variety of calls for assistance, prepare reports, and still maintain the semblance of watchman service which is a traditional responsibility of police patrols. The motorized patrolman should be superbly trained by both formal and direct supervisory methods; he should be closely supervised as a part of that training; and he should be carefully observed to assure administration that the public safety is being properly served.

Essential Equipment

While the most common bars to effective street supervision are unwillingness and inability, a few cities have additional obstacles to effective supervision of motorized patrols. In San Francisco, California, none of the street supervisors of the uniformed force even have an assigned car. While that city permits the supervisor some latitude in supervisory technique, it has denied the captains, lieutenants, and sergeants of the districts the primary tool of radio car supervision: a radio-equipped sedan for the supervisors. In consequence the captains and lieutenants characteristically remain in the district station throughout.the watch performing nonessential police functions at best. By and large the street sergeants in the districts perform routine foot patrol, ignorant of the activities of the motorized patrolmen who are at least nominally subordinates subject to their control and supervision. Perhaps needless to mention, San Francisco experiences serious disciplinary and performance problems in the uniformed force.

Other cities such as Chicago assign street sergeants to regular patrol vehicles to work with a patrolman on normal and routine calls. While under favorable conditions the assignment of a supervisor to work with a patrolman may yield excellent results, it is clear that the supervisor-subordinate relationship must be maintained. This relationship cannot be retained if the sergeant must work with the same officer without rotation, and if he is not free to leave his patrol to supervise other members of his command at will. In practice, street supervision in Chicago has become nonexistent.

The more normal equipment for street supervisors is a radio-equipped sedan for the street sergeant or lieutenant. With transportation and communication the supervisor can observe the activities of foot and motorized patrols, and with the radio he can communicate with his motorized patrols. In addition, the supervisor can hear and respond to calls for police service. He can call cars to him by radio for consultation, or he can establish a point for observation while protected from inclement weather and while still in radio contact with all that occurs.

Common Modus operandi of Supervisors

Throughout the nation the operational pattern of the street supervisors is often the same. At roll call the supervisor checks the attendance, reads a list of stolen auto plates and missing persons, and relates any incidents in the area (such as a recovered bicycle, break in, or vandalism) and dismisses his patrols to their posts. Then, climbing into a radio-equipped car alone, most street supervisors devote the remainder of their tour to cruising as especially privileged patrolmen; driving about the streets awaiting a radio dispatch to summon one of their patrols to perform a service. If a call stirs his curiosity, the street supervisor may also respond to assist the patrol car if required. At the end of a tour few street supevisors take any definite action to assure that all personnel are still fit for duty. In fact, a common practice is for street supervisors to end their day's work before their subordinates end theirs, placing reliance for dismissal upon the supervisor of the oncoming tour.

Common Failings of Supervisors

The most common failings of street supervisors are:

a. Neglect of their responsibility to see that subordinates carry out their assignments. Supervisors often take over such duties themselves, making all the arrests, issuing the summons, or directing traffic. This is a denial of all that justifies higher pay and privileges for the supervisor.

b. Favoritism is common, and justice between subordinates is fitful.

Punishment is often administered to the group rather than to the individual responsible for the infringement of the rules.

c. No real effort is made to assure that the assignment is understood and that it is properly carried out by subordinates. This is characteristic of all levels of police command, up to and including many police chiefs.

d. Few will take responsibility for their actions, especially in the higher command ranks; thus destroying the bond of loyalty.

e. Lack of emotional control by supervisors, evidenced by intemperate outbursts of anger.

f. Protection of subordinates from deserved disciplinary action.

Although supervisors are selected by the most various means, and for diverse reasons, all consider themselves competent leaders of men. Further, all supervisors assume that they are liked by their men, and that they know their men. Since few persons in or out of the police service will disabuse a supervisor of his competence, an appeal for proper supervision too often falls on deaf ears.

Direction of subordinates is the core of supervision, it is the reason for supervision, and it is the only justification for the higher pay accorded supervisors. Yet the street supervisor who actually directs his subordinates by any means is rare. Granted that there is wide latitude allowable in supervisory technique; that some supervisors might lead through personal example, while others might prefer group conferences, friendly suggestion, or direct orders; still by whatever method, the supervisor to justify his rank should make his will apparent.

If the supervisor can increase the effectiveness of each of ten men by 10 per cent, he has thereby increased the public safety far more than if he had himself been the most effective patrolman. This direction of others is difficult, however, and the vast majority of street supervisors find it an easier and more congenial self-assignment to continue to be the patrolman-watchman.

The second serious shortcoming of supervisors is their failure to assure that the assignment is understood and that it is properly carried out by subordinates. It is an especial weakness in the higher levels of command: police chiefs often utilize periodic staff conferences as a substitute for on-the-street observations of the day-to-day operations of subordinates. It is aggravated by an inclination at all levels of command to issue orders which cannot be properly executed: the order being intended purely to pass responsibility downward. An excellent example of this latter inclination is shown at hundreds of roll calls in police departments around the country when patrolmen are instructed to be on the lookout for a too great multitude of occurrences. Were the crews to receive these orders as binding, and to faithfully execute them until directed to desist, the entire police patrol effort would be negated by special service watches. The use of discretion in issuing orders is essential to establish their importance, and thorough follow-up is essential to assure that orders are executed.

The cardinal requirement of leadership is fair dealing with subordinates. In police practice favoritism most frequently shows itself through assigning desirable details to friends, and the unwanted "special details" to non-favorites. Many police departments accord a daytime assignment to favorites, with or without regard to seniority or the need for the assignment; while others arrange the hours of assignment of favorites to coincide with their needs in connection with outside work or interests.

The supervisor who exercises his powers with discrimination in favor of his friends is being politic. On the surface it might appear that to help one's friends, at the expense of other members of the command, is good practice. Actually, it is the reverse, for the gratitude of friends may be weak as compared to the ire of the offended. In addition, favoritism renders the supervisor open to charges or innuendo of political bias.

The three remaining enumerated shortcomings are failure to assume responsibility, lack of emotional control, and protection of subordinates from deserved disciplinary action. Basically they represent an unhealthy attitude on the part of supervisors—an attitude which can and should be corrected by their superior. The first and the last stem from a fear of upsetting present conditions, while emotional instability is a psychological problem which can be suppressed.

Some Exceptional Supervisors

While the majority of police street supervisors are unwilling or unable to exercise supervisory control, a few have developed the desire and the methods for good supervision. It is to these leaders that we may look for the progress and professional development of the municipal police.

While no two leaders will ever use identical techniques, there are noticeable similarities between successful police leaders. These similarities may be categorized as: personal character which inspires respect "as a man"; ambition to excel; a determination to accept full responsibility as a supervisor and "get the job done properly"; and the fortitude to withstand the attendant criticism.

The personal character of an effective leader of policemen inspires respect in the men. Added to the usual honesty, sobriety, courage, tact, humility, and so forth is the need for fair dealing with all men, and the ability to meet all men on an equal footing. The very essence of professional policing is an impartial administration of justice. A man with a naturally subservient personality is not qualified for either leadership or enforcement. Men who are too talkative do not appear to become good and respected leaders, nor do those who show nervous impatience, or who court favor openly with superiors and subordinates. The very nature of leadership seems to require a character compatible with some personal self-sufficiency: a willingness to stand alone against odds.

The drive to get the job done shows itself in several ways. Effective leaders of policemen train themselves through reading and personal observation. Accepting such formal training as their department may provide, successful leaders are energetic in improving their own professional knowledge. An inquiring turn of mind and a healthy skepticism reveal to the supervisor the falsity of numerous commonly accepted bits of "knowledge." By the same token, however, the effective leader knows sound procedure, details of the traffic and criminal codes, and specific requirements for the policing of his own municipality or area.

To utilize available manpower effectively, an active supervisor determines in advance of the need the time required to properly patrol a shopping center, housing project, or traffic hazard. Such knowledge cannot be acquired from texts; it is the result of personal observation and trial. This useful knowledge is difficult to acquire, but it is collected by supervisors who really have the drive to get the job done.

Training of subordinates is a second aspect of the drive to get the job done. Effective supervisors have utilized roll call as a brief period for training, although most rely upon on-the-street conferences. One successful street sergeant (later promoted to night supervisor) arranged to meet subordinates periodically during their tour, using the police radio as necessary, and thus spent fifteen or twenty minutes with several subordinates during each tour. This sergeant directed his subordinate to park his radio car and to sit with the sergeant with the latter's police radio in service. The training then might be based upon a specific problem: such as what should be done if an armed man were in a particular warehouse. The discussion which followed would be both instructive and constructive. Teamwork in an emergency was being assured by advance planning and instruction.

Another active supervisor, a lieutenant (later a captain), utilized the routine visits to district stations as an opportunity for the training of desk officers in the requirements of arrest. By reviewing the known evidence against prisoners in the lockup he was protecting the department against charges of improper detention at some future date.

To train subordinates in observation and patrol technique one street sergeant spent an appreciable time riding with each man. In the course of normal motorized patrol the subordinate would be trained to observe those things which police experience suggests deserve special observation and investigation. A motorized patrolman can be taught to observe auto license plates, arrangements of business establishments, suspicious persons, and so forth.

The handling of complainants or criminals on calls is taught by supervisors who are concerned with effective operations. The usual procedure is for the supervisor to respond to a call to observe the procedures of the assigned subordinate. Though the temptation may be strong to correct mistakes as they are made, experience has demonstrated that better results may be expected if the critique is handled later and in privacy between the supervisor and his subordinate. Difficult or dangerous calls may be handled by the supervisor directly, his manner serving as training for subordinates by example.

An essential aspect of getting the job done is the inspection to assure that it is done properly. A supervisor who instructs his men to check a parking lot periodically, himself may wait near the lot to see whether his order is carried out. There is nothing difficult or complex in checking on a subordinate's performance of an assignment, but it is essential to effective supervision. The lack of follow-through on assignments is especially noticeable in the higher ranks, lieutenants and captains too often being content to direct sergeants to execute all aspects of supervision. In at least one southern city a director of public safety has achieved commendable results working through his police chief yet still retaining the faculty of personal observation and evaluation of results.

A part of getting the job done is the identification of, and proper action against, subordinates who violate laws or rules. In a smoothly functioning department this aspect of supervision will receive continuous attention by administration. The pattern of discipline seems to be universal: after a period of years of slack supervision the number of major disciplinary cases falls to the vanishing point. With a new leadership the number of disciplinary cases may increase ten or twentyfold in response to tighter supervision. In time (perhaps two or three years) the number of major disciplinary cases declines to a normal level; the worst offenders having been weeded out, and the remaining personnel convinced that a violation of a rule involves a risk of disciplinary action.

The methods used by successful leaders to prevent infractions of the rules, or violations of laws, are merely a repetition of the direct inspection to assure compliance. Subordinates are inspected daily before and after their tour to assure sobriety and appearance. They may be observed covertly to determine their honesty, and they can be observed in the course of normal supervision for alertness. Successful leaders do these things regularly and purposefully, as a part of the effort required to get the police job done, to assure the public safety.

It was a state police trooper in Pennsylvania who named the lethargy which paralyzes individual initiative in large organizations: he called it "being herd-bound." The term is startlingly accurate, and it describes a too prevalent condition. Whatever his attitude at recruitment, the policeman gradually may become convinced that the safest course is to follow the group in anonymity, never rising above the level of contemporaries sufficiently to be noticed. If through the workings of the promotional process he is placed in command, too many still fear to be outstanding in any respect.

Effective leaders are subjected to social pressures by the herd, by some superiors, and often by politicians. Pressures may take the form of "friendly" advice, of derogatory remarks, or of family ostracism. Much of the fear of social pressures from the herd is unfounded. The group recognizes the need for leadership and respects members who assert it. Politicians, too, can recognize devotion to duty as a merit, and virtually all of the effective supervisors with whom we have been acquainted have received promotions and recognition. The fire of ambition is essential to create and maintain a true supervisor.

Organization for Supervision

The role of organization in accomplishing supervisory control is confusing and controversial, principally because sound organization cannot assure performance results. Still, the grouping of men and activities into a controllable unit is necessary to aid otherwise competent supervisors to achieve control. The balancing of the factors which enter into a workable scheme of organization is dependent upon detailed knowledge of the municipality and the state of training of its personnel. It thus follows that no one pattern of organization for the uniformed patrol will be satisfactory in each city, but rather that the scheme of organization can be suited to the need.

While the larger police departments in this country characteristically assign enough or more than enough sergeants, lieutenants, or captains to office positions, by and large these departments assign too few positions to street supervision. It is not uncommon for one street supervisor to have ten to twenty assigned subordinates, distributed about an area of many square miles. In the most populous precincts of the largest cities, such as New York and Chicago, the area assigned to one street supervisor is small. However, the police problems of the most active precincts still demand a full measure of supervisory effort; they are seldom oversupervised.

Too many subordinates, too scattered in terms of travel time, minimize the effectiveness of supervisors. Probably there is no definite limit to the span of control, either in terms of the number of subordinates, or in terms of area. Clearly a supervisor can adequately control more foot patrolmen than men in radio cars, more men in two-men cars than in one-man cars, and more men in quiet patrol areas than in active areas. On the other hand, rivers, railroads with but few crossings, open spaces, and even a congested traffic area may all work to reduce the effective span of control of a street supervisor.

A related trend in the reduction of street supervision has been the reduction in district or precinct stations. The reasoning behind the closing of many precinct stations was sound: they were expensive in upkeep, they absorbed a disproportionate share of manpower for desk assignments, and the decentralized facilities for citizen service, police gathering, and criminal lockup were minimized by the telephone and the radio-equipped sedan. No doubt in many cases the number of patrolmen on the street from small precincts was so small that street supervisors would be severely tested to invent supervisory activities which would occupy their tour.

In consolidating districts or precincts at least some cities have at the same time reduced street supervision. A counter trend is now appearing in such progressive departments as that in Richmond, Virginia. In that city the patrol area has been divided into segments, each segment being assigned to a street sergeant, and patrolled by four to six patrolmen in one-man radio cars. Thus five or six street sergeants may be working on each tour, in a city of a little over 200,000 population; though the city of Richmond has but two precinct stations.

An important aspect of organization is the rotation of tours by supervisors and patrolmen, commonly accomplished each month or twice a month. A practice has developed, often under the urging of politicians, of allowing an individual supervisor to devote only a third of his time to a particular group of patrolmen. This is accomplished by rotating the supervisors at different times or in a different direction from that of the patrolmen (when the patrolmen change biweekly from the evening tour to the day tour, their supervisor would be changing to the midnight tour). The argument for rotating supervisors counter to the patrolmen has been that it prevents frictions between supervisor and subordinate from festering for too long. Unfortunately, counter-rotation of tours also breaks any semblance of a supervisory relationship: sergeants are reluctant to correct and train patrolmen who are not their especial responsibility. Capable supervisors can and will exercise supervision only if they are to spend an appreciable period of time with the same group of men: say a year or more. Unusual friction between supervisors and subordinates can be handled by individual consultation and sometimes transfer.

Supervising the Supervisors

Often obscured in discussions of street supervision is the role of the men who supervise the supervisors: the lieutenants, captains, and other officers up to the police chief. The common work pattern in large departments is for lieutenants to be considered in command of each tour, the street sergeants being subordinate. In practice, however, the mode of supervision of many lieutenants is to remain in the station house, sometimes acting as desk officer, at other times without assignment. A few active lieutenants do attempt the street supervision, but largely in duplication of the work of the street sergeants. The principle that station lieutenants are responsible for the training in supervision of their subordinate sergeants has not even occurred to most lieutenants. Yet the entire concept of a chain of command rests upon the acceptance of responsibility at each level of command: without the responsibility there is no justification for the command level.

In large departments the uniformed force is divided into districts or precincts, while in smaller departments the uniformed force will be under the command of the police chief or one of his immediate subordinates. In either event, the pattern in American policing is for the district captain or police chief to work only on the day tour, limiting night supervision to occasional visits to his command during the evening hours.

A police supervisor in command of an activity or area is not limited in his responsibility by the time of day. For so long as the police problem exists the supervisor is responsible for the steps taken by subordinates to meet the problem. It is on this basis that the common lack of night supervision by district captains and police chiefs is to be condemned. Again, a district captain, an activity commander, or a police chief who ignores the operations of his command for two-thirds of the time has broken the chain of command which is assumed to flow from the highest officers in the city to the newest patrolmen.

To circumvent captains and lieutenants who will not supervise their subordinates many medium-sized and large departments have resorted to staff supervision from the chief's office. Whether called inspectors, deputy chiefs, night chiefs, or by some other appellation, the purpose of these staff supervisors is to provide around-the-clock supervision which is not being secured through the normal command channels. As a stopgap measure the positions are often both necessary and justified; but they tend to weaken the levels of command which they are intended to circumvent. Given adequate line supervision, the staff supervisors should be utilized only as silent observers to the chief: never to issue orders, never to assume command, but rather to serve as representatives of the chief of police in an inspection capacity.

Special Unit Control

The preceding discussion of street supervision is concerned primarily with the uniformed patrol, as that arm normally constitutes at least half of total department manpower. Also, the uniformed patrol force is involved in all of the police activities, including those which also receive attention from specialized squads or bureaus.

The spectacular increase in automotive traffic during the past fifty years has led virtually all police departments into establishing a specialized traffic division to direct traffic, to enforce moving and parking regulations, and to investigate auto accidents. Some traffic divisions also undertake traffic engineering and related studies. Likewise the fear of sensational disclosures of vice conditions has prompted virtually all police departments of even moderate size to establish vice squads to suppress gambling, narcotics, liquor, and sex violations. The pressure of local social agencies and sometimes the local juvenile court have forced the creation of youth or juvenile bureaus to investigate offenders in particular age brackets, and to conduct patrols into locations of juvenile congregation. The specialized detective division is, of course, a unit of traditional standing.

The problem of organization and supervision of these specialized units: traffic, vice, juvenile, and detective, is aggravated by the relatively small number of personnel involved, and the fact that they will at least nominally be assigned to a large area. The division of a city into traffic, vice, juvenile, or detective districts is a seldom used approach to supervision, although the activities may be appended to the normal uniformed force district station organization. More frequently these activities are broken down into squads, such as accident investigation, solo motorcycle, three-wheel motorcycle, and intersection control (for traffic); or (for detectives) homicide, burglary, robbery, pawnshop, stolen auto, and so forth, on into combinations which are different in every city. Unfortunately the subdivision of specialized units seldom achieves an increase in supervision. Unit chiefs almost universally surround themselves with clerical details and telephones, thus precluding any effective work on the street supervision of their assigned activities.

Adequate supervision of specialized units appears to depend upon frequent personal observation of the subordinate by the supervisor, and continuing evaluations of the work produced by the subordinate. The techniques of personal observation of specialized units may be substantially the same as those utilized in supervising the uniformed force. The evaluation of work accomplished can be done on a comparison basis with other subordinates with similar assignments, but only if the supervisor has the underlying knowledge of the subordinates acquired through personal observation. Investigating officers may have their success in conducting and clearing investigations reviewed against national averages; but these statistics are not conclusive. A burglary detective might possibly be credited with a fantastic "cleared by arrest" record if a criminal confessed a series of burglaries to other investigators, perhaps in another city. On the other hand, an excellent investigator who was assigned to the most difficult cases might appear statistically to have a poor arrest record; though a review of the case investigations might well indicate commendable thoroughness and technique.

The Future

Looking to the future of municipal police street supervision there appear but few rays of hope for improvement. No college or university teaches even the rudiments of supervision, nor does any academy or professional school. Superior officers, whose primary duty is the training of subordinate supervisors, all but universally ignore their responsibility: treating rank as one of the good things in life, not to be marred by the assumption of responsibility.

On the hopeful side of supervision is the rising recognition of need, by police administrators as well as some police association chapters. A few individual supervisors have had the fortitude to develop and apply sound street supervision techniques; and in several departments active supervisors have been rewarded with promotion and increased responsibility.

CHAPTER 10

CENTRAL SERVICES

At the first general meeting of American police administrators, held in St. Louis in 1871, effort was made "to procure and digest statistics for the use of police departments,[1] . . . to provide for a systematic plan of transmitting Detective Information throughout the several States of the Union,[2] . . . to adopt a system of [telegraphic] cypher for the use of police throughout the country,"[3] to arrange for a more complete interchange, among police departments, of the photographs of criminals[4] and to effect the permanent organization of the National Police Association.[5] Thus, at the very outset of formalized relations among the police forces of this country, emphasis was placed upon ways and means for performing certain common services for the benefit of all. It is both interesting and instructive to observe that these initial efforts aimed at cooperative action were concerned with criminal investigation, identification, police communications, and criminal statistics. These four fields still constitute major objects of cooperative activity, though a fifth, and equally important, item has been added to the list of common services, in the form of the great training centers now emerging.

The ninety years that have elapsed since American police forces first sought a way through and around the jurisdictional barriers still separating them do not mark a period of consistent growth in cooperative police action. On the contrary, little was accomplished for

[1] *Official Proceedings of the National Police Convention*, St. Louis, Mo. (1871), p. 30.
[2] *Ibid.*, p. 55.
[3] *Ibid.*, p. 69.
[4] *Ibid.*, pp. 73, 97-98.
[5] *Ibid.*, pp. 80-83.

several decades beyond the formation of a number of state federations of police and a gradual strengthening of the national body.[6] These did not in themselves constitute significant departures. During their early years they contributed almost nothing to the policeman's art, nor did they undertake to solve the interjurisdictional problems arising on every hand. It was not until the turn of the century that joint police action became a reality. The new means of transportation then coming into general use were dispersing and intermingling the criminal population in ever-widening arcs, and it was becoming apparent that the old method of distributing criminal information by means of printed handbills could never hope to cover a patchwork of police forces numbered by the tens of thousands.

The First Central Service

To meet this situation the International Association of Chiefs of Police in 1896 set up a national clearinghouse for criminal identification records. Originally located in Chicago, it was transferred some years later to Washington, D.C. The primary purpose was to provide central filing facilities for the photographic portraits of known criminals and for the system of anthropometric measurements devised by Alphonse Bertillon in 1882. Gradual abandonment of *Bertillonage* after 1904 and the substitution of fingerprint classifications greatly handicapped the growth of the new bureau, which was thus constrained to cultivate new fields without abandoning the old. Nevertheless, it enjoyed mounting annual accretions as more and more cities contributed their identification data to the central office. During these early years the National Bureau of Criminal Identification was supported by the annual fees paid by less than 150 police forces, supplemented by an occasional appropriation of $500 by Congress. Its budget seems never to have exceeded $5,000 per annum and often fell far below even this modest figure. With the continuing support of a mere handful of police forces it somehow persisted. The point is important because it is illustrative of the fact that some of the specialized federal, state, and regional police services which have since sprung up in such great numbers have

[6] In 1893, the National Police Conference was reorganized as the International Association of Chiefs of Police, in which an overwhelming proportion of the membership is drawn from the United States and Canada. The active membership exceeds a thousand police officials, with representatives drawn from every state.

been developed largely through police initiative and effort or in response to demands made vocal by a few of the official police agencies. Thus the national clearinghouse for criminal identification has a dual significance: it represents the first systematic attempt at cooperative activity in American police work, and in its origin at least was solely the result of local police enterprise.

1. CRIMINAL IDENTIFICATION AND POLICE SCIENCE

Sheer overriding necessity produced the first clearinghouse for fingerprint identification. Here was a program depending upon unity of action over a wide area. Only the fingerprint collections of the great cities were sufficiently large to justify management by identification experts. The great mass of persons in police custody either were not fingerprinted at all, or the prints when made were placed in collections so small as to lack significance and value.

This was the situation when the International Association of Chiefs of Police entered the field. The importance of this first venture into cooperative activity can scarcely be exaggerated, because it marked the end of the suspicious isolation that had characterized local police operations from the earliest times. At the moment of their inception the new facilities were not too impressive. As already noted, their financial support was uncertain and could only be maintained at inadequate levels by a more or less continuous membership campaign. The central collection during this period was not of a size to compare with those of the largest cities, so it had no comprehensive service to offer to prospective members in return for their fees and voluntary contributions of fingerprint records. Some of the largest cities kept severely aloof during this period of testing and thereby diminished the new venture's already small chances of success.[7] While it did not then succeed in establishing itself as a truly national clearinghouse, it managed to survive during this testing period so that recourse could be had to it when more favorable conditions prevailed.

Such conditions were in the making. A few states were already appropriating funds for central identification systems, consisting

[7] The New York City Police Department at that time wished to operate the nation-wide clearinghouse for identification. Precedent was to be found in the Criminal Record Office for England and Wales, which is operated in London by the Metropolitan Police.

chiefly of the prints taken from prisoners in the various prisons, penitentiaries, and reformatories, but supplemented also by such other records as local police administrators could be cajoled into contributing to the central files. Being tax-supported, there were no large uncertainties concerning the financial outlook to plague them, and in some cases their positions as state-wide clearinghouses were confirmed by enactments requiring all penal, correctional, and police agencies to file identification records at the several state bureaus. Their powers were thereby broadened to a point where the only restrictions rested upon territorial jurisdiction. Carried to its logical conclusion, this method would have produced forty-eight state identification bureaus, which then might possibly have banded together in opposition to any nationwide program.

A National Clearinghouse for Identification

While these various state developments were taking place, the police chiefs' association was engaged in negotiating with federal authorities to the end that the latter should maintain and operate the rudimentary clearinghouse already established for the country as a whole. This was accomplished in 1924, and shortly thereafter the association's identification records and files were consolidated with those of federal prisoners maintained at Leavenworth, Kansas, and both systems thereupon transferred to the Bureau of Investigation[8] in the Department of Justice. The prestige of the new setting, and the vigor with which federal officials administered the work and publicized its results, soon revitalized the whole undertaking. Illustrated pamphlets and popular treatises on fingerprint identification techniques were distributed broadcast to even the smallest police unit. Free identification forms and franked envelopes for their return removed the last apparent obstacle to full local participation, with the result that fingerprint identification is now firmly established as an essential police function, even among sheriffs, constables, and other police of brief official tenure.

In addition to its criminal files, the national identification division maintains noncriminal fingerprint records voluntarily contributed to police forces throughout the country by law-abiding persons who

---

[8] Now known as the Federal Bureau of Investigation. It received formal statutory authority for conducting the central identification work by act of Congress in 1930.

seek in this way to show their support of "universal fingerprinting."[9] Also important for purposes of central record are the single fingerprint records of many thousands of known kidnapers, extortionists, bank robbers, and notorious gangsters. These are of special value in identifying persons who leave the "latent" print of perhaps only one finger at the scene of a crime, and hence cannot be traced through the regular classifications of ten fingertip impressions maintained for general identification purposes. Other data include a classified collection of unidentified ammunition and various descriptive files of missing persons and certain types of stolen property. Thus the basis is being laid for a central exchange for many types of information of value to police inquiries.

Growth of the national identification system under federal auspices has since been so extraordinarily rapid that in the course of but a few years it became the largest fingerprint collection in the world.[10] All this was accomplished without the aid of federal statutory provisions imposing upon local police officials the duty to submit identification records to the national agency—a compulsory feature which is barred in any case by the limits of federal jurisdiction. Some states, however, require that police shall file their fingerprint records with both state and federal clearinghouses, and even in those instances where such formal requirements are lacking most police forces are alert to contribute, while the several state identification units generally undertake to keep the federal files supplied with the data which comes to each of them individually. Thus nationwide consolidation of our identification resources, involving many tactical difficulties and a few technical problems, has been accomplished in substance through cooperative efforts by federal, state, and local authorities.

State vs. Regional Clearinghouses

Some problems still remain. For example, it is not yet clear what is to be the ultimate role of the state bureaus, such as are maintained in some form by thirty-four states. About one-half of these conduct a full criminal identification program within their own territorial

---

[9] These civil identification records in 1934 numbered only 600. Fifteen years later they exceeded 5 million.

[10] The FBI Division of Identification has a total of almost 34 million prints in its criminal file, plus 120 million others of a noncriminal character.

jurisdictions and as far outside thereof as they can attract contributions to their files. To that extent each of them duplicates the work of the federal clearinghouse. Whether in the long view this will prove to be a desirable course in all states is debatable. It may be argued, though not too convincingly, that all state bureaus should be retained, since otherwise any abandonment of the federal facilities would leave the states and the country as a whole in the situation existing fifty years ago. It does not seem reasonable, however, that the state governments should burden themselves to insure against so remote, improbable, and wholly incalculable an event. The disciplinary effect of the state bureaus should also be considered. As already indicated, they alone apply the compulsory reporting statutes to the various police agencies, and their departure from the scene might conceivably result in less satisfactory reporting to the central agency, though this likewise is highly speculative. Again, there is the fact that eighteen of the state bureaus are operated by active state police forces maintaining hundreds of men on patrol and conducting investigations throughout the length and breadth of their several jurisdictions. They would in any case operate their own identification services, even though they did not have the addiitonal responsibility for conducting a state-wide clearinghouse. Hence the cash economies to be effected by abandoning them would probably be so inconsequential as to argue their continuance under any ordered scheme.

Finally, there is the very special situation of the states located at a great distance from the seat of government at Washington, which upon occasion may experience unavoidable delay in securing the visual proof of identity from the national files. Some states now seek to minimize the effects of distance by operating their own identification systems so that local police forces within their boundaries may be less dependent upon the remote federal agency. Whether this expedient is justifiable may be questioned, since modern means of communication offer many ways, which are in fact often employed, of quickly reporting the results of identification searches to police authorities. The full visual proof of such identifications need not be immediately forthcoming.

Still another angle of approach has received some consideration. It would require the federal identification system to operate one or more regional offices, thereby obviating the disadvantages arising either from delay or from incomplete state records. Whatever merit this recourse may possess, it would not seem to be justified unless the states in the region to be specially served were to abandon their own identification systems. Otherwise, the present overlapping of clearinghouse facilities would be aggravated still further, with national, regional, and state bureaus all seeking to serve the same area. Absurd as this situation may appear to be, it is unlikely that the rival interests which have sprung up on all sides will easily give way, so that there is a possibility that the nation, from having too few central identification facilities, someday may find itself embarrassed with too many.

Identification Services for Groups of Communities

Regional approaches to the question of identification have also been made at the local police level, but rather for the purpose of rendering the basic local identification services than to provide regional clearinghouses. Thus, when the Cincinnati Police Department undertook to provide central identification facilities for the police forces in Hamilton, Butler, Warren, and Clermont counties in Ohio and in Campbell and Kenton counties in Kentucky, only five police forces in the region maintained fingerprint and photograph files, and 142 forces were wholly without them. A regional identification bureau conducted under police auspices was naturally welcomed, and has since flourished.[11] It has doubtless prevented many of the local forces from attempting to maintain their own identification services on a piecemeal basis.

The advantages of substituting one identification unit for many are obvious. Hundreds upon hundreds of such regional identification services might be set up throughout the country if the local police forces in each county or region could be prevailed upon to use central facilities rather than try to maintain their own. Thus the regional identification service, now no longer a new device, promises to provide a test of the adaptability of our traditional police system.

Central Laboratory Services

Closely related to personal identification is the matter of determining the quality and significance of various traces left at the

[11] Bruce Smith, *A Regional Police Plan for Cincinnati and Its Environs* (1931), pp. 24-26.

scene of a crime. It is only within the past generation that chemistry and physics have been brought to the aid of criminal inquiries. Numerous unrelated laboratory procedures, known on the Continent as *Police Scientifique* and in English-speaking countries as *Police Science,* now have been developed to a point where they are of major importance in the investigation of certain types of crimes.

Police laboratories had their origin in Europe, sometimes operating in conjunction with medicolegal institutes which in turn were affiliated with the universities, sometimes being conducted under the direct auspices of police. But in Great Britain and the United States police were slow to accept the new methods, partly because of the decentralized police systems prevailing in both countries, partly from a profound skepticism of the value of such refined methods of inquiry. Hence the first well-equipped police science laboratory to be set up on this continent was not established by police, but by private interests in Chicago, working through Northwestern University. This was in 1929.[12] In the course of the next ten years, the entire status of police science in the United States was radically revised, and its prospects for future development greatly enlarged. The Northwestern University laboratory was acquired by the Chicago Police Department, and police forces throughout the length and breadth of the land now vie with each other in the acquisition of laboratory equipment and technical staff. In short, police science is now widely, and often generously, supported from public funds.

So much at least is true of most of the large forces and of many others of moderate size. In the small units, however, there is no prospect of developing the new techniques of investigation, and hence there is continuing need for more central facilities. The crime laboratories set up by the large forces, both municipal and state, represent the most convenient means of satisfying that demand and since 1933 the Federal Bureau of Investigation has placed the unusually extensive facilities of its own laboratory at the disposal of investigating and prosecuting officers.[13] The service of the state laboratories, like those of the FBI agency, are available without cost to local police forces within their several jurisdictions.

[12] For a description of the events leading up to the establishment of the Scientific Crime Detection Laboratory, see the *American Journal of Police Science,* Vol. I (1930), No. 1, pp. 3-4.

[13] The scope of the FBI Technical Laboratory, and the facilities which it emphasizes, is indicated by the summary of its work for the year ending June 30, 1958, found on page 268.

Members of the laboratory staffs necessarily serve as expert witnesses upon occasion, and since such services are rendered without cost to the prosecuting authorities, the practice tends to raise the dignity and increase the reliability of expert testimony, the disinterested character of which may otherwise be clouded by pecuniary considerations.

Thus the situation with respect to laboratory science in the service of criminal investigation is somewhat similar to that of the older identification techniques. Where local enterprise is lacking or there is only irregular or insufficient demand for laboratory examinations, the police of some of the large cities, and particularly those of the states and of the federal government, have been quick to satisfy the need. As the extension of formal training programs to the smaller forces brings more and more of the local police to an understanding of what laboratory tests can do in aid of the investigator, the demand for such services may be expected to increase appreciably. It may then become necessary to fix responsibility for performing laboratory analyses more clearly than is now the case. However, the probabilities are that the state and federal laboratories will continue to operate over wide areas, with the laboratory services of the great cities largely confining their operations to the metropolitan districts immediately surrounding them.

There has been a growing trend among the medium-sized state and municipal police departments to establish their own crime lab-

[13] (Continued.)

Biochemical	2,572	Petrographic or geologic	3,419
Biological	779	Pharmacological	248
Charred paper	23	Photographic	161
Explosives	374	Portrait parle	16
Fibers	2,804	Radio and electrical	57
General chemical	1,099	Secret writing	147
Glass fractures	53	Shoe print	633
Gunpowder	318	Spectrographic analyses	4,406
Guns and ammunition	2,691	Tire tread	219
Handwriting and hand		Toolmarks	3,176
printing	75,833	Toxicological	287
Indented writing	304	Translation and special	
Ink and pencil	309	examinations	43,925
Metallurgical	282	Typewriting and other	
Number restoration	83	mechanical impressions	7,518
Obliterated writing	1,336	Miscellaneous	10,564
Paper	1,826	Total	165,462

(These involved examination of 137,142 specimens of evidence.)

oratories. Using either centralized laboratory facilities, or trucks out-fitted as mobile laboratories, many departments present the appear-ance of technical preparedness to investigate crime. A more careful analysis, however, reveals that with few exceptions crime laboratories other than those of the FBI and City of Chicago are of limited cap-ability, are in fact largely sham and show.

The reasons for the low capability of most state and municipal crime laboratories may be summarized somewhat as follows:

1. In prosecuting major cases only the best expert testimony is good enough.

2. Crime laboratories may be asked to conduct analyses which cover a wide range of scientific and near-scientific fields.

3. The scientific fields require advanced training, a professional status.

4. However, virtually all departments fill their crime laboratories with men selected from the force, whose scientific training was con-sidered as of secondary importance when they were recruited as pa-trolmen or troopers.

5. State and municipal crime laboratories do not receive sufficient requests for analyses and determinations to justify the employment of the large number of specialists in learned and semi-learned pro-fessions which truly complete and expert analysis requires.

Mobile crime laboratories have been purchased and manned by several municipal police departments. Ostensibly intended to bring scientific analysis directly to the crime scene, the mobile crime labora-tory is expensive and nearly useless. The City of Chicago, which has an excellent crime laboratory, does not burden itself with showy but useless equipment; instead, the mobile section of the crime lab-oratory uses ordinary sedan automobiles, the operators carrying their cameras, fingerprint equipment, and evidence containers in a satchel. When the City of San Francisco purchased a special truck and equipped it as a mobile crime laboratory the department re-ceived the desired newspaper publicity; but in the first six months "in service" the mobile crime laboratory was not used even once.

In nearly all departments it has been found that for crime lab-oratory service it is best to rely upon the facilities of the FBI, and such special talents as are available in their own and nearby police departments, governmental agencies, and private persons and insti-tutions, as fortune may provide.

II. CRIMINAL INVESTIGATION

Criminal identification and police science are among the most important of the modern aids to investigation. Both have been the subject of considerable effort directed at centralization, and impressive progress has been made toward that end. The question therefore naturally arises, why inquiry into all major crimes, or into certain types of crimes, should not be the proper sphere of a central criminal investigation agency, which could thus supplement the local police, not merely with collections of specialized data (as is now done by the central identification bureaus and crime laboratories) but also with a specialized personnel trained in the art and science of criminal investigation.

A superficial consideration of the plan seems to disclose so many advantageous features as to invite the conclusion that here is the shortest route to police efficiency in America—one which will leave our decentralized police system undisturbed but will provide technical competence from a central source whenever and wherever it is needed. In this way, it is argued, the shortcomings of a localized police system may be offset, while avoiding any violence to the traditions of local police control. On behalf of the plan, attention is also directed to the fact that all the more highly developed police forces have their own specialized investigating squads which are shifted hither and yon in supplementing the uniformed and plain-clothes police regularly engaged in localized field service. Hence it is contended that the establishment of central investigating facilities for the aid of local police forces is merely an application, on a larger scale, of a scheme of police organization long employed by such forces themselves.

Recourse also is had to practice abroad—to the *Police judiciaire* of Belgium, a national detective force charged with the investigation of crimes of first magnitude; and to the *Sûreté Générale* of France, which provides central detective service through its agents located permanently at various points throughout the country, and supplements them, when need arises, with its *Brigade mobile*. The examples furnished by Scotland Yard, by the Federal Bureau of Investigation, and by some of our state police forces are likewise marshaled on behalf of the plan. Despite so many varied reasons for its adoption, the scheme of central investigation does not spread with great rapidity, and in some of the jurisdictions where it has been tried the results have been disappointing. The causes for such failures are easily identified.

Lessons from Experience Abroad

In the first place, the illustrations so widely drawn from police experience are not strictly comparable. There are, on the one hand, the examples provided by the central detective services so commonly found in Europe. Such as these are part and parcel of nation-wide police organizations which exercise almost complete administrative control over provincial police, reaching down to the smallest municipalities and communes. In other words, the local police and the central detective services are both subject to the same superior administrative authority, and are therefore related parts of the same organization. Hence they are not counterparts of the proposal for detective service conducted by a separate central authority.

Scotland Yard offers a more nearly parallel case because it deals with local police forces which are in fact independent of it and of each other, and (except for the annual grant from the Exchequer upon the recommendation of His Majesty's Inspectors of Constabulary) are also independent of the national government. Yet certain facts concerning Scotland Yard as a national detective service receive too little attention from those who cite it as a model especially adapted to American police requirements. It is necessary to recognize at the outset that "Scotland Yard" is a term of several, and sometimes confusing, connotations. It happens that the general offices of the Metropolitan Police are located on a short street or court, which lies between the Thames Embankment and Whitehall, and known as New Scotland Yard.[14] In plain American parlance that is nothing more nor less than a popular name for the street address of police headquarters. "Scotland Yard" has therefore become a generally descriptive team which may be loosely and indiscriminatively applied to (a) the Metropolitan Police force, (b) the general headquarters offices of that force, or (c) the criminal investigation department (or "CID" as it is commonly known) of that force. This third meaning in its application to the detective headquarters

---

[14] For an interesting account of the early usage of the term "Old Scotland Yard," in its application to the original site of the headquarters of the Metropolitan Police, see Prothero, *History of the Criminal Investigation Department at Scotland Yard*, pp. 103, 141-149.

of the Metropolitan Police has become so deeply embedded in legendary fact and fiction that it often obscures the real relationships existing between the Metropolitan Police and the police of the cities, boroughs, and counties. Ignoring the fiction, and sifting out the pertinent facts, the situation is as follows:

The Metropolitan Police force is primarily responsible for the protection of life and property and for the general maintenance of order within the limits of the Metropolitan Police District, an area within a radius of about fifteen miles from Charing Cross as a center.[15] This force, like all other police forces in England and Wales, is supported from both national and local funds. It is essentially a local police unit, although its control is lodged in the Home Office. It is also distinguished from the others by (1) its numerical strength of 20,000 officers and men, (2) its world-wide fame, (3) its exercise of certain imperial and national functions, in return for which a special contribution from the Exchequer of £100,000 a year is made by the national government, and (4) its obligation to assist in the investigation of crimes throughout England and Wales, *upon the request of the local authorities.*

Here at last we come to the concept of "Scotland Yard" as a national detective force. Yet it will be noted that in the investigation of crimes committed outside the Metropolitan Police District, the CID does not operate as a free agent.[16] It does not take charge unless requested to do so by the local authorities. If these make their demand within twenty-four hours of the commission of the crime, the treasury defrays the expenses of the CID in the local investigation; if that demand is delayed, the local government must pay. Thus there is the promise of free service upon prompt notice or service-at-cost if the locality chooses to employ its own agents exclusively during the early stages of the investigation.

There has been so much contentious discussion concerning the extent to which the CID from Scotland Yard is engaged upon such extradistrict investigations that only the highest authority should be permitted to settle the question once and for all. Let Sir John

---

[15] It does not, however, include the ancient city of London, which still retains its separate police force.

[16] In common with other police units, the CID of the Metropolitan Police dispatches its agents wherever it is necessary for them to go in order to investigate crimes committed within its own jurisdiction.

Moylan, Receiver General for the Metropolitan Police District, provide the answer. He says:

Two mistaken notions are current with regard to the actual relations of Scotland Yard to the police of England and Wales. One is that Scotland Yard has some sort of general jurisdiction in police matters; the other that the Metropolitan Police stand apart from and above other forces. Both ideas are erroneous. Scotland Yard does not control and has no desire to impinge in any way upon the local independence or management of any other force; its position as one member of what might be called the police commonwealth of England and Wales is only that of *primus inter pares*. There is not and there should not be any isolation, splendid or otherwise. . . .

. . . It must not however be supposed that Scotland Yard has a roving commission which enables its detectives to go anywhere; they can take up a provincial case only if asked to do so by the local Chief Constable. Any officer lent in response to such a request is, for the time being, attached to the local force, and keeps the Chief Constable informed of all he does, but he remains under the direct control of the Commissioner of the Metropolitan Police. The cases in which Scotland Yard's assistance is invoked by the provincial police are usually murders, and are very few; it is only in detective stories that an officer from "the Yard" will be found at the scene of a country burglary, or clearing up a country house mystery. Those police forces which have no detective branches of their own, or only small ones, are encouraged by the Home Office to call in the CID in difficult cases, not because Scotland Yard has any monopoly of detective brains but to obtain the benefit of its wider experience and greater resources, which naturally far exceed those of any other detective establishment in Great Britain. It is clearly desirable that detectives of the greatest skill and experience should be available to conduct a criminal investigation in any part of the country. Such need as there may be for a national detective service is partly met and could be met still further by local forces making the fullest use of Scotland Yard's resources, or of those of some other force in the position to provide expert assistance.[17]

It therefore should be clear that the role of Scotland Yard in provincial investigations is not very different from that which would prevail in this country if the metropolitan police of Washington, or the New York City Police Department, were obligated to investigate crimes committed beyond their own boundaries, when local authori-

[17] J. F. Moylan, *Scotland Yard*, pp. x-xi, 197-198.

ties requested them so to intervene. Under such circumstances there would be quite as little "intervention" here as there now is in England and Wales.

Lessons from American Experience

In point of fact there are in this country various criminal investigation agencies exercising a broad territorial jurisdiction without too much regard for the predilections of local authorities. Some of them are, however, easily distinguishable from centralized units designed to supplement local police authorities. Thus in the federal government, the Secret Service, the Bureau of Narcotics, the Post Office Inspectors, the Customs and Immigration Border Patrols, and other police units described in a previous chapter,[18] range up and down the land, and the Coast Guard patrols our shores, in the course of investigating infractions of the particular federal statutes with which each is concerned. They do this freely, and without regard to the sensibilities of local authorities, because they are operating in a different medium or sphere—that of the federal criminal law. The Federal Bureau of Investigation likewise performs its functions with primary reference to a rather lengthy list of federal penal statutes, and in addition is authorized to investigate state crimes committed under circumstances which may possibly bring them within federal jurisdiction. All these national investigating units necessarily come into contact with local police bodies, and where the desirability of cooperative action is indicated, proposals to that effect are made by one side or the other. Such proposals are sometimes rejected. Even if accepted, joint cooperative investigation by federal and local agencies may fail because the will to cooperate is not present, or because private quarrels develop among the investigators, or because corps rivalries prevent mutual trust and common action. These are widely prevalent human failings, and are demonstrated in many activities other than police. If they are to be corrected or suppressed in connection with federal–local investigations, it can be done only through the application of a disciplinary power common to all forces engaged. No such superior administrative authority now exists, and it is difficult to see how it could be provided for the purpose of coordinating federal–local criminal investigations without undermining and ultimately destroying the foundations of

[18] Chapter 6.

our local police systems. Yet it is the future integrity and independence of these same local systems that the new central investigation agencies are intended to assure.

The relationships existing between local and state police units are generally similar. Here are found but few distinctions as to the kind of criminal jurisdiction exercised. State and local police alike enforce the state criminal law, which prescribes one set of criminal definitions, one scale of penalties, one general code of criminal procedure, applicable to all who, by whatever means, come within its purview. Such uniform provisions have no disciplinary effect, however, where interforce rivalries are concerned. That is the experience of our state, county, city, town, and village police at the present time, and there is no reason to believe that the patterns would be essentially different if one or more of them were designated as central investigation agencies. That has already been tried in some states, and the results are nowhere impressive.

For even the most successful of the state police forces have not been able to break down the defenses of self-sufficiency erected by many local police units. Accordingly, state police are careful not to encroach upon the territorial jurisdiction of city police, and have been known to move with considerable caution even in some rural counties, because of the sheriffs' antipathy to them. When state bureaus of criminal investigation have been set up, they can operate freely only in those areas that enjoy virtually no other form of organized police protection. In short, they are notably more effective when they operate as supplements to the regular state police patrols. In such circumstances they are in no real danger of being viewed as intruders. Elsewhere they are either dependent upon the good will of the local police or of the prosecutor, or they must assume the risks incident to their appearance at the crime scene as uninvited and duplicating investigative agencies.

Relations between county, town, and village police remain to be considered. Here there is seldom much opportunity for friction because so many of these agencies are mere paper organizations, without much manpower or pretense at high investigative skill. If part-time constables, village marshals, and deputy sheriffs are all projected into the investigation of a criminal case, they operate as equals. The issue as to which of them represents the expert and specialized investigating unit is not often raised, because none possesses such qualities. But when it is raised, the results seem to be generally consistent with those already described.

Reference has been made to the Nassau County (New York) police as one of the unique county forces in the nation. Over the years the Nassau County police have increased in strength and acceptance, both in their own normal patrol district, and as a service agency to municipal police forces within the county. Today three-quarters of all criminal investigations within the country are performed by the county police, while only a fourth are performed by the municipal police. The practice is for the municipal police in the smaller towns of the county to perform only routine police patrol and protection, referring criminal investigations directly to the county detectives. Apparently there exists some dissatisfaction with the scheme, primarily on the grounds that county detectives do not report the results of their investigation to the referring municipal police department.

III.   UNIFORM CRIME REPORTING

In his *Autobiography* Lincoln Steffens recounts with gusto the circumstances under which he and Jacob Riis, as rival news reporters at New York police headquarters, produced a crime wave to the great embarrassment of Theodore Roosevelt, who was then president of the board of police commissioners. It was eventually established that there was in fact no wave of crime at all, but a wave of crime news created by the activity of these friendly rivals, and that Riis was securing his information from the crime reports suppressed by the police department itself.[19] This might easily have become the occasion for opening the "squeal book" to the popular gaze, in which event the development of crime reporting and of criminal statistics might have been advanced by several decades. But the official files of crime reports were moved to a less accessible part of police headquarters, and the "crime wave" subsided.

Other police forces have quite generally adhered to a policy similar to that which then prevailed, and still prevails, in many cities. There is a certain justification for it. Although crime complaints and police investigations are merely colorful features of the routine of public business in connection with which the press has an important function to perform, they also partake of a character which

[19] *The Autobiography of Lincoln Steffens*, Vol. I, pp. 285-291.

often requires that, in the public interest, secrecy shall be observed. Police for many years confused these considerations with others of a quite different nature. For however important secrecy may be during certain stages of a criminal investigation, it has no place in appraising the results of police activity. So the closing of the "squeal book" effectively prevented measurement of the amount and incidence of crime.

An alert and resourceful press was not slow in developing substitutes in the form of independent investigations, which produced reports of varying accuracy. Others turned to compiled summaries of arrest reports which most police forces issue, or to the statistics of persons prosecuted, or convicted, or admitted to penal institutions. Whatever their value for other purposes, these failed as measures of the amount and incidence of crime.

The best index and in the strict sense the only index of the amount of crime consists in what is described in this country as "offenses known to the police."[20] These are crimes which come to the

[20] Statistics of arrests, prosecutions, convictions, or of prisoners in penal institutions can never be reliable indices of the volume of fluctuation of *criminal acts*, for they are clouded by the varying policies of enforcement and incarceration pursued by police, prosecutors, courts and juries, and prison administrators, and in any case include only those persons who were apprehended, tried, convicted, or imprisoned. Therefore, it is almost self-evident that as the collection of criminal statistics becomes more and more remote, in a procedural sense, from the commission of the criminal act itself, the less value does it have as an index to the actual volume and incidence of crime. This does not mean, of course, that records of arrests, or judicial or penal statistics, do not have great value in measuring the *processes* of criminal justice.

As stated by Thorsten Sellin, "An index based on crimes reported to or known to the police is superior to others, and an index based on statistics of penal treatment, particularly prison statistics, is the poorest." (Encyclopaedia of the Social Sciences, Vol. IV, p. 565.)

In discussing the significance of its penal treatment data, the Bureau of the Census takes a similar stand. In each year's report, beginning with 1931, the following caveat has been issued:

"Statistics showing the number of sentenced prisoners, even if obtained from all classes of penal institutions, cannot be taken as an index either of the extent of crime or of the punishment of those convicted. Many offenders are never arrested. Of those arrested, many are never tried; and of those tried, a substantial proportion are not convicted. While most convictions result in a sentence of punishment or treatment of some kind, the penalty is not always imprisonment. Many of those convicted receive suspended sentences, are placed on probation, or are punished by fines rather than by imprisonment." (Bureau of the Census, *Prisoners in State and Federal Prisons and Reformatories;* 1931-1932, 1933, 1934, 1935, 1936.)

attention of the police through reports and complaints made to them by the general public, plus those which the police discover through their own initiative and in the routine performance of police duty. Since the original report of a crime may either be inaccurate as to the nature of the act committed or even entirely false as to the commission of any offense whatever, the computation and classification of offenses actually committed must be adjusted in the light of subsequent police inquiries. Likewise the varied provisions of the criminal codes of fifty states, the District of Columbia, Puerto Rico, and the Canal Zone, involve considerations of the most complex and difficult character. Such adjustments require the systematic application of certain principles of crime accounting which must be widely and uniformly applied before any broad compilations of "known offenses" can be attempted. Thus a central supervisory authority is necessary if the collection of crime statistics on a large scale is to succeed.

Approach to a Unified System

In 1870 a statute passed by Congress sought at a single stroke to provide a national system. By its terms the attorney general was directed to collect statistics of crime under the laws of the several states as well as of the United States.[21] No groundwork had been laid, however, for the active participation and support of the police forces of the country which could be expected to contribute the data on which great nationwide compilations might be based. It soon became evident that such support would not be extended on a voluntary basis, and since no means were at hand to compel it, the plan was abandoned. In the very next year the newly formed National Police Association itself attempted to collect crime data from its members, but again without result.[22] Thus the technical problems involved and the complexities of our decentralized police sys-

---

Likewise, the Committee on Uniform Crime Records of the International Association of Chiefs of Police, in presenting the system of crime reporting which has been in operation since 1930, declared that "Lack of any constant relation between the number of arrests, convictions, and prisoners, on the one hand, and criminal acts on the other, must always prevent measurement of the extent of crime by any such changing standards." (*Uniform Crime Reporting*, p. 3.)

[21] *Second Session of the Forty-first Congress*, Act of June 22, 1870, Sec. 12.

[22] *Official Proceedings of the National Police Convention*, St. Louis, 1871, p. 30 and appendix.

tem combined to make crime reporting on either a local or a national basis an unpromising field of endeavor.

The crime statistics of the country remained in this unsatisfactory condition until most other nations had provided at least the foundations of crime-reporting systems. Then ,in 1927, through the collaboration of various private interests with the International Association of Chiefs of Police, the Committee on Uniform Crime Records was organized. It consisted in part of police administrators, and in part of a widely representative group of persons having an official or professional interest in criminal statistics.[23] The most important feature of the whole undertaking was, however, its implicit support by the police administrators of the country. Lack of such support had marked all earlier efforts and had been the chief contributing cause of their ultimate failure.

Encouraged by police acquiescence, in the space of two years the Committee on Uniform Crime Records produced a new classification of offenses particularly adapted to police needs, analyzed the criminal statutes of the various state, territorial, and other jurisdictions; effected a reconciliation of the crime classification and the criminal statutes by a series of detailed schedules; produced a system for scoring offenses; defined administrative procedures for crime recording, for compiling, and for publishing the results; and for seven months collected and published the returns from the various reporting police agencies. The response of the police forces exceeded all estimates. For January 1930 the first returns included 400 police jurisdictions located in .43 states. One-half of all cities over 30,000 population were represented. From this impressive beginning the reporting communities were almost tripled in number before the close of the first year of operation. The growth of the reporting area has since been more orderly, but nonetheless impressive.

With all cities over 25,000 population included, together with well over 3,000 cities, villages and rural townships of varying size, it is clear that the data must be fairly representative of the complex pattern of police jurisdictions. Here is striking evidence of the capacity of our decentralized police systems to participate in at least certain kinds of cooperative effort.

[23] For a detailed account of the committee's work, see *Ten Years of Uniform Crime Reporting, 1930-1939,* Federal Bureau of Investigation, Washington.

Role of the Federal Government

An especially interesting feature of the whole enterprise has been the role of the federal government. The crime reports had only just been fairly launched when the Committee on Uniform Crime Records announced that its technical and promotional work was completed and that the Federal Bureau of Investigation would thereafter collect, compile, and publish the *Uniform Crime Reports*.[24] That agency has since been charged with the delicate task of leading some thousands of state and local police forces through the technical details of crime reporting. It has performed this task with tact, skill, and decision. When carelessly prepared returns are submitted, they are rejected for publication until challenged features are corrected. If the carelessness continues, the offending police unit is dropped from the crime-reporting system. That such episodes have not been of common occurrence is a tribute to the good intentions of the local police forces and also to the firmness with which the Federal Bureau of Investigation has performed its disciplinary role. There is, of course, no formal basis for such authority, since the crime-reporting system is wholly voluntary in character. Nevertheless, disciplinary action is implicit in the power to edit and compile the returns, and both the International Association of Chiefs of Police and individual police administrators have been quick to support federal authorities in any corrective action taken by the latter.

Thus the crime-reporting system has followed a course closely similar to that pursued by the central identification facilities. Each found its origin in local police work, each was cultivated by the police chiefs' association, and was then transferred to the Federal Bureau of Investigation as operating agency.

Scope of the Uniform Crime Reports

As they stand today, the *Uniform Crime Reports*[25] are a primary source of data concerning crimes and police operations in the United

[24] *Uniform Crime Reports*, July, 1930.

[25] The first series of the *Uniform Crime Reports* was edited and published monthly by the Committee on Uniform Crime Records from January through July of 1930. With the transfer of the entire system to the federal government, as of July 31, 1930, the present series of reports was established. From August, 1930, to December, 1931, these appeared monthly and have since been published on a quarterly or semiannual basis.

States, its territories and possessions. The tabulations of known offenses are still their most important feature. Owing to a wide variety of influences, many criminal offenses of a minor character are not regularly reported to the police by the public at large. The official record of such crimes therefore can never be even approximately complete. Hence the formal tabulations of "offenses known to the police" omit a large number of crimes of varying degrees of gravity, and are restricted to a limited list of crimes which experience has shown to be most consistently reported by the public.[26] A supplementary list of offenses is then employed for the reporting of arrests and dispositions.

Next in importance is the record of "crimes cleared by arrest" in

[26] These "reportable offenses" are as follows:
1. *Criminal homicide*
   (a) Murder and nonnegligent manslaughter. Includes all felonious homicides except those caused by negligence; does not include attempts to kill, assaults to kill, justifiable homicides, suicides, or accidental deaths;
   (b) Manslaughter by negligence. Includes only those homicides in which death is caused by culpable negligence which is so clearly evident that if the person responsible for the death were apprehended he would be prosecuted for manslaughter.
2. *Rape*
   Includes forcible rape, statutory rape of female under age of consent, assault to rape, and attempted rape.
3. *Robbery*
   Includes stealing or taking anything of value from the person by force or violence or by inspiring fear; includes also assault to rob and attempt to rob.
4. *Aggravated assault*
   Includes assault with intent to kill, attempt to kill, and assault by shooting, cutting, stabbing, maiming, poisoning, scalding, or by the use of acids; does not include simple assault and battery, or related offenses in which no lethal weapon or other deadly means is employed.
5. *Burglary; breaking or entering*
   Includes burglary, housebreaking, safecracking, or any unlawful entry to commit a felony or theft; includes also attempted burglary and assault to commit a burglary.
6. *Larceny; theft (exclusive of auto theft)*
   (a) Fifty dollars and over, in value;
   (b) Under fifty dollars in value.
   These subclassifications include pocket picking, purse snatching, shoplifting, or any theft of property or thing of value which is not effected by force or by fraud; specifically excluded are auto theft, embezzlement, "confidence games," forgery, passing worthless checks, etc.
7. *Auto theft*
   Includes all offenses in which a motor vehicle is stolen, or driven away and abandoned; does not include taking for temporary use when actually returned by the taker, or mere unauthorized use by those having lawful access to the vehicle.

which the success or failure of the police in conducting investigations, collecting evidence, and effecting the arrest of persons who are later formally charged with crime is more clearly reflected than in any other type of statistical compilation. Other tabulations deal with the social characteristics of persons arrested and fingerprinted, and with some of the major categories of their disposition by the courts.

From time to time the *Uniform Crime Reports* also contain special treatments of material relating to the operation of police forces, the number of police employees, their distribution among the various phases of police work, the types of major police equipment in use and the method of their employment. These and similar features provide basic police data on an extensive scale, which lend more clearly defined outlines to our police defenses and more concrete knowledge on emerging police problems than was ever before available.

IV. TRAINING

Even the most casual observer of police training facilities must be impressed by their confused relationships and by the chaotic disturbances which afflict them at frequent intervals. One is likely to be made more aware of the noise and the disorder than of the striving for improvement that produces them. For it is only a few decades since the first systematic police training was applied by the Pennsylvania State Police to its original recruits, and only since 1920 that the application of training procedures has been at all common. Even today entire states are without a single police training unit worthy of the name, and others with police schools conducted on such a casual basis, and for such brief uncertain periods, as to have little influence in raising the general level of police service. In most instances the fault lies in the fact that small forces cannot support training facilities of any kind, and that even in some of the larger police establishments recruits are inducted at irregular and unpredictable intervals. With the facilities inoperative for long periods, they are either dismantled or neglected. Thus each recruiting campaign must be followed by an administrative reconstruction of the police school, attended by much wasted effort and loss of effectiveness.

That American police administrators have continued in their

efforts to establish training programs in the face of so many discouragements is evidence of the general conviction now prevailing that police should be disciplined and instructed in their duties before they are turned loose on the community. Inexperienced administrators rush recruits through a brief training program in order that they may the sooner be available for the protection of life and property. Such as these forget that, if inadequately trained, the policeman's value as an agent of civil peace and order is likely to be overestimated. Meanwhile the problem arises of finding and developing capable police instructors who not only are experienced in police work, but are also adept at transmitting the results of that experience to others.

These and related questions have produced much of the confusion now attending the expansion of police training in the United States. Federal, state, and local police vie with each other in producing new types of elementary and advanced courses for their own recruits, state associations of police and sheriffs may sponsor a series of lectures for brief periods, colleges and universities conduct institutes which may operate for a week or more in each year, while full-time, pre-service courses for prospective police are beginning to appear at some of the state colleges. Collisions of interest are frequent, and there is occasional duplication of effort. Hence it is natural that consideration should be given by public officers to various types of central facilities for police training, which shall tend to eliminate wasteful duplication, provide more adequate programs, and introduce a higher quality of instruction. Such facilities are of three general types.

State and Local Police Training Programs

The first central training was accorded by certain state and local police schools to other than their own personnel. The arrangements underlying such services are usually of the most informal nature, the visiting police officers merely attending with the regular instruction groups, and receiving evidence of attendance in the form of a certificate.

Although the number of police who have received in-service training in this way has never been large, and there is no demand for or possibility of extending the scheme by administrative order, the system has a significance all its own. For the very informality of the arrangements, and the lack of any broad official recognition, actually serve to emphasize the spontaneous and voluntary character of the undertaking. Here is police training in its most disinterested form —with police officers subjecting themselves to its disciplines without hope of immediate or tangible reward.

The local and state police schools have another significance in connection with central training facilities, since it was in these schools that the techniques of police instruction were first developed and in them that the curricula were produced and expanded. If their work had not been well done, the whole concept of police training would be less advanced than it is. Indeed, this type of police training school had every desirable feature save one: it was not well adapted to the training of men from many other police forces. The procedures taught were those of the police agency conducting the school for its own recruits; the schooling in official conduct was based upon the rules and regulations of the local force, and the instruction in penal law, ordinances, and criminal procedure also was naturally confined to the local jurisdiction. Hence police from other forces were sometimes trained in matters which would prove a positive hindrance to them when they returned to their own commands.

Systems of Zone Schools

Central police training developments during the decade which followed the First World War were chiefly of this casual character. They were succeeded by other efforts, originating in New York and later widely adopted in other states, to set up a state-wide system of zone schools. For the most part these are conducted by the police forces which already have the largest resources and the best conducted training programs. They may involve no real increase in the number of training units, but a more extensive use of those already in operation. Likewise there is little change from the informal stage of central instruction just described, except that the courses offered in the several zones are likely to be more uniform in scope and character, and there is a certain amount of interchange of teaching staffs, supplemented in some instances by traveling instructors who present their several specialties at all of the zone schools.

This second type of central training was initiated by state police, state leagues of municipalities and state associations of police chiefs, but participation has remained optional for the local police forces in the several states. In 1938, the federal government entered the lists by appropriations in aid of police education.[27] Standards were formulated which have since been applied by the Office of Education in extending financial support to police training programs throughout the country. Such aid is provided from federal funds if the state training programs meet certain conditions. These are quantitative rather than qualitative in character. The courses are not lengthy, consisting of less than one hundred hours of instruction in most instances, and even these may be distributed over a considerable period. The vocational education agencies of the state and federal governments share responsibility for any central guidance and inspection that may be attempted, thus introducing into the situation a factor of dual control. Backed by the power to grant or withhold federal and state funds, this may inflict considerable damage upon the new police training techniques. As yet one looks in vain for anything comparable to the great training centers that were independently developed by state police in Pennsylvania, New York, Massachusetts, New Jersey, and Michigan, among others, or by local police forces in New York, Detroit, Los Angeles, Berkeley, and Wichita. The obvious answer to such questions is that the new arrangements deal primarily with a host of small police forces. Even when these act in concert they cannot be expected to develop their training programs as rapidly as the large, compact police forces have done. Nevertheless it seems reasonable to demand that the federal aid program shall reach levels comparable to the best produced under the independent auspices of state and city police forces. If the new facilities do not in fact achieve some such standard of excellence, they may ultimately destroy the great training schools by providing a cheap substitute for them—one which can be attended with less expenditure of time and money but with the acquisition of equal distinction and prestige.

A far more promising central training service is rendered by the Federal Bureau of Investigation. It undertakes upon request to provide instructors in special subjects for the wide variety of state, local, and zone schools. Such instructors are in particular demand for courses in the techniques of investigation and of arrest, in firearms practice, and in fingerprint identification procedures. They are drawn from the active personnel attached to the field offices of the bureau but receive special preparation before being assigned to such work. The country is divided into thirteen "field training zones" for

[27] Under the George-Deen Act of 1936.

the more convenient administration of this service to local police.

The schools thus sponsored by the FBI include both recruit and in-service general training plus various specialized courses in traffic law enforcement, fingerprint identification, police administration, photography, firearms, and other subjects. While many of the schools extend over periods that are necessarily brief, well over 2,500 of them are held annually, with a grand total of more than 60,000 policemen in attendance.

In such a brilliantly planned and executed program the FBI exercises an influence for the improvement of police service that defies close measurement. Equally impressive is the fact that the instructing staffs are drawn from federal, state, and local forces alike, but with local autonomy and control maintained at all times.

While all such expedients are admirably calculated to increase the extent of police training by bringing various well-developed facilities to the very doorsteps of the local police, there is as yet no assurance that the rather brief courses are of sufficient bulk to occupy a large place in the real training needs of small communities. Some of the most elementary of police techniques require much time for their proper description and demonstration. Hence the outlook for training in the smaller police units, while measurably improved by the various central facilities extended in the name of the state or federal governments, cannot as yet be said to be assured. In a situation complicated by so many diverse factors it is perhaps best to adhere to two self-evident propositions. The first is that some tens of thousands of minor police units cannot be raised to full stature by any courses of instruction in which they can be prevailed upon to enroll; the second, that these microscopic units are not the necessary concern of the federal government and soon or late must stand or fall by their own unsupported merits.

Like the British police, New York State municipal policemen now receive state sponsored training at a newly authorized academy. While other states, notably Pennsylvania, have offered training to municipal officers through state police facilities, New York has pioneered in establishing the state-wide academy. No doubt, the influence of the academy will be to standardize doctrine and procedures throughout the state, and to greatly improve the training in the smaller forces which, until this time, have been at a disadvantage in securing adequate training.

The National Police Academy

A superior type of central police training is provided by the Federal Bureau of Investigation through its National Police Academy. The academy was established in 1935 for the training of state and local police executives, police instructors, and other police officers who are preparing for specialized types of work. The course absorbs the full time and effort of the student for a period of twelve weeks. It is presented three times each year to a student body of thirty-five to forty police officers selected from all parts of the country. Once each year the acamedy conducts a ten-day session for such of its graduates as can attend, at which advanced studies are pursued. In common with the other central training facilities already described, no tuition is charged. The instructing staff is drawn not only from the service schools of the Federal Bureau of Investigation itself, but also from state and local police, the universities, and other sources.[28]

The primary purpose of the National Police Academy is to train instructors who are attached to state and local police schools. More than half its graduates are so employed. The balance has consisted chiefly of men from the higher administrative posts or whose native ability marks them for early preferment. Thus the academy not only has given fresh impetus to local police schools, but exercises a profound influence upon the methods and processes of local forces, by raising the standards of general administration and of training.

It accomplishes this without becoming involved in the delicate interjurisdictional relationships characterizing some of the other central services.

Courses in Institutions of Higher Learning

The various types of central facilities thus far described are all supported from public funds and are therefore strictly of an official nature. An increasing number of police courses also is offered by universities and colleges. These partake of a central character only because they are general and their operations are not confined to one jurisdiction. Being unofficial, they exercise no coordinating influ-

[28] In addition to the basic police subjects common to most police schools, the National Police Academy offers instruction in patrol and investigation methods, signal systems and communications, crime reporting, police organization and administration, safety education, traffic regulation and accident control, and teaching methods for police instructors.

ence and attempt none. Still they are important because they introduce into the field of police training a factor representing public
interest in police development and in the preparation of the men
who join the police service. Most of the courses are brief affairs, and
therefore of no great significance in themselves.[29] A few, however,
deserve special mention. At Yale[30] and at Northwestern[31] extensive
training programs are conducted for the study of traffic engineering
problems and more adequate methods of accident investigation and
control. These are highly specialized curricula of first quality and
are not intended for the recent police recruit. At California graduate
work in police administration is well established, operating in conjunction with the Berkeley Police Department, while the courses
for undergraduates at Michigan State College (in collaboration with
the Michigan State Police and the Detroit Police Department), at
San Jose State College, and the College of the City of New York, to
name but a few widely separated efforts, indicate the future direction of pre-service training in the police field.[32]

Police work is attracting an ever larger quota of college men, who
naturally seek to acquire some preliminary police training within
academic halls. An even larger proportion of college students would
systematically prepare for police work in this fashion were it not
for the artificial barriers raised in many quarters by hard-and-fast
residence requirements, and by the active and deleterious forms of
political influence.

---

[29] There is in fact great uncertainty among colleges and universities concerning the extent to which such institutions should participate in police
preparation. A commentator observes: "The future role of the university in
public service training of this type is difficult to define. Many universities
feel that, once they have demonstrated training possibilities by organizing a
police school, the planning of future schools should be left to the officers
themselves. Other universities have felt that the organizing and conducting
of pre-service and retraining courses for public officials is one of the functions
of the university, and that adequate facilities should be made available for
this purpose." William O. Hall in *The Commonwealth Review*, November,
1939, p. 231.

[30] Yale University Bureau of Highway Traffic.

[31] Northwestern University Traffic Institute.

[32] Other institutions conducting general training or traffic courses include
the universities of Indiana, Kentucky, Michigan, Minnesota, North Carolina,
Ohio State, Purdue, Rutgers, and Southern California, Tennessee, Utah, and
Pennsylvania State College. Cf., also, James M. Williams, *The Six County
Police School; An Experiment in Adult Education at Hobart College* (Geneva,
New York, 1935).

The New York City Police Department initiated a special program in police science and other courses within the Bernard M. Baruch School of Business and Public Administration of the City College in 1955. Courses are offered leading to Bachelor of Business Administration and to Master of Public Administration degrees. There are in excess of 1,150 enrolled undergraduates as this is written, and more than 100 enrolled in the graduate program. Provision is made in scheduling classes so that men on all duty tours may participate in all subjects. Courses are offered in such fields as: English, foreign languages, mathematics, natural science, psychology, social science, art, physical education, police organization, police supervision, police administration, police personnel administration, investigation, law, and the American legal system. There is no instructional fee for New York City residents. In thus encouraging policemen to participate in education at the college level the city no doubt facilitates premature separations from the service to pursue more attractive employment, but it also is assuring that trained personnel will always be available for the more responsible administrative positions.

The Future Development of Police Training

With so many different factors at work, it is difficult to determine what the future scope of police training may prove to be. A large number of local, state, and federal police, together with the state and federal vocational training agencies also, have been engaged in pursuing independent programs of police training. Each has set up its own standards. Some are impressively high; others are so low as to strengthen the belief that the interest of the sponsors is more concerned with promotional and publicity features than with improving the policeman's art.

The informed and disinterested observer will continue to hope that the distinction between the two major types of police training will be maintained. For pre-service training, police need the independence and academic prestige of the colleges and the universities. As to in-service training, on the other hand, police should be careful not to lose that complete administrative control which is properly theirs. In the training of the recruit and of the higher ranks and grades alike, police should provide their own courses of instruction, and to a large extent the instructors also. Those forces which are large enough to warrant the maintenance of independent training programs will properly insist on doing this work for themselves. The smaller police units will have to band together for the purpose as has already been done in many cases. If they retain control over the management of such general courses, there seems to be no reason why the corps discipline of the in-service training course conducted for groups of police forces should be lost or impaired. That control will be secure, however, only if the administrative boards in charge are in large measure composed of police officials. The latter may not in any given instance represent the highest pedagogical standards, but they should prove to be the best guardians of in-service training as a measure of constructive discipline. The quasi-military character of police service requires that full professional controls be maintained at all stages subsequent to recruitment.

V. STATE AND REGIONAL COMMUNICATION SYSTEMS[33]

The whole purpose of police communication systems is the distribution of police intelligence. Hence the various means by which one force establishes contact with another have a direct influence upon interforce relations and the success of joint operations. Almost necessarily they involve the use of common facilities, which raises new types of problems in connection with central services.

[33] The following facilities are employed for internal, as distinguished from interforce, communication, though not all are available, nor necessary, in any given force:
Between headquarters and stations:
  1. Telegraph (Morse Code)
  2. Telephone
  3. Teletype
  4. Radio-telephone
  5. Radio-type
  6. Radio-telegraph
From station to patrolman:
  1. Recall signals (electrically controlled horns, lights or bells)
  2. Radio-telephone (one-way or two-way systems)
  3. Radio-type
From patrolman to station:
  Call-box systems (automatic telegraph and/or telephone; the automatic telegraph code being registered on a record tape at the station)
  2. Radio-telephone (two-way system)
  3. Public telephones
From patrol car to patrol car
  1. Radio telephone (three-way system)

Until the advent of the radio and the teletype, improvements in police communication rarely possessed any but local significance. With these two major facilities once installed, however, each technical development and improvement involves a larger and larger circle of police forces. Some are so revolutionary in their effect that they have profoundly influenced not merely the functioning, but even the design and structure of police forces, by producing new points of contact for the police and giving them constant administrative relationships with police agencies located at a great distance. These changes are so numerous and so important that the patterns of existing police communications systems are subjected to extensive revisions. To appreciate the full impact of this revolution it is only necessary to recall that it was not until 1928 that Detroit set up the first publicly owned police radio system; that as late as 1935 there were but 184 municipal police radio transmitters in operation; that within three years thereafter the number had more than tripled, and had passed the 700 mark in 1939. Today all organized police agencies have some form of radio communication.[34]

District and State Radio Systems

With a thousand police radio transmitters crammed into a few limited broadcast bands, the problems of station interference multiply even more rapidly than the number of stations. These have been met by various devices familiar to radio engineers, with limited power output and consequent limited range proving to be the most common recourse. Such measures restrict, though they do not destroy, the effectiveness of the local systems, but they also raise serious questions in the suburban districts surrounding great cities where scores of small municipalities engage in a scramble for police broadcast licenses. Within congested areas, no limitation of power output or juggling of wave lengths could prevent an eventual confusion of tongues in the ambient ether rivaling that of the Tower of Babel.

While plans for sharing common signal facilities have been the result of sheer necessity in most instances, they also carry with

---

[34] The following schedules are issued from time to time by the Federal Communications Commission: (1) *List of Interzone and Zone Police (Radio) Stations Authorized;* (2) *Municipal Police (Radio) Stations;* (3) *State Police (Radio) Stations.*

them certain advantages of their own. There is, for one thing, the matter of economy of installation and operation—with but one capital outlay and one annual maintenance and operating cost where there might have been scores. Equally important is the advantage attaching to a unified system of communication that leaps across narrow local boundaries without dependence upon formal cooperative relationships. Such relationships have, of course, sprung up in response to this new state of interdependence among neighboring police agencies, with large and sometimes active regional police associations now operating in such widely different settings as the metropolitan districts of Chicago, Detroit, Cincinnati, Los Angeles, and the San Francisco Bay area.

Also worthy of special note is the fact that few disturbing questions concerning the cost of the central broadcast facilities are ever raised. The central municipality generally assumes the full burden of construction and operation, without contribution by any of the surrounding satellite towns. This interesting situation is due in part to a realization of the difficulty of apportioning such costs on an equitable basis, and in part to the fact that the police force that operates the radio facilities enjoys by far the greatest and most accessible use of them, and in addition can broadcast its own alarms to the police of surrounding towns without delay. Such advantages are not of a minor nature, particularly as an extension of radio service to the whole metropolitan area only slightly affects the cost of operation. At the same time the nearby communities do not escape all financial burden under these arrangements, since they must install and maintain their own receivers, together with the direct-line telephone or teletype facilities that connect them with the regional broadcasting station.

The state-wide radio systems operated by state police and highway patrol forces likewise bring crime broadcasts to many towns and village police who would otherwise lie beyond the normal range of the city radio stations. Thus new networks of communication are woven, and with them new demands are made upon the coordination of police work.

Interstate Teletype and Radio Systems

The developments briefly described with respect to radio communication are paralleled by similar arrangements for central teletype service. Here no compulsion is imposed by limited broadcast bands or by station interference. Rather the various teletype hookups increase in response to a growing belief in police circles that permanent facilities for interforce communication are necessary to successful operations. The great teletype chains now operating have been so completely cooperative in their inspiration that they represent one of the most significant features of central police services.

As in the case of radio, the first uses of teletype in police work were confined to intraforce communication between headquarters and outlying stations in the larger cities. Gradually the suburban towns tied in with the central systems and it was not long before intercity lines formed an intricate network across many states. The aid of state governments was invoked at this stage, under arrangements which generally involve lease of the long lines by the state and the operation of regional control stations by the state police. Thus any community desiring to avail itself of widely ranging teletype facilities need only lease a teletype receiver and a relatively short tie line to the nearest junction point of the state system.

Next stage in development was the interstate police teletype system linking together the states of Vermont, New Hampshire, Massachusetts, Rhode Island, Connecticut, New York, New Jersey, Maryland, Delaware, Pennsylvania, the District of Columbia, Virginia, North Carolina, and Ohio. In the Far West, California, Washington, Oregon, and Nevada have similar ties.

The intrastate stations of such systems often operate through a hierarchy of state and zone headquarters with several score receiving stations located in the police headquarters of cities, towns, and villages throughout the state. Such arrangements are held together quite easily by the fact that the state government defrays the largest share of the expense, which is far from being a minor item. In the interstate tie-ups, however, there must be not only a sharing of cost of the tie lines between states, but also a considerable self-discipline in the proper use of such far-flung resources. As means to these ends, the eastern interstate teletype conference has proved invaluable as a cooperative enterprise, through which the police representatives of the several states adopt rules and regulations for the use of teletype facilities which are observed by the hundreds of state and local forces concerned.

Radio also is employed as a medium for interstate distribution of criminal intelligence. The most ambitious of these schemes is the radiotelegraph system operating on a selective scale of ten frequencies. Direct police contact is thereby maintained among the states of Ohio, Michigan, Indiana, Illinois, Kansas, New Mexico, Texas, Missouri, Wisconsin, Kentucky, Tennessee, Louisiana, Georgia, Oklahoma, Minnesota, and New York. Similarly the periphery of the United States is linked together by the radiophone facilities of the Immigration Border Patrol. As supplemented by 36 state hookups and numerous local systems of radiophone and teletype communications, the country is covered by a network that is very nearly complete. There are few populous sections which are not a part of the major systems when occasion demands, and only the smallest police establishments are still confronted by communication difficulties which appear to be insuperable.

Carried one step further, not only is there exchange of information but also, in major cases, some degree of concurrent action by the police of neighboring states—an arrangement which has thus far reached its highest development in the cooperative blockade systems adopted by the state police of Indiana, Illinois, Kentucky, Michigan, and Ohio, and in the closely articulated police region surrounding Cincinnati.

Decentralizing Influences

With the resources of a major industry supporting research and technical development in distant communication, no one can forecast the nature of the adaptations which may yet be made to police work. The examples of cooperative action here given, however, should make it clear that communication systems will continue to be an important aid to police operations over a wide area, and that few administrative difficulties will be encountered in connection therewith. Yet it does not follow that all such developments will operate to increase the number and scope of central facilities required by our decentralized police system. On the contrary, the low-powered, high-frequency radio transmitters employed in two-way communication, such as have been installed by a host of police establishments, tend strongly in the opposite direction. They represent high-grade communication facilities so inexpensive that even the smaller forces can afford them and in addition involve less difficult problems of station interference than the transmitters with lower frequencies once produced. Still their very number contributes to serious congestion of local broadcasts in some instances, and there is a disquieting tendency for small suburban forces operating such facilities to collaborate in their exchange of information, to the virtual exclusion of the larger police departments operating over a much wider area. Thus the influence of the large-scale regional services may eventually be much reduced by the growth of relatively small and independent police radio networks within their normal range.

Perhaps other changes are impending which likewise will further tend to make police units self-sufficient rather than interdependent. Even so, there will be continuing need for great clearinghouses of criminal intelligence which can be made quickly available over large areas and to all police agencies within such areas. Only facilities that serve not one but many forces can perform that kind of service. Such as these may be expected to increase in number, variety, and importance as the years pass.

VI. CENTRAL SERVICES IN A DECENTRALIZED POLICE SYSTEM

If they accomplish nothing else, the foregoing brief descriptions of central services should make clear the diverse character of the motives and influences that brought these services into existence. Some have been produced by the initiative of local police, some have been developed by state and federal agencies, while at various points the effect of the plans and encouragement of private interests is apparent. This diversity of origin has certain consequences. There is unnecessary and wasted effort as a matter of course; there is duplication of activity even while certain possible areas of activity lie neglected; and there is competitive spirit which results in much constructive effort and sometimes produces bitter rivalries.

Thus the history of our central police services and of the cooperative action which has encouraged and developed them does not revolve around any central theme or master plan of defined scope and purpose. On the contrary, these central facilities have sprung up here and there whenever the need for them became apparent, and wherever there could be found some individual or agency able and willing to spend the time, money, and effort required to cultivate and systematize the new interrelationships. Just as our police growth has been unregulated and unplanned, so the new central services created to bring order out of impending administration chaos are themselves often without systematic programs.

When matters of such absorbing interest suffer from the effects of unregulated expansion and random development, the critical observer is tempted to suggest ways and means for avoiding the conflicts by eliminating the competition and for stimulating the establishment of new central services in the areas now lacking them. Whether in the long view this would produce a more satisfactory result is at best doubtful. For it must be remembered that the central services are not an end in themselves, and that they exist chiefly as a means for filling the geographical and functional interstices between a multitude of police organisms. If, as is possible, these independent police bodies should ultimately fuse in such fashion as to reduce their number, the need for some of the regional, state, and federal auxiliary services will be sharply reduced. But there is no way of determining which of the central facilities now rendering aid to some tens of thousands of police agencies would be required for the needs of a less complex police system. Hence definitive plans must await such basic changes.

The Conditions of Centralization

If this approach to an admittedly difficult situation is sound, the process of centralizing cooperative action should be confined to those activities which by their very nature require uniformity of treatment, or which are far more valuable when their management is centralized than when it is decentralized. For example, the various means of criminal identification acquire increased value with each increase in the size of the collection, while the use and significance of statistics of crimes and of police operations are enhanced if these are recorded, compiled, and distributed through a single, far-flung, and uniform system. On the other hand, the advantages to be derived from uniformity or from large-scale operations are not so apparent in the field of police training, nor in the large but as yet rather vague collection of relationships clustering about radio and teletype communication. Imposition by some central authority of uniform standards of pre-service or in-service training might in the course of time wander far from the practical needs of the police forces, which would have to employ the services of the men after they were trained. Similarly, the management of systems of communication strikes too close to the core of police administration to justify any general program that would involve their *ex parte* consolidation. It is for these reasons that any unifying influences applied to auxiliary services for police training and communications should secure their results through cooperative action, rather than by control or direction. In this way the experimental advantages of such activities may be enlarged, and the participation of private technical interests encouraged.

Even where uniformity is a prime requisite, it may often be secured through noncompulsory regulations prepared by a central agency and observed by police forces. If mild regulation of this character fails to achieve its purpose, one can always have recourse to the support of statutory enactments by the several states. Such moderate pressures prove wholly adequate to the needs of any type of uniform requirement imposed by a central service.

There is some danger that the compulsions of law may be too freely employed, and used more for the gratification of someone's sense of order or from a desire to insure general compliance, than for the advancement of the real objectives of the central services. After all, these have been created because they have or are assumed to have substantial value for local police forces; but if regularly organized police must be compelled by statute to avail themselves of such services, it may well be that the practical values involved are more apparent than real.

So far as rudimentary police bodies are concerned, no statutory pressure and no scale of penalties can be established to make them fully effective units in a cooperative police program. Their difficulties do not spring from deliberate avoidance of outside relationships so much as from their incapacity to maintain them. A unicellular organism cannot perform specialized functions.

Success and Failure of Central Services

Another matter which the foregoing descriptions should help to illuminate is the underlying reason why some types of central services are so freely employed by local police, while others are resorted to only with the greatest reluctance. Although the interests of police forces often clash in the course of an investigation, there is ample evidence that they can work together toward a common objective, provided each is allowed to operate freely within its own normal jurisdiction, without direct competition from a rival police organization. Thus it is not alone the large number of police forces that handicaps cooperative action, but also the overlapping of their jurisdictions. When police who owe different loyalties are all required to function within a given hundred square feet of area, as occurs in duplicating investigations, ruinous conflicts may arise; but when they can operate at arm's length and each within its own normal and defined territorial jurisdiction, as in close pursuit of offenders, the maintenance of road blockades, or through relations with central identification offices, an impressively close coordination is obtained.

Still another factor contributing to the success of central services is the ease with which the required procedures can be reduced to a routine varying but little from year to year. For example, the process of taking fingerprints and forwarding them to a central bureau on a standardized form is by its nature a simple matter and one which never varies. The submission of summaries on reportable offenses, and their clearance by arrest, is likewise mere routine once the basic records are set up and necessary procedures are put in operation. The same is true of communication systems, which could not be enjoyed at all by many police units unless provided by some central source, and which throw but slight administrative burdens upon those participating in this group service. Such activities are easily adapted to central operation because, once the procedures are defined and understood, they involve little adjustment between the various police forces concerned. For where large numbers of administrative units are involved, the mere effort at coordination may be so great as to be a principal influence in determining whether the area central service administration shall be large or small; whether it can succeed under precise regulations laid down in the interest of uniformity, or must be subject to a multitude of official and personal adjustments from day to day. This underlying condition is produced in large measure by the multiplicity of our police forces. It helps to explain why central investigating squads, laboratory experts, and common facilities for police training move ahead on a narrower front than do those services which are easily reducible to routine. While the future of the small police force would seem to depend upon the extent to which it is able and willing to employ the central services now becoming so freely available to all, the fact remains that the very number of small forces creates administrative problems that will seriously retard the growth and impede the functioning of such services. Thus the problem of the small forces, for whose benefit many of the central services are chiefly devised, is to adapt themselves to the disciplines of uniformity in ever larger areas and in more complex relationships of cooperative effort.

Uniform Laws and Interstate Compacts

These in substance are the influences that are leading or driving police into dependence upon various central services. Running through nearly all of them is one common denominator: uniformity. The striving for uniform standards and procedures actually extends far beyond even the outermost limits of the police field into criminal procedure and judicial and penal administration. The most successful of the efforts to this end have been conducted by the National Conference of Commissioners on Uniform State Laws and by the Interstate Commission on Crime. Through the efforts put forth by these agencies and others, 41 states have enacted the uniform narcotic drug act either in terms or in effect, and 37 states now provide new and improved methods for interstate rendition of witnesses in criminal proceedings. Other matters brought within the sphere of joint crime control include simplified procedures for extradition (30 states), interstate supervision of parolees and probationers (33 states); empowering duly authorized peace officers to engage in fresh pursuit of criminals across state lines (31 states), and the uniform pistol act regulating the sale, transfer, and possession of certain firearms (9 states) .[35]

Thus it is apparent that police are not by any means alone in their efforts to secure united action along certain of the crime fronts. They are but parts of a general movement that seeks to lower jurisdictional barriers and to coordinate activities over wider and wider areas. But when such as these are viewed from the administrative as well as the legislative standpoint, it becomes clear that police cooperation is the most varied and the most extensive to be found in the entire range of crime control.

[35] The Commissioners on Uniform State Laws are designated by the constituted authorities of the several states. The Interstate Commission on Crime was organized in 1935, and consists of representatives of the states and of the federal government. Cf. its Handbook of Interstate Crime Control.

CHAPTER 11

OUTLINES OF FUTURE
DEVELOPMENT

It has been the aim of the foregoing chapters to present a general view of the police systems of the federal, state, and local governments and to provide the basic data necessary to an understanding of American police problems. These take many forms in the intricate mosaic of police forces now covering the United States. Yet there are certain cardinal points which are more or less common to all, while the rapidly growing interrelationships of police at all levels of government tend to bring many police operations into a common focus. Thus despite the number and diversity of police establishments certain broad generalizations can be drawn.

These are of two kinds. The first is concerned with the efficiency of the police machine as a device for enforcing the criminal law and a host of minor regulations, and for extending protection to all legitimate interests. Such problems revolve largely about questions of administrative technique—of organization, personnel, matériel and leadership—questions which, while sometimes baffling, often do elicit positive answers.

The second aspect of the American police problem is less clearly defined. It is concerned with questions of popular control over the police mechanism. These are difficult to formulate and do not readily lend themselves to treatment by systematic procedures. Under such circumstances there is danger that the whole matter will become the subject of vain speculation—without plan, method, or objective. So on this general aspect of control, the present chapter will attempt first to define the question, and then to indicate the approaches to its solution shown by experience to be most promising.

Centralization vs. Decentralization

Attention has been drawn repeatedly to the decentralization and fragmentation featuring our police defenses. These are the most striking characteristics of American police patterns, since no other part of the world has carried local autonomy in police management to such extreme lengths. If every local government, no matter how weak or how small, is to maintain its own police facilities, the latter become so numerous that their interrelationships are unduly complex and burdensome. When to sheer complexity is added the confusion and destructive rivalries arising out of overlapping enforcement powers, the discouragement that so often overtakes police administrators is readily understood. Nor does the process of dispersion stop there. Our city, county, state, and federal governments are replete with examples of police forces created for special and limited purposes and existing side by side in the service of one single government. Thus a second dimension is introduced which further confuses an already complex situation.

Table IV is a graphic representation of the results of this process of uncontrolled and unguided development. Column 2 shows that so far as police forces of general authority are concerned, the matter of duplication is primarily an aspect of our multiple layers of government, even though two police forces with coordinate general powers occasionally will be found in the service of a given township or county. The situation with respect to forces exercising only a restricted police authority is of the latter type. Column 3 shows how the more common of them are distributed. The duplications and conflicts which they produce are for the most part within the level of government in which each of them operates. Thus the general forces overlap chiefly in a vertical plane, while those of limited authority produce greatest friction from contacts in the horizontal plane.

The various central services now flourishing in so many specialized police fields are really no offset to this process of minute particularization. They cannot solve the constantly recurrent problems arising from a duplication here or hiatus there. While they make it possible for the clumsy and ill-articulated police organism to perform its tasks, that is not their proper function. Central services in identification, and in criminal statistics, communications and training are a

TABLE IV

DISTRIBUTION OF LAW ENFORCEMENT AGENCIES; CLASSIFIED ACCORDING TO THE TYPE OF GOVERNMENT SERVED, AND EXTENT OF POLICE AUTHORITY WITH WHICH THEY ARE GENERALLY ENTRUSTED

Type of Government Served (1)	Police with General Authority (2)	Police Units with Restricted Authority or of Limited Use (Maintained in Certain Jurisdictions Only) (3)						
Village	Village Marshal, Constable or Police Department							
Township, County-District or Magisterial District	(a) Township or District Constables AND/OR (b) Township or District Police Department		Fish and Game Wardens					
City	City Police Department	City Park and Parkway Police						Other City Law Enforcement Units
Special District	Special District Police	Boulevard and Park District Police						
County	(a) Sheriff and Deputies AND/OR (b) County Police	County Parkway Police	Fish and Game Wardens		Prosecutor's Detectives and Raiding Squads			
State	State Police	State Highway Patrol AND/OR Motor Vehicle Inspection	Fish and Game Wardens	Alcoholic Beverage Control	State Bureau of Investigation AND/OR Identification	Attorney General's Investigators	State Fire Marshal (Investigations)	Other State Law Enforcement Units
Federal	Federal Bureau of Investigation (Justice)	Immigration Border Patrol (Justice)	Customs Border Patrol (Treasury)	Enforcement Division; Alcohol Tax Unit (Treasury)	Secret Service Division (Treasury)	Bureau of Narcotics (Treasury)	Post Office Inspectors	Other Federal Law Enforcement Units

necessary feature of any police pattern covering an extensive area. They perform a role wholly distinct from that of binding together into an appearance of unity the tens of thousands of unrelated police agencies which are found in cities, counties, towns, and villages and in every hedgerow. Even a greatly simplified scheme of police would require the aid of central intelligence facilities of some kind, and in large measure these would be the very ones now maintained. Yet as matters stand the central services sometimes actually operate to revive and to stimulate into new activity various police instrumentalities which are so ill-adapted to modern conditions that they might better be allowed to decline and disintegrate. Sheriffs, constables, and a host of other nonprofessional police in the service of local, state, and federal governments alike are put through so-called training courses, which may extend from a few days to a week, or may consist in occasional lectures offered on a regional basis to police who have never enjoyed even the rudiments of police instruction. To some this appears as progress toward better police service, simply because an ancient police arm has been given a modicum of exercise after decades or centuries of comparative inactivity. But who wants popularly elected policemen to continue as part of the American scene? Who believes that the sheriff, the constable, and the short-term village marshal are necessary or even desirable parts of our police defenses? The answers to these questions should go far toward determining the proper sphere of central services and cooperative arrangements.

So it is perhaps just as well if our central police services are not now too closely knit, nor too carefully adapted to the large organic relationships and technical problems. For there is as yet no certainty, nor even clear intimation, of the form which the reconstruction of our police systems will take, though all who are familiar with its ramifications seem to agree that some rearrangement is in the making. When this anticipated realignment of police defense is effected, it will probably result from a piecemeal process, springing up here and there in groups of communities and spreading across larger and larger areas. A flexible and competitive arrangement of central facilities for laboratory services, criminal investigation, communication, and training will easily conform to such changes as they occur, whereas an orderly scheme of centralized services to be performed within defined areas of federal, state, and local jurisdiction might find itself somewhat disorganized by each shift in the underlying pattern of police relationships. Hence, while it seems reasonable to suppose that the identification of criminals and uniform crime reporting will become more and more highly centralized (since their value depends upon unity of design and the completeness of the data concerned), other common aids to police work will probably follow a more selective program adjusted to the special needs of each technique and each group of police forces involved. If such services continue to display the vitality and adaptability they have shown over varying portions of the last fifty years, they will be able to grow and develop without serious dislocations due to changes in the basic patterns of local police systems.

The Issue of Local Autonomy

To all this it may be objected that the ancient police setup is part and parcel of our system of local government, and that any process of centralization, if pursued to its logical conclusion, perhaps would end in extensive control by the higher levels of government and might thus destroy the foundations of local autonomy. That this proves to be a persuasive argument it is impossible to doubt, since so many of our local police arrangements persist in the face of developments which have radically changed the conditions of local government.[1] When new police forces are set up by counties, states, or the federal government, it is often in response to a demand for a kind and a degree of protection which existing agencies have proved incapable of providing; but almost never is any effort made to destroy the old instrumentalities which the new devices are intended to displace. On the contrary, the ineffective units are carefully preserved and sometimes even enlarged. Thus a succession of inadequate forces is piled one on the other, at unnecessary expense, and in the vain hope that by some synthetic process the fractions can be added together and so produce unity in the end.

It is but a little more than a century since Robert Peel sought a larger degree of unity for the police of England and Wales. While he failed to accomplish this during his own lifetime, he did succeed in establishing the Metropolitan Police on a secure foundation, even though to this day the police force of the ancient City of London

[1] The shift from local to state or federal control is especially striking in education, highways, and welfare.

preserves its separate identity within the historic square mile on the banks of the Thames. Later police reformers led public opinion in an assault upon the parish constables and the police authority of sheriffs. Both were finally swept away, and in their place was inaugurated a uniform system of county constabularies which operates throughout all rural areas and in those urban districts not maintaining separate city or borough police establishments. Some of the forces thus absorbed by county constabularies were large and important units serving municipalities of two or three hundred thousand population. Meanwhile the process of consolidating the smaller police units is still proceeding, with current plans which call for the eventual absorption of the police of all noncounty boroughs having less than thirty thousand population. Even so, there is no stampede toward centralization, as is illustrated by the action of a parliamentary committee which declined to recommend merging the police forces of all boroughs having less than seventy-five thousand population with the county constabularies.

In the first place [argued this body] nineteen of the police authorities concerned are county boroughs. Your Committee are not aware of any precedent for depriving a county borough, however small, of any powers it already possesses. Some of the boroughs concerned have enjoyed the dignity of being counties or cities since the Middle Ages, and their long experience in police administration entitles them to favorable consideration.[2]

Thus the police system of England and Wales, while it has made real progress toward coherence and unity, still rests upon the antonomy of the local governments. Under unusually able and farseeing leadership within the Home Office, implemented by the investigations and appraisals conducted by His Majesty's Inspectors of Constabulary, there has been improvement in some of the weaker jurisdictions, and by the Police Act of 1946 most of the smaller forces were consolidated with neighboring police establishments. Only 133 forces are retained in the service of almost 500 cities, boroughs, and counties.

One other highly important feature should be noted: Nowhere in England, Wales, nor for that matter in Scotland, is there the slightest

[2] *Report from the Select Committee on Police Forces (Amalgamation)* (1932), pp. 5, 14.

duplication of police authority. The police establishments of city, borough, and county governments do not overlap in any way. Their powers are identical, and they exercise a territorial jurisdiction that is distinct and exclusive. This highly desirable result has been achieved by the abandonment of outworn police agencies and their consolidation with those retained. Though small police units are being merged with the county constabularies only gradually, it is not difficult to foresee the day which will mark the complete disappearance of all police units having less than 100 or 150 men.

Here on this side the suggestion is occasionally advanced that the states, or even the federal government itself, might likewise assist toward a more satisfactory system of policing, through grants-in-aid to the various county, city, township, and village governments. By use of such a device at least the appearance of a narrowly restricted local autonomy in police affairs could be preserved for many years, since the local governments would then cling even more tenaciously to their several police forces in order to collect the subsidy, though wholly without regard for considerations of economy or the prospect of better protection by other means. Another and equally unfavorable result would emerge from the fact that state or national support would almost necessarily be conditioned upon some measure of state or national control. This would not be exercised through the natural avenues of command, but rather through rules and regulations which could not conceivably be adapted to our highly varied patterns of police agencies. Thus the hand of a remote bureaucracy would be laid upon local police forces both large and small, and the free and untrammeled development of our police institutions, now almost the sole outstanding virtue of the present scheme, would find itself restricted more and more as the years lengthened into decades.

Impending Revision of Police Patterns

Such a plan of police aid would also miss the real objective, because it is not financial support that local police forces chiefly lack, but rather an increased measure of order and simplicity in the relations existing between them. For even while the number and variety of independent units are still rapidly increasing, there is as yet no disposition to collect the administrative debris of the ages. We construct new police devices without so much as a gesture toward removing the ancient ruins. Still the evidence multiplies that this process will not be continued indefinitely. Interforce rivalries are becoming more and more destructive in their effect upon field operations, the task of coordinating the work of so many agencies reaches impossible proportions, while the cost of maintaining overlapping and conflicting agencies has carried America's bill for police protection to an all-time, all-continent high. When these and other factors combine to compel a reconstruction of our police defenses, it seems most probable that the initiative will be taken by the several states, which alone have any considerable power to delegate and retract the exercise of police authority.

Although simplicity of plan is a desirable feature of police organization and management, it is unlikely that impending revisions will adhere to any one pattern. On the contrary, the local differences that characterize existing arrangements almost assure adaptations to such special needs in the future. This need not mean a perpetuation of the confusing outlines that now prevail. The mere process of reducing the number of police agencies will operate to simplify the structure. In commonwealths like Vermont and New Hampshire, which are small in area, predominantly rural, and have few urban complications, the state could effectively operate a single force without delegating any large powers of enforcement to local units. Likewise in Rhode Island, a single state-controlled police establishment would encounter no uncommon difficulties in protecting the urban core and the narrow margin of rural area that adjoins it. Even some of the far-flung western states, featured by large areas, low population density, and a total absence of complex urban centers, represent situations which may easily be met in the same fashion. These offer the most promising opportunities for thoroughgoing police unification.

Other and more difficult situations arise in the industrial states or in those having numerous and important commercial centers. These offer less attractive prospects for simplification, not primarily because they are too large to lend themselves to single police control, but because the clash of cultural interests and differing standards of law enforcement which have inspired the ill-fated struggles for state control of local police in the past do not forecast a more successful result under the guise of unification. Such intricate situations will continue to challenge our ingenuity in devising new mechanisms geared to the current requirements of police protection. The police of the great cities will probably undergo only slight adaptations, if for no better reason than that they are large enough and strong enough to defend and maintain their separate existences. In suburban areas, however, and in other composite urban districts, consolidation of police resources holds high promise for improved service at lowered cost. In some instances the county will be the appropriate unit, in others an *ad hoc* district may have to be created, or common police facilities provided by intergovernmental contract.[3]

Throughout the open countryside the state police, as now constituted in some of the northeastern and north central states, should be able to take over the entire task of rural law enforcement without major changes of organization or impressively large increases in their numbers. But the small urban centers and market towns which are found wherever rail and highway transport facilities favor their existence introduce a baffling element into the situation. They are neither large enough to warrant a separate police establishment, nor so small and simple that they require only occasional patrol surveillance such as is customarily offered by state police. They may need intensive traffic regulation during certain hours of each day, as well as a multitude of minor regulatory services. Such as these could not be provided by state police without large additions to their manpower, and various adaptations of their several schemes of organization. Still no serious problem is here presented, particularly as the surrender of police authority by small towns steeped in local pride will not be so rapid as to test the powers of the state police to adjust themselves to the new conditions.[4]

There remains the possibility that small urban communities may

[3] In England it is not at all unusual for two or three small forces—whether of boroughs or counties—to be placed under the single command of one chief constable who is made responsible for their joint direction, even though the forces themselves remain independent in all other respects. Similarly in New York, there has been some experimentation with contracts between small communities and the state police, whereby local areas receive the exclusive services of one or more state troopers. While such devices offer no large-scale solutions, they may have at least temporary value in specific situations.

[4] In some instances small towns and villages are already disbanding their local police establishments because of the unnecessary financial burdens they entail, and are placing themselves under the protection of state or county police forces.

be deprived of their police authority by legislative fiat, in order to provide more adequate and economical facilities. In this connection it should be remembered that the local governments of some of our smaller communities even now are virtually being supported in one way or another by state funds, and that the next great national emergency demanding new and larger sources of revenue for the support of military services might profoundly and unfavorably change the tax bases of state and local governments. In that event, the governmental areas now limping along with the assistance of state aid and state distributions of tax proceeds may find themselves unable to continue. Immediately there would be need for additional state-supported police facilities in such areas, due to the disappearance of local police.

Barring such eventualities it seems probable that the police of the small cities and those of the larger villages lying outside the sphere of metropolitan influences will be the last of the rudimentary forces to disappear. They will outlast the sheriff and the constable because they are making a greater and a more intelligent effort to adapt themselves to current needs in police protection, and also because they are part and parcel of institutions of local government which are native to our soil. On both counts their chances for survival are excellent, even though their unwieldy numbers and wide distribution will greatly complicate the police mechanisms of the future.

Civil Defense in Major Emergencies

The mechanisms themselves are already so complex that it is doubtful whether they could carry, in anything like their present form, the burdens certain to be imposed by a great national emergency. Federal agencies such as the military and naval intelligence units and the FBI would play a decisive role in preventive activity, but neither their numbers nor their organization structures will prove adaptable to the repression of organized violence. Only compact bodies of large numbers of men can do that, and with the National Guard in federal service, and the Home Guards undergoing rudimentary military training, the entire burden will necessarily fall upon state and local police.

Meanwhile, any threat of actual attack would so greatly increase their responsibilities that the absurd patchwork of overlapping protection would probably be abandoned overnight, and a new and more cohesive scheme quickly improvised. To many who have become impatient with the lost motion and inefficiency of our present dispositions, a clean sweep of major proportions would doubtless represent a welcome departure. Yet it should be remembered that any such radical and hasty readjustment would be compelled to ignore a multitude of local situations meriting careful preliminary study if time permitted, and in any event would do such violence to some of our institutions of local government that they might not survive the blow. After all, police relationships are complex partly because intergovernmental relationships in general are complex, with police so deeply embedded in the basic philosophies of local autonomy as to make their separation a delicate matter at best. The ruthless manner in which old patterns are likely to be revised under the pressure of emergency conditions does not promise any such careful adjustment of means to end, as the difficult nature of the question clearly requires. Hence it seems far preferable that pending an evolution of local police systems, some appropriate action should be taken which will anticipate emergency conditions through formal plans for the direction of interforce activities whenever need may arise.

A highly desirable feature of such an emergency plan of civil defense consists in assurance to all local authorities that the statutory basis and organization structure of their police will not thereby be affected, and that each local force will remain free to conduct the normal routine of police work without abrupt interference from authorities operating under the guise of emergency powers, or with the justification of some compelling necessity. This moderate course is followed not only because it is required by the existing statutory framework of our police system, but also because it is the best way to secure the active support of state and local police administrators for a scheme of emergency relationships which, to be effective, must elicit a considerable measure of cooperative action.

Mobilization of Police Resources

With some 40,000 police forces totaling nearly 300,000 men in the nation as a whole, it is apparent that the typical American force is far too small to possess either primary striking power or reserve strength. Yet in all of the larger cities, and in some of the counties, there are regular police establishments having a sufficient numerical strength to provide a nucleus for a regional police organism, while in extensive rural areas, with no great urban centers, state police forces when supplemented by the police of small cities and villages can usually provide enough manpower to permit tactical operations by a compact body. If to such forces is added the fragmentary and unorganized police facilities represented by rural constables and an occasional sheriff, the effect—though perhaps not imposing in all states—is certainly superior to the wide dispersion of police effectives under uncontrolled local autonomy. For even though some of the part-time and untrained police have no great value in tactical operations against subversive or destructive elements, they prove to be welcome aides in the conduct of routine protection of a community when a part of its regular and disciplined force is engaged in emergency duty. Conversely, rural and semirural areas with vulnerable or extrahazardous locations enjoy emergency protection by police facilities such as they could not hope to be able to support as part of a normal program.

With mobilization officers designated by the governor from among the regular police officials of each region, a focus of leadership and of temporary authority has been provided in several states. Such regional supervisors are responsible not only for the initiation and direction of emergency operations, but also for laying plans for civil defense in all its branches, for mobilization schedules of men and machines, for the reserve recruitment of able-bodied police who are on the retired list, provision of connecting links in police communication systems, procurement and safe storage of automatic rifles, gas and smoke bombs, the training of mounted police, and conduct of close-order drill and extended order maneuvers. Sheriffs within each region can be held responsible for the continuing protection of especially hazardous points by full-time special deputies, for providing temporary shelters for prisoners and others, and for guarding confiscated property.

The mobilization districts are large enough to embrace a total police complement of substantial proportions, though not so far-flung as unduly to slow up the process of mobilization. In this as in other aspects of modern police work, speed is an important factor. Fortunately, most state and local forces are well provided with transport and communication facilities. These prove essential to prompt and effective action. In any event the number of mobilization districts is kept as small as the hard facts of manpower, miles, and minutes will permit, in order that the governor's span of control may not be subjected to unnecessary structural strains.

The control exercised by the governor, and his full responsibility in ordering a mobilization of police resources, must be maintained from the outset and at all times; otherwise there is possibility that the large and highly organized social instrument represented by the mobilized force may fall into irresponsible hands, with attendant danger of its misapplication. Hence the governor should select as mobilization officers only police executives who possess special qualifications and in whom he has full confidence. Further, he should require from the officers so designated an adequate report on the nature and extent of the disturbed conditions, and of the need for outside aid, before giving his consent to a mobilization in any given instance.

Whether mobilization areas should follow the district lines employed by state police for their own administrative purposes, with the state police commander of each such district serving as mobilization officer, or should describe wide arcs around cities and metropolitan areas, with mobilization officers designated from among the leading police executives within the area, or some combination of both methods, are matters which can best be determined with primary reference to the geography of the state, the distribution of its police effectives, and with due consideration for various imponderables of strictly local application and significance.

A rather difficult question also is presented by the matter of actual command at the scene of the emergency. Local authorities are likely to expect this as a right, despite the fact that they have had to call in outside assistance and may not themselves be greatly experienced in policing riots or disasters. All things considered, it appears preferable that active command should be lodged in the hands of the local police commander since he is thoroughly familiar with local geography, and has been in active charge from the very outset of the disturbance. Any attempted transfer of general control after the arrival of mobilized reserves might cause confusion. So much, at least, would be true if the local police leadership were experienced in directing large-scale operations. In the larger centers and in the better organized state forces, such leadership is available.

Hence if a rule of general application appears to be necessary or desirable, one of the following procedures might be adopted by the governor in allocating responsibility: If any disorder requiring outside police aid occurs within the corporate limits of one of the larger cities, the local chief of police shall command the police reserves made available by the district mobilization officer, who in turn acts under the orders of the governor. Outside of such major centers, however, the governor should himself designate the active police commander (for example, a captain of state police, or an experienced local chief of police) , for each emergency as it arises. Thus a distinction is drawn between the duties of mobilization officers and those of field commanders, thereby permitting a considerable degree of adjustment to varied local conditions.

Dangers Arising from Volunteer Police

These and related questions are now included in few police plans because the disasters which give rise to them are not of frequent occurrence, while civil problems of national defense have only recently become the concern of either police or public.

When such problems have arisen, it has been common practice to turn to the law-abiding elements of the community for emergency aid. Recourse of this nature is deeply ingrained in local government procedures, which in turn rest upon fundamental philosophies of self-help and self-protection. If the regularly organized agencies of society are hard pressed or overwhelmed, every householder is likely to feel impelled to offer his services for civil defense and the common welfare. The civic consciousness which inspires voluntary community action is such a desirable and even precious thing, that public authorities who are dependent upon popular good will are naturally reluctant to thwart its exercise. Nevertheless it is at best a rather hazardous expedient, and one which at worst may threaten the integrity of our institutions. Examples are not wanting in our own history, nor in that of other lands, of civic groups entrusted with police powers under the stress of emergency conditions, ultimately employing them as instruments of private malice and of political, racial, or class oppression.

Unhappy results of this character have been so common that the executive officers of state and local government should consider carefully and well before deputizing private citizens as special agents for law enforcement. Volunteer police are necessarily untrained and undisciplined, though they are vested with an authority which can be exercised with prudence only under the established forms of law. Even the best disposed elements of a community must assume severe handicaps in performing emergency police duties. But experience has shown that it is not alone the sober defenders of hearth and home who clamor for an opportunity to serve. Truculent, disorderly, intolerant, and downright vicious elements also flock to police standards at such times, from motives of their own and with objectives foreign to the maintenance of civil peace. These form a menacing bloc within the ranks of hastily improvised citizen reserves. Thus it seems clear that the regular police establishments, quickly mobilized with the aid of communication and transportation facilities such as they generally possess in full abundance, are the only safe and sure recourse for civil defense. Some of them are highly trained and disciplined bodies, with actual experience in the firm though restrained suppression of public disorders. Even the least of them is accustomed to acting under the guidance of procedural rules laid down by legislatures and courts. From whatever angle viewed, they will prove more responsible guardians of private rights and civil liberties than even the best intentioned of vigilantes.

The states do not lack trained police to deal effectively with isolated threats and outbreaks; but they need a current inventory of police resources, and a mobilization plan which will make them available wherever needed. Practically all of such a program can be carried out without special statutory authority, although once the patterns of police action on a regional basis are clearly defined, it may prove desirable to provide the support of legislative enactments, particularly in allocating responsibilities and in extending or clarifying the powers of local police to act outside their usual geographical limits. Thus there may be established in each state both a normal and an emergency system of police protection, with the latter featured by the compactness and coherence which non-routine and unanticipated operations require.

Varied Approaches to Integration

Meanwhile the problems arising in connection with day-to-day police routine are no less exacting in their demands upon police organization and administration. The foregoing pages may have indicated how diffused are these questions, and how desirable it is to adapt the ways and means of the consolidation process to the special requirements of each community. Such varied approaches to the problems of police unification may evoke objections that they do not fall into simple patterns, nor present clear-cut issues which can be met by general rules. It is unfortunate that this is so, because simplicity of design is an important quality for any program that involves thoroughgoing reform. Here are posed not one or two problems, but half a dozen, each with its own type of solution, and no general rule which can readily be made applicable to all. Before such possible criticisms are taken too seriously, however, it should be remembered that it has been the application of general rules—such as statutes permitting the unrestricted creation of police agencies by local governments regardless of size, location, or character—which have put us into the troublesome position in which we now find ourselves. With this experience so prominently before us, care should be taken that the new arrangements are not so general in their scope that they do not fit actual conditions. Simplicity of design we must strive to achieve, but not by a distortion of the underlying facts.

These seem to represent the basic needs for a unification program, whether its realization be a matter of years, decades or generations. Pending such developments the common tendency to produce specialized police bodies for the enforcement of particular statutes by the federal and state governments, or for performing other fragmentary services for counties and cities, will have to be halted and its direction reversed. The need for unifying police authority in this horizontal plane is especially urgent, because so many of the narrowly specialized police forces in counties and cities are created in response to demands for political patronage. They are accordingly a severe handicap to the development of professional standards in police administration.

New Personnel Procedures

Such standards are even now emerging. When federal, state, and local forces set higher educational qualifications for recruits, they are weakening the unfavorable influence of cut-and-dried information tests on police recruiting for the past fifty years; when they conduct searching investigations into the personal histories of applicants for appointment, they raise the prestige and dignity of police service everywhere; when pre-service and in-service training programs are established, police acquire a consciousness of the dignity of professional status that is out of all proportion to the pedagogical standards or intrinsic values of such training; and when police administrators are able to apply a rigorous discipline to the rank and file, and to dismiss those who for any reason are unsuited to police work, they afford convincing demonstration that the protective forces of the community can police their own ranks.

It is a highly impressive and significant fact that many such advances are being made by police agencies lying wholly outside the sphere of civil service control, and result in the application of methods produced out of police experience. With the civil service commissions rapidly extending their domain, a crisis therefore approaches which will severely test the ability of police to devise and introduce their own distinctive procedures. For unless such inventions and applications are made in ever-increasing volume, there is real danger that the renewed march of civil service reform will again be featured by slipshod personnel methods—methods which are better than nothing where clerical and other routine employments are concerned, but may be worse than nothing when applied to a quasi-military arm such as police. If positive qualifications are not adapted to police needs, our civil service regimes represent merely the dead hand of negative control. When applied through hard-and-fast limitations upon the exercise of executive judgment and discretion, the initiative and resourcefulness of the entire police service suffers.

Political Spoils vs. the Merit System

Such strictures commonly elicit two rejoinders. The first is that whatever the faults of the merit system, it is superior in every respect to the spoils system which it sometimes displaces. If the comparison be accepted to mean that the merit system at its best is better than the spoils system at its worst, there can be little ground for disagreement. The reverse is equally true; even a politically controlled public service at its best is better than the merit system at its worst. But there are more than just these two alternatives—spoils system and merit system. There is the demonstrated fact that a number of federal, state, and municipal police forces have always operated entirely outside the sphere of civil service control and without partisan domination over the rank and file. Included in this category are some of the outstanding police units in this country—forces enjoying a high position on the rather short list of police establishments which may be compared favorably with the protective agencies developed in Great Britain and on the Continent. Such departures provide adequate ground for the hope that a new standard of public service is possible, and that the political patterns and traditions upon which such standards ultimately rest are now in process of drastic revision.

A second rejoinder is that the merit system should not be condemned *in toto* for the obvious faults developed under special circumstances and under particular regimes; that promising changes in personnel administration under civil service auspices are constantly being adopted by the more competent civil service commissions; and that where there is demonstrated capacity for growth and change, there is also the possibility of improvement. This viewpoint can be accepted only with reserve, because the general picture presented by the practical workings of the merit system is so dismal and so little relieved by the highlights of occasional success. Yet it may possibly offer some prospect for an evolution of the merit system which will gradually shift its primary emphasis away from those negative controls designed to thwart administrative direction and discipline, and in time place it squarely upon a basis of technical assistance to the police administrator.

The Need for Major Changes

If this end is to be achieved, the partisans of the merit system will find it necessary to cast aside the bureaucratic aloofness which has so often characterized them in the past, and to concern themselves with the problems of management. They will have to determine more accurately than they now do what the police administrator wants in his recruits and then actively cooperate with him in devising ways and means for attracting such recruits to the public service and for identifying their special qualifications when they do apply. It will be necessary also to enlarge the administrator's disciplinary control over the rank and file, in order that the errors which are inevitable in large-scale recruiting may be corrected by prompt and vigorous action.

The burden of veterans' preference acts probably cannot be thrown off, and will continue as a reproach to our civil service systems as defined by law. But there are other burdens and obstacles which can be removed more easily. Prominent in the latter category are the local residence requirements. If police service is to be viewed as just another form of work relief there may be some justification for their continuance, but there is no warrant for applying them to a group which should meet varied and exacting standards of qualification. Civil service commissions can join hands with police administrators in securing the repeal of these narrow and artificial residence restrictions, and in some instances can destroy the local residence rule without recourse to legislation, by the simple expedient of amending their own regulations. They can conduct more thorough character examinations. They can speed up the examination process, so that the more desirable applicants will not be snapped up by private employers before unavoidable delays permit appointments to be made. And finally, they can make some positive provision for recruiting administrators without subjecting them to the long and unremunerative process of promotion from the lower ranks.

Recruiting Police Administrators

This last deserves further consideration. One of the greatest handicaps suffered by the merit system as now practiced is that its mechanisms and processes are largely concerned with a personnel of mediocrity. Rarely is there provision for ways and means by which a real career in the higher administrative posts can be quickly achieved by qualified men. Hence ambitious and qualified youth must spend years in the lower ranks and grades, in the course of which it acquires no practical experience or training in administrative leadership, before it can hope to share the responsibilities and enjoy the prerogatives of high command.

Under our prevailing patterns, really ambitious youths often avoid the toil and drudgery of the merit system, by devoting themselves to a career in police administration that is tinctured by politics. There is some loss of political independence and less security, it is true, but the major result is usually attained with more certainty and at an earlier stage than under the old style of merit system. If and when the latter finally produces its leader, the weight of years is already upon him, the erosive effects of routine have worn him down, and an ultimate promotion to high administrative rank is likely to mean only that his retirement annuity will be the larger for it.

The Army and the Navy do not commit such blunders. They recruit and discharge without fear or favor, on the basis of merit alone, and without the aid of any civil service commission. They also—and this is an especially important point—recruit officer personnel which is thoroughly trained at the great service academies at West Point and Annapolis. In other words, they provide a separate career service for military and naval leadership. So do the police systems on the Continent, with their special educational requirements for officers. So does the Royal Canadian Mounted Police, which draws its commissioned personnel in part from the graduates of the Royal Military College and from the commissioned grades of the militia.

If American police can also produce a larger proportion of trained officer personnel, a long step will have been taken toward establishing professional standards in police work. That this can be accomplished on a large scale by general training of the rank and file is highly improbable. In fact the thin pretense that all police employees can ultimately be raised to full professional status is getting us nowhere. We need to recognize quite frankly that some types of police service do not offer the prospect for brilliant careers, and to recruit our police forces accordingly. Perhaps then we shall be able to concentrate our thinking and our inventiveness upon those members of the force who hold real promise for advancement into the higher ranks and grades, and to supplement them with police cadets who receive a broad preparatory training for police command. As more and more leaders of true professional quality are thereby produced, the influence of partisan ties will perforce be weakened, and in quarters favorable to civil service controls there will be less suspicion of the free play of executive discretion when entrusted to such highly trained hands. It will be easier also to attract an occasional police leader from commerce, industry, or the learned professions, because capable officers will be ready to assist him at every turn. When the maintenance of popular controls seems to require the introduction of an administrator from civil life, it can be accomplished without throwing the rank and file into confusion or launching the force upon expedients that already have been proved fruitless.

Some state and municipal forces accept the principle of pre-service training for recruits, and others have laid secure foundations for in-service training of aspirants to the higher ranks and grades. We need now to mark the road to promotion by the establishment of pre-service training of true professional grade as a standard for direct admission to the administrative level. It is an undertaking which should evoke, as it will surely demand, the full cooperation of police commanders, personnel administrators, universities, and state colleges. These have it within their power to provide new administrative careers in the police service that are generally comparable with those already available in the Army and Navy, and in education, public health, engineering, forestry and other professional fields.

Whither Police Unions?

Recent years have witnessed a considerable increase of interest in police unions among the rank and file. While the number of such associations is still small, the question bulks large in the minds of police administrators throughout the land.[5] The Boston police strike of 1919 raised so many disturbing issues it is not surprising that the prospect of further unsettlement should produce grave concern in official circles.

Considering the benevolent attitude of federal and state governments toward organized labor, it is startling to find them arrayed in such uncompromising attitudes against police unions. By police regulation, attorney general's opinion, executive order or judicial decree the unions have been turned back so frequently and emphatically that one is tempted to conclude the issue is approaching final decision. Certainly the precedents established in the course of the past thirty years offer little to encourage the police union leadership.

Despite the well-established trend, it is necessary to recognize that however easy it may be to distinguish police employment from other public and private forms, there will always be local issues of compensation, working conditions and job security that will in-

---

[5] International Association of Chiefs of Police, *Police Unions and Other Police Organizations* (1944).

volve the police rank and file. Since unions do not offer an appropriate means for police representation at city halls and state capitols, other methods must be developed through which city patrolmen and state troopers on occasion may give voice to their needs.

Thus far two devices have been adopted. One of them appeared during the early years of state police development and consisted in enlisting troopers for terms of two or three years. This avoided any obligation by the state and rested the trooper's service squarely upon military precedents.

The other device has been adopted by police employees and consists in the support of police benevolent associations that are free and independent of the national labor unions. Such independent associations are generally welcomed by elected executives, career administrators, and the various ranks of policemen alike. They accordingly offer the greater promise for a satisfactory solution of some of the disturbing questions of police employment that loom ahead.

Applied Science in Police Work

From such difficult and often baffling features of the police problem one turns with more assurance to an appraisal of mechanical aids in police work, and to the prospect for application of laboratory techniques in criminal investigations. The aptitude recently shown by American police in these fields stands in striking contrast with their rather dreary record of mediocrity where administrative skill is concerned. For we have here in the United States the most impressive collection of police gadgets that has ever been assembled anywhere. Our systems of local and regional intercommunication by radio, teletype, and other means are clearly superior to those employed in other parts of the world. Signal devices for the regulation of traffic acquire new and more ingenious features with each passing year. Motorized facilities are made available to an extent elsewhere unknown, while in a single generation our police have won a leading place for themselves in the employment of laboratory science as an aid to investigation. Nor is the end in sight. There is as yet no indication that American police are relaxing their interest in the physical resources which an age of science has so freely placed at their disposal. On the contrary there is every reason to conclude that the competitive spirit now animating them in adopting the latest in electrical and mechanical devices will continue to flourish.

A considerable part of this acquisitiveness is desirable and useful, since it keeps police abreast of inventions and adaptations likely to be of value in police work. Some of it, however, merely results in the accumulation and operation of mechanical toys which absorb the time and attention of an increasing proportion of the force without contributing much to the business of protection. Even more serious, in the larger view, is the disposition of many police commanders to measure their own effectiveness, and that of their respective forces, by the amount and variety of the paraphernalia thus marshaled. The use of such measures of efficiency implies a feebleness in true administrative capacity that is all too often substantiated by the results of firsthand investigation. Moreover, a public necessarily unschooled in the realities of police duty often finds it easier to appraise its police defenses in terms of mere physical resources than in terms of the quality and discipline of officers and men. Here then is the problem represented by the mechanical device in police service: while it makes only minor and secondary contributions to police efficiency, it serves to divert the attention of police and public alike away from those large issues of personnel management upon which success in police protection ultimately depends.

Despite the fact that we are a gadget-minded people, there are police administrators who understand the importance and bearing of these considerations, and who would welcome a change of the popular criteria from mechanisms to men. Their attitudes will remain unimportant, however, so long as the press and other agencies of public enlightenment emphasize the more superficial aspects of police performance, and measure effectiveness by the ingenuity of traffic signals or the range of radio transmitters. If popular controls are to be effective, some more relevant data than these must be made available. Although abstract tabular summaries of certain end results such as crimes committed and cases cleared by arrest do not hold the same interest for the general public that they do for the alert administrator and close student of police activity, a long step in advance will be taken if the emphasis in appraising police operations can be shifted away from the machines and back to the men involved. There are many angles of human interest in the recruiting, training, promotion and discipline of police forces which are as yet undeveloped. Still a promising beginning has been made, and it is perhaps not too much to hope that popular appraisals in the future may be more concerned with the human factor than they now are.

The Objectives of Popular Control

Meanwhile American police problems will continue to revolve not only about matters which relate to efficiency in keeping the peace, in suppressing crime, and apprehending offenders. They will also be concerned with the due observance of private rights by all law enforcement officers. On this point public attitudes can be so confusing that to police they seem to threaten the effectiveness of the entire police establishment. Thousands of the men who day and night patrol our thoroughfares, who strenuously contend with criminal activities and risk their lives in the public service, are fully convinced that they do not have full popular support in these operations, and that the public stands ready to condemn them for conditions not of their making. Some police are also critical of the attitudes of bench and bar in emphasizing various technicalities of criminal law and procedure, largely because their training as police has not made it clear that personal liberty is protected and broadened by just such expedients. No one has ever explained to them why it is that, although they may be well-intentioned servants of the public will, their police authority needs to be carefully defined, and its limitations scrupulously observed, if it is to be made secure from misapplication and abuse.

The public, on its side, seems to lack even an elementary knowledge of the unfavorable conditions under which police work is performed, and of the practical difficulties confronting it. Citizens understand in a vague and general way that their civil liberties must be respected by police, but they do not appreciate that this protection necessarily extends both to those who consider themselves to be law observers and to those who are law violators. The upshot of it all is that a large segment of the public demands that police shall be meticulously careful in their handling of some persons, while others are to receive short shrift with no formalities. How such nice discriminations are to be effected, either in fact or in law, is not made clear, and so the basis is laid for serious misunderstandings between police and public.

Changing the Rules of the Game

Although there is no well-defined path out of this morass of uncertainty and confusion, avenues of escape may be provided if sufficient time and patient labor are devoted to their construction. One of them consists in a revision of our state codes of criminal procedure with reference to the law of arrest and of preliminary examination, to the end that a more liberal framework of statutory provisions surrounding performance of police duty may be established. Thus, in a land where carrying concealed weapons is still common, the authority of uniformed police to make superficial searches by "frisking" suspects should be formally recognized. Similarly there should be an extension of their power to make valid arrests without a warrant.[6] Such departures would signalize the substitution of trained police for informal community action in law enforcement and could be effected without encroaching upon any private right or interest worthy of the law's protection.

On the other hand, police are under obligation to assist in removing the tangled mass of unlawful practices by which they sometimes offset statutory safeguards of great importance. Most common of such practices and holding the gravest consequences for police service are the ill-defined abuses of police authority known collectively as the third degree. On this score enough evidence is at hand to warrant the conclusion that police subject persons in custody and under interrogation to many kinds of force and intimidation. That they often do so in the sincere belief that they are thereby serving the public interest merely serves to emphasize the gravity of the situation. Events have now reached a point where something effective must be done about extralegal practices. Bench and bar, pulpit and press are allied against them,[7] while legislative bodies

---

[6] See, for example, State of New York, Report of the Commission on the Administration of Justice; "Revision of the Code of Criminal Procedure" (Legislative Document, 1939, No. 76), pp. 23-26; 43-46; and *American Bar Association Journal*, Vol. XXVI, No. 2 (February, 1940,) pp. 151-155.

[7] It is of course difficult to secure reliable and extensive data on third-degree practices, or to measure the precise extent in which they infringe upon personal liberty. All special treatments of the subject tend to exaggerate the frequency of third-degree abuses. The best source is: National

are beginning to lend an attentive ear to the chorus of condemnation. Two angles of attack have thus far been proposed and both are rapidly enlisting support. One would by statutory enactment destroy the probative value of all confessions made to the police; the other would remove the occasion for such confessions by requiring that persons in custody shall be taken immediately before a magistrate without even a brief preliminary detention in a police lockup.

Either device would aid materially in suppressing third-degree practices, though at grave risk of limiting police effectiveness. By outlawing confessions made to the police, some of the most valuable results of successful investigations would be thwarted. By requiring immediate examination before a magistrate, police would be deprived of all opportunity to establish the identity of the prisoner, to search for a previous criminal record, or to determine whether he was wanted in another jurisdiction for a crime, an escape, or a parole violation. Hence, so long as the procedural codes of many of our states are content to limit the magistrate's examination to a *pro forma* proceeding, without placing the defendant under oath, or penalizing him for failure to make even an exculpatory statement, or in any other way making him accountable for his actions, there can be little hope for an adequate substitute for interrogation by police and prosecutors.

The Issue of Lawful Enforcement

This throws full responsibility back upon police administrators to require that interrogations shall be conducted with decent restraint. In fact theirs has been the responsibility all along and there is no good reason why they should continue to avoid full assumption of it. The general disciplinary powers which they already possess are in most cases entirely adequate for controlling objectionable practices and excesses of authority. Once let investigating officers clearly understand that the physical or mental abuse of prisoners

---

Commission on Law Observance and Enforcement: *Report on Lawlessness in Law Enforcement* (Washington, 1931). We are still too far removed from the standards of civil liberties observance which are so well established in Great Britain for the police procedures and restraints there employed to have more than an inspirational value for us at the present time. In this connection, the monumental *Report of the Royal Commission on Police Powers and Procedure, dated 16th March, 1929,* Vols. I-IV, is invaluable.

will be followed both by disciplinary action and also by such criminal prosecution as the facts may warrant, and use of the third degree will end, and end abruptly. Though the prosecution of certain cases might fail owing to the use of this method, it would be more than offset by the changed attitude of the public as represented in jury boxes.

In the long run it will be these public attitudes which determine the strength and nature of popular controls, as well as the circumstances and frequency of their application. For if the general attitude is one of trust and confidence, then lay and inexpert interference with the essential process of law enforcement should be of rare occurrence. In that event, police might hope to enjoy long periods of uninterrupted development, in the course of which the arts of civil protection could flourish, and the basis for an even-handed justice in police operations would become more firmly established.

There will be scores and perhaps hundreds of police administrators who will respond to this with the declaration that they themselves unremittingly emphasize to the rank and file the importance of "courtesy" in dealing with the general public, and will contend that the frequency and gravity of third-degree episodes are greatly exaggerated. Such as these miss the point of popular dissatisfaction. It is not courtesy, but civility, that our uniformed forces should cultivate, while the actual extent of civil rights violations and third-degree practices is largely irrelevant so long as they do exist and are popularly believed to be both frequent and general. That belief will persist until the full, equal, and lawful enforcement of the law is freely accepted by police as their standard of performance and is consistently applied, year in and year out, as a matter of corps discipline and administrative routine.

The words of Rufus Choate are pertinent in this connection. In describing the essential qualities in the character of a judge, he said that "he must possess the perfect confidence of the community, that he bear not the sword in vain. To be honest, to be no respecter of persons, is not yet enough—*he must be believed such.*" Police are subjected to a somewhat similar test by the communities which they serve, and accordingly are under a special duty and obligation to take the initiative by establishing humane policies in dealing with their prisoners, and in their scrupulous observance of civil liberties. No mere declaration of intentions will suffice, nor will any standard of performance not in complete accord with the most exacting of the community's attitudes. Even a relatively good record is still not good enough. No matter from what angle the civil liberties question is viewed, always there is the problem of police observance. Unless that is complete and unqualified, the confidence of the community will be withheld.

This, in substance, seems to be the meaning of American experience. These are the reasons why the declarations of police are not accepted at face value. When they protest that civil liberties are protected "except in emergencies," they weaken popular support in many unanticipated ways. When they extend assurances that "no decent citizen is ever 'beaten up' in a police station," public uneasiness rises to the point of actual alarm. When governors, mayors, and police administrators threaten hoodlums and gangsters with informal punitive measures, rather than the full measure of justice under law, citizens begin to wonder just how such a condition of outlawry is to be established.

The strong indications are that police believe in observance of civil liberties quite as much as does the general public.[8] Both groups are prone to depart from the accepted standard under the stress of what at the time are believed to be compelling circumstances. Thus police violations of civil liberties and the application of various restrictions upon police as means of popular control become segments of a vicious circle. Popular distrust is not a favorable climate for the consistent development of police techniques, and when these are pushed aside in favor of short-cut procedures a lawless enforcement of the law is produced which in turn arouses new public antipathies. While this aspect of the police problem varies with each jurisdiction, and therefore presumably requires varied treatment, police administrators would do well to weigh the advantages to be realized from a clean break with the old slipshod police tradition. The administrator who lays down hard-and-fast rules of police conduct which are enforced to the letter may lose his official head in the political guillotine, but if he survives this danger the chances are good that he will break through the circle of inter-

---

[8] See, for example, Beyle and Parratt, "Approval and Disapproval of Specific Third Degree Practices," in *Journal of Criminal Law and Criminology*, Vol. 28, No. 4, pp. 526-550 (1937-1938).

acting cause and effect now preventing the extension of so many major improvements in police service.

The Price of Greater Efficiency

We pay high for our law enforcement—more in cash per capita than does any other part of the world, and our police enjoy compensation scales, disability benefits, and retirement pensions having no parallels elsewhere. In return for such costly standards in the conditions of employment, there is a natural expectation of more and more police efficiency. That end, however, can never be achieved so long as popular controls take the form of ever higher obstacles to vigorous police administration; all on the theory that since we cannot have law-abiding police, we can at least weaken their capacity for abusing the authority entrusted to them.

Here is a complete cycle of futility produced at the cost of much blood and treasure. There is ground for hope in the fact that police of all ranks show an increasing concern with the trend of public opinion, and are more and more disposed to re-examine some of the basic assumptions concerning exercise of their authority. If this attitude of self-criticism continues, we may yet effect a close approach to a police regime which is vigorous without being oppressive, and scrupulous in its observance of civil liberties without losing its effectiveness in law enforcement. Thus far these various objectives rarely have been found in combination, nor is it likely that they will become more common until police are able to establish themselves as enforcers rather than as evaders of our criminal codes. In the last analysis this promises to be the real test of the emergence of a police profession, which will thenceforth proceed to regulate and control its members without corrective action by the public on any but rare occasions. When that day comes, the problems of police administration can be approached in more systematic fashion than is now possible. With the vicious circle of popular distrust and lawless enforcement broken, police management will be able to move more directly and with increased assurance toward its truly great objectives.

INDEX